ROUTLEDGE LIBRARY EDITIONS: INEQUALITY

Volume 7

POVERTY AND SOCIAL INEQUALITY IN WALES

POVERTY AND SOCIAL INEQUALITY IN WALES

Edited by
GARETH REES and TERESA L. REES

Routledge
Taylor & Francis Group
LONDON AND NEW YORK

First published in 1980 by Croom Helm Ltd

This edition first published in 2023
by Routledge
4 Park Square, Milton Park, Abingdon, Oxon OX14 4RN

and by Routledge
605 Third Avenue, New York, NY 10158

Routledge is an imprint of the Taylor & Francis Group, an informa business

British Library Cataloguing in Publication Data
A catalogue record for this book is available from the British Library

ISBN: 978-1-032-43329-5 (Set)
ISBN: 978-1-032-43750-7 (Volume 7) (hbk)
ISBN: 978-1-032-43781-1 (Volume 7) (pbk)
ISBN: 978-1-003-36882-3 (Volume 7) (ebk)

DOI: 10.4324/9781003368823

Publisher's Note
The publisher has gone to great lengths to ensure the quality of this reprint but points out that some imperfections in the original copies may be apparent.

Disclaimer
The publisher has made every effort to trace copyright holders and would welcome correspondence from those they have been unable to trace.

POVERTY AND SOCIAL INEQUALITY IN WALES

Edited by
GARETH REES and TERESA L. REES

CROOM HELM LONDON

© 1980 Gareth Rees and Teresa L. Rees
Croom Helm Ltd, 2-10 St John's Road, London SW11

British Library Cataloguing in Publication Data

Poverty and social inequality in Wales.
   1. Wales – Social conditions
   2. Equality
   I. Rees, Gareth   II. Rees, Teresa L
   301.44'09429   HN398.W26

   ISBN 0-7099-2200-0
   ISBN 0-7099-2205-1 Pbk

Printed and bound in Great Britain by
Redwood Burn Limited, Trowbridge & Esher

To All Our Parents

CONTENTS

TABLES

MAPS

ACKNOWLEDGEMENTS

This collection of essays has been a long time in preparation and we have incurred a correspondingly large number of debts. We should like to thank Paul Atkinson, Sara Delamont and Paul Wilding for the general advice and encouragement that they have given us. Colleagues in the BSA Sociology of Wales study group have contributed significantly to the development of the ways in which we think about Welsh society.

No less significantly, we should like to acknowledge the contribution to the production of this book by Mr Winston Gough and the technical staff at the Department of Town Planning, UWIST; in particular, we should thank Gareth Jones for the expert preparation of the maps. Myrtle Robbins has typed successive drafts with a speed and accuracy far beyond the call of duty and we are indebted to the Sociological Research Unit of University College, Cardiff for making her services available to us.

Finally, we thank our publishers not only for advice, but also for unfailing patience in the face of our unerring ability to miss deadlines.

Gareth Rees
Teresa L. Rees

Map 1: County Boundaries and Major Towns of Wales.

Part One

DIMENSIONS OF SOCIAL INEQUALITY IN WALES

1 POVERTY AT THE PERIPHERY: THE OUTLINE OF A PERSPECTIVE ON WALES

Gareth Rees and Teresa L. Rees

It is an obvious truth that there are wide disparities between the different regions of Britain. To see this, all we need to do is compare, say, the Highlands of Scotland with the urban-industrial sprawl of the English Midlands; or the former mining areas of Durham and Northumberland with the 'commuter belt' of the Home Counties. In short, economic development generates divergent patterns of industrialisation and urbanisation. In consequence, regions experience widely varying levels of material prosperity. These general conditions, in turn, set the context for a diversity of cultures and political traditions.

Moreover, as Day (1979) has recently pointed out, trends towards the development of *supra*national organisations in both economic and political spheres (multinationals, the EEC, etc.) have – paradoxically – coincided with renewed concern over such *intra*national (i.e. inter-regional) disparities. In fact, whilst these latter issues have been a recurrent theme of politics in Britain, seldom has there been a more intense debate than in the past decade or two. The obstinate geographical unevenness of economic prosperity, in spite of the long post-war boom, yielded during the 1960s a widespread concern not only with the technicalities of regional economic planning, but also with the wider limitations of what had come to be seen as a highly centralised system of government and administration. The former is perhaps best exemplified in (now Lord) George Brown's ill-fated National Plan; the latter in the ultimately equally ill-fated Royal Commission on the Constitution. Clearly, these concerns were brought into sharp focus by the political successes of the nationalist parties in Scotland and Wales during the late 1960s and 1970s. The ensuing debate over the Labour Government's devolution proposals ensured that 'regionalism' and, more particularly, the grievances and aspirations of the Scottish and the Welsh occupied – albeit briefly – the very centre of the political stage.

However, what has seldom been made explicit is the context which made these political controversies possible. It seems to us that this context comprises not only a distinct structure of inequalities, but also a very specific notion of the obligations of government in respect of those inequalities. It is to this context, then, that we turn in the next section.

17

Inequalities and the Welfare State

Following Westergaard (1978), it can be argued that the structure of
unequal material prosperity in a capitalist economy is determined
according to two principles of distribution (or, as some would have it,
exploitation).

> The first principle is that property gives its owner a recognised claim
> to a share in resource output . . . if private profit is to drive the
> wheels of production, it and the property from which it derives must
> constitute a means of private consumption. (p.72)

> The second principle is . . . that the majority who do not own sub-
> stantial income-yielding property must rely for their livelihood in
> the first instance on the labour market: they have either to hire out
> their own labour or to depend on others — usually related members
> of their own household — who do the same. (Westergaard, 1978, p.73)

Clearly, the vast majority live by the latter principle and are severely
disadvantaged as compared with the small minority into whose hands
property which yields substantial income (according to the first principle)
is concentrated (see, for example, Westergaard and Resler, 1975).
   This is not to suggest, of course, that this is all there is to say about
inequality under capitalism. It is quite clear that within the classes defined in terms of these two distributional principles there are distinct
patterns of inequality (and it is these latter which seem to attract most
attention). Obviously, different groups of 'workers' are able to hire out
their labour on widely varying terms: compare, for example, the situation of the established 'professions' or even certain craftsmen groups
with that of unskilled, manual workers. However, whilst a great many
questions need to be asked about the determination of these differentials, the significance of the distinction between property income and
employment income remains.
   Nevertheless, inequality cannot be understood simply by reference
to these 'market' mechanisms. We refer here, of course, to the fact that
there emerged in Britain (and elsewhere), for the most part during and
immediately after the Second World War, a state which was committed
to the mitigation of the worst distributional consequences of the market
and, thereby, to effecting a lessening of inequality. What was involved
in this — to use Miliband's (1978) term — 'settlement of 1945' was,
firstly, a general acceptance of the principle that governments should

guarantee for all citizens, as of right, a minimum standard of living. This implied both protection of people against the consequences of certain contingencies in life – retirement in old age, sickness, 'involuntary' unemployment – and recognition of the entitlement of those who could demonstrate their *bona fide* need. Secondly, it involved undertaking to ensure some form of 'equality of access' to certain 'essential' goods, irrespective of ability to pay for them: hence, for example, all children were to be provided with the opportunity to fulfil their educational potential; adequate medical care was to be freely available; and, in a much more complex way, housing of an acceptable standard was to be the right of every household.

Just as fundamentally, however, the 'settlement of 1945' involved the acceptance of a much higher level of state intervention in economic life than had previously been the case. In brief, conditions of production were to be modified in such a way as to achieve both full employment and economic growth. The principal means of ensuring these goals were the familiar budgetary and fiscal instruments of Keynesian economic management: the control of 'total demand'. However, more direct intervention in production was also important: most obviously, the nationalisations carried out by the immediate post-war Labour Government, but also the local controls exerted through regional economic policy, the sponsorship of research and development, and so forth.

The point which is of immediate concern here is that these elements of the post-war state's role also have distributional consequences. Quite simply, distribution cannot be separated from economic production. Hence, the commitment to the maintenance of full employment should be interpreted against the background of the economic crisis of the 1930s. Whilst Keynesianism was clearly primarily aimed at ensuring high levels of economic activity and hence growth, this necessarily involved the avoidance of the severe inequalities and material poverty occasioned by economic recession. Similarly, regional aid and employment creation programmes, whatever their primary objectives, by altering the geographical balance of supply and demand for labour have inevitable consequences in terms of the distribution of income. Of course, the rationales for these sorts of policies have frequently been couched in terms of their effects on income distribution. Economic growth has likewise been closely connected with issues of social inequality. Thus, only in conditions of a thriving and expanding economy would the necessary surplus be available to finance, via the taxation system, the welfare provisions which we described earlier.

What we are saying here, then, is that there has been a considerable measure of consensus over this view of the proper role of government during the post-war period — at least, that is, until the crises of the 1970s (for one view of these, see Miliband, 1978). This consensus has unquestionably straddled the boundary between the two major political parties and was, of course, most clearly illustrated in the policies of so-called 'Butskellism'. In other words, we suggest that there has been widespread agreement that the development of the interventionist Welfare State has mitigated the consequences of the distributional principles characteristic of a capitalist economy.

Clearly, there can be little question that this is, in fact, the case. Although the precise effects of particular policies may be controversial, the impact of the system as a whole is undeniable. For example, no one could argue that the least well-off in contemporary Britain are not in more favourable circumstances than they would be without state intervention. Moreover, even the most reluctant are bound to conclude that 'public policy clearly does to some degree mitigate class inequality' (Westergaard, 1978, p.83). In other words, the state does constitute a source of provision which modifies the impact of 'market' mechanisms.[1]

However, there seem to us to be other consequences of the 'settlement of 1945', which, in conjunction with those which we have just sketched, have given rise to political tensions and instability. Clearly, the emergence of the Welfare State was in some sense premised upon a set of expectations as to the obligations of government, expectations which were relatively widely held amongst the citizens; the growth of state intervention was, to an extent at least, a response to popular aspirations. Moreover, we suggest that the actual commitment of successive governments to the principles embodied in the 'settlement of 1945' reinforced and strengthened these expectations. In other words, undertakings by the state to ensure full employment, to eradicate poverty, to provide equality of opportunity had the effect of consolidating the belief that governments were actually obligated to achieve these objectives.

Crucially, however, the state has actually been unable to fulfil these expectations. In spite of its real impact upon the structure of distributional inequality (to which we referred earlier), the state has fallen a long way short of discharging its commitments or, to put this another way, of satisfying the demands increasingly made upon it. Unemployment has remained a naggingly persistent feature of the life of many areas; economic growth has been, at best, only very sluggish; the welfare services have been a persistent object of controversy as a result of

their perceived inability to meet 'needs'. It is here that the origins of
political tensions and instability lie.

Therefore, we suggest that the political controversies over 'regionalism' and nationalism during the late 1960s and 1970s are attributable,
at least partly, to these failures of the state to fulfil commitments and,
thereby, to satisfy expectations. It is extremely instructive, for example,
that Butt Philip (1975) should demonstrate the close connection between
Plaid Cymru electoral successes in South Wales and the dislocation
(redundancies, unemployment, etc.) caused by the restructuring of the
region's traditional industries. Similarly, it is significant that much of the
debate over devolution in Wales was focused upon what the proposed
Assembly would (or would not) do to improve Wales's economic condition and to increase the efficiency of its welfare provision. Clearly,
similar points could be made about events in Scotland and, indeed, other
parts of non-metropolitan Britain during this period. None of this would
make any sense, however, were it not for the fact that the 'settlement
of 1945' prescribed for the state a role that was central to our economic
and social life. It is only against this background that demands for political and administrative solutions to these kinds of problem can be
understood.

Two further points should be made here: firstly, these 'failures' of
government were defined in this context as 'regional' issues; and,
secondly, there was an unusually vigorous political mobilisation around
this particular view of the problems, especially in the nations of Scotland
and Wales. It is the latter which is the distinguishing feature of the
1960s and 1970s (at least as far as twentieth-century history is concerned). Clearly, we are much more used to conflicts over questions such
as these being organised on some non-spatial basis. Most familiar, of
course, is the ritualised struggle between organised labour and capital,
mediated through the state. But we have also become accustomed to the
struggles for some measure of equality in employment and other key
markets of the ethnic minorities and in particular those distinguishable
by their skin colour. Whilst of special relevance here, perhaps, is the
political activity premised upon the so-called 'rediscovery of poverty'
(see, for example, Wedderburn, 1974): the discovery that in the midst
of the Welfare State, particular groups – the aged, the disabled, the sick,
the unemployed and the low paid – were acutely disadvantaged. As
Westergaard and Resler (1975) put it:

> Poverty – dismissed as an increasingly residual phenomenon in the
> 1950s – was rediscovered with a vengeance in the 1960s. It has

become part of the verbal stock in trade of politicians and commentators of nearly all shades of opinion; and the subject of a major
growth industry in social and economic research. (p.122-3)

Moreover, these alternative bases of political mobilisation parallel
alternative perspectives on the nature of the state's shortcomings. Hence,
these latter can be viewed as primarily a matter of inter-regional inequalities, or as a failure adequately to regulate the conflicting interests
of workers and capitalists, or as the disadvantages experienced by
particular population groups. For example, in terms of academic traditions, much of regional economics has been based on the first view;
labour relations experts have frequently adopted the second; whilst a
good proportion of the race relations and poverty 'industries' are based
upon the last view.

However, to conceive of social inequalities exclusively in this way is
to ignore the point made earlier that the state only modifies – and, of
course, only sets out to modify – the impact of the basic distributional
principles of capitalism. Even if governments had been wholly successful in achieving their stated aims, a considerable measure of inequality
would have been left over. The sorts of specific disadvantage identified
above are attributable not only to the 'failures' of the state, but also to
the basic structure of inequality which is the product of the mode of
economic organisation itself. As we have indicated, a basic distinction
can be drawn between classes in terms of the inequalities generated in
the distribution of income according to the principles of property
ownership and wage earning. However, we also noted earlier that superimposed upon this simple structure are a variety of within-class differentials, thus yielding a highly complex empirical pattern. In effect, the
consequence of the commitments implied in the 'settlement of 1945'
and, more particularly, the failure to fulfil them has been to focus
attention on certain of the particular circumstances which generate
especial difficulties for working-class people (i.e. retirement in old age,
sickness, regional unemployment, etc.). However, in doing so, attention
has been diverted from the general structure of inequality itself. Although
this argument does raise questions about the nature of the state, the
weakness of those political mobilisations which we described earlier is
precisely that they seek remedies only in political and administrative
reform and fail to see the much more general context. Westergaard and
Resler (1975) put the point well for the example of the assault upon
'poverty':

'Poverty' has been rediscovered . . . But to single out 'the poor' for special attention in practice runs the risk of emphasising the specific to the neglect of the general. The spotlight picks out the variety of particular circumstances – old age, sickness, large family size, single parenthood, unemployment, especially low pay – which push working class people under an arbitrarily defined poverty line. It leaves only dimly lit the wider structure of inequality, and the overall condition of dependence which exposes workers at large to the risk of 'poverty' in such circumstances. Remedies proposed tend to be correspondingly discrete, directed separately to each set of particular circumstances. (p.19)

In talking of 'poverty', then, we are highlighting a particular manifestation of the social inequality that is endemic to capitalism. The same could be said of the other specific phenomena to which we have referred. What emerges is that we need to grasp the nature of the general structure of inequality, which is rooted in the very characteristics of a capitalist economy. However, within this general structure there is a highly complex differentiation between groups defined by their particular circumstances; and here the state plays an especially significant role.

Class Inequality versus Regional Inequality?

For the purposes of this discussion, we shall focus upon only one issue which arises from this complex distributional structure: namely, the tension between class inequalities and regional inequalities. As we have seen, there are manifest inequalities between 'regions' (see also, for example, Taylor and Ayres, 1969; Coates and Rawstrom, 1971). In turn the relative disadvantages of certain 'regions' – attributed to 'failures' of the state to cope adequately – have provided the foundation for significant political activity during the recent past. To what extent, then, do these inequalities constitute fundamental divisions within British society?

Again, Westergaard and Resler (1975) deliver a characteristically forthright judgement:

common class situations produce similar – not identical – circumstances in life: in London much as in the provinces, in one region much as in another. And class for class, on a number of scores, geographical variations are probably less than they were. It is the

horizontal divisions of class, not the vertical divisions of region,
which are the crucial breaks in British society by criteria of welfare,
opportunity and influence. As when Disraeli first used the phrase,
the line between the 'two nations' divides privilege and power from
dependence throughout the country; not south from north, or metropolis from provinces. (p.356)

This seems to us to be a clear oversimplification. Crucially, it ignores the
point that the key processes of industrialisation and urbanisation
necessarily take place unevenly over geographical space. To put it
simply, it is a fact that the sorts of distinction to which we referred in
the opening paragraph of this chapter do exist. More formally, capital is
constantly seeking out the most profitable locations for its activities; as
the nature of those activities change — again under pressure to keep up
profitability — so these most profitable locations also change. Most
clearly, for example, as manufacturing production became less dependent upon coal power, so coalfield locations became less advantageous.
Therefore, there is a constantly shifting spatial pattern of economic
activity, with particular local economies being the product of both old
and new locational priorities (Massey, 1978; also Chapter 10 below).
    The point here is that this shifting spatial pattern of economic activity
produces, in effect, a locally differentiated class structure. Hence,
Gramsci (1977; quoted in Massey, 1978) describes Turin as 'the proletarian city, *par excellence* . . . precisely because of this powerfully
united character of the city's industry'. Would it be stretching things
too much to suggest that Industrial South Wales in, say, 1910 was the
'proletarian region' *par excellence?* Similarly, of course, there are
spatial variations in patterns of property ownership: for instance, land
holding in East Anglia is radically different from that in rural Wales
(compare Newby, Bell, Rose and Saunders, 1978 with Chapter 9, below).
In short, then, it is possible to talk in terms of local (or regional) configurations of classes. These, in turn, have distributional patterns predi-
cated upon them. In this way, we can conceive of 'poor' and 'wealthy'
regions.
    Moreover, the unevenness of economic development determines the
amount and type of employment that is available, again with clear
distributional consequences; compare, for example, South Wales during
the 1930s with the South East and Midlands of England. It may also
determine the prices at which workers are able to sell their labour,
although the growing role of nationally negotiated rates of pay has
lessened the significance of local demand here.

These effects of the spatial unevenness of economic activity cannot be separated from those of the parallel unevenness of urbanisation. There is clearly a close relationship between the economy of an area and its population density, pattern of settlement, housing provision, transportation network, etc. Hence, for example, the growth of British industry during the nineteenth century was matched by an equally massive movement of population and the consequent mushrooming of whole regions of urban development. Many of these regions have more recently been in economic decline; although – and this is significant – it has been much more difficult to 'balance' this decline in terms of population movement, etc. Other areas, of course, have an economic structure which has never required concentrations of population and associated urban development: indeed, this is so of much of the upland areas of Britain.

The critical point here is again that quite distinct distributional effects flow from this geographical unevenness. Quite simply, urbanisation generates a structure of differential access to a wide variety of scarce resources. Harvey (1973) puts the point well (see also Chapter 12, below):

inherent in social processes (of distribution) lies the question of spatial organisation. Externality effects are localised, so are job and housing opportunities, resource benefits, communication links, etc. Political power is partly areally based. Many of the hidden mechanisms for redistributing income come to fruition in the act of location. (p.86)

This is to say, then, that where we live has a significant impact upon, for example, the sort of housing available to us, the healthiness of our environment, our access to a wide range of service facilities. In short, location is a major determinant of total real income. This is not to suggest, of course, that these effects are independent of class inequalities in distribution; rather, the spatial differentiation between regions renders these class inequalities much more complex than they otherwise would be.

Finally, we should acknowledge the fact that the state exerts a widely differing impact upon different regions. Clearly this is the case in terms of its attempts to 'manage' the British economy. Although the effects of regional policies are a matter of some controversy (Keeble, 1976; Massey, 1979), no one would claim that they have actually achieved the 'balanced economic growth' at which they aimed (see, for example, Moore and Rhodes, 1976). In consequence of these persistent inter-regional differentials, the state's more general intervention via, for example, budgetary and fiscal measures have had divergent impacts upon different areas: for instance, a deflation means something quite different for regions of relatively high and low unemployment. Less obviously, there is a growing body of evidence that governmental provision of essential items of consumption – housing, education, health care, transport, etc. – is also far from evenly spread geographically (for example, Taylor and Ayres, 1969; Davies, 1968). In other words, people in different parts of the country have unequal access to facilities of this kind. Indeed, some commentators have suggested that these inequalities are systematically distributed according to an 'inverse care law': the most disadvantaged are accorded the least satisfactory services (Hart, 1971a; Duncan, 1974). Whether this is so or not, it remains the case that certain regions are 'poor' in these terms and others decidedly 'rich'.

Our conclusion, then, is a simple one. The unevenness of industrialisation and urbanisation generates a framework within which basic class inequalities are also unevenly expressed across space. A highly complex distribution of social inequality and poverty between both population groups and the regions in which they live is thereby generated. If we are to understand the conditions in which disadvantaged people actually find themselves, we need theories that will comprehend this complexity.

Alternative Perspectives: the Contribution of this Volume

The intention of this collection of essays is to contribute to the task of developing such theories. As will be clear to most readers, the preliminary analysis of the dimensions of social inequality and disadvantage which we have presented in this chapter is grounded in a particular perspective of British society. As Day's contribution to this volume makes explicit, a variety of alternatives are possible, although by no means equally satisfactory (see Chapter 12, below). Many would argue (including some of our contributors!) that we have been premature in giving the account that we have. However, we have begun the volume in this way not only because we ourselves find this perspective the most convincing, but also because it illustrates in a concrete fashion certain essential themes which, we believe, are indispensable to the sort of theory which we seek – themes which accordingly run through all of the various essays which follow.

Firstly, we have placed a prime emphasis upon the consequences in terms of distributional inequality of an economy which is essentially capitalist. In brief, it is an inevitable consequence of such a mode of economic organisation that some members of society are relatively disadvantaged. We have suggested that this disadvantage is best understood in terms of the fundamental division between classes; others, of course, have argued for different criteria of differentiation (hence, for example, an 'internal colony' model stresses the inequalities between ethnic groups: see Chapter 12). Nevertheless, understanding the capitalist economy remains integral to understanding inequality. This implies, of course, that state intervention to modify the distributional inequalities deriving from the 'market' has not changed the essential character of capitalism. Yet, our second major emphasis *has* been upon the activities of the state. In effect, our argument has been that, in spite of the extent of government intervention, it has not operated to rectify class inequalities in any thoroughgoing way – although this intervention has been significant in the political sphere. (A fuller account of our analysis of state intervention is given in Chapter 10; see also Chapters 9, 11 and 12.) Once again, it should be clear that contrasting views are possible: for example, advocacy of intervention in the economy remains a cornerstone of those analyses which are based ultimately in Keynesianism (see Chapters 2, 7, 12 below). However, an account of the state's activities remains a *sine qua non* of a viable theory of whatever kind. Thirdly, the geographical unevenness of industrialisation and urbanisation (as well as the impact of the state's activities) emerged as an essential element in our discussion of the real structure of social inequality and poverty. Our location of this unevenness in the changing requirements of capitalist production can be contrasted with theories of the 'development of underdevelopment' or 'core-periphery relations' (see Chapters 9 and 12). The necessity of providing some form of explanation is however, a common feature of all approaches. Admittedly, these three essential aspects of our desired theory are very general ones: even so, they provide a more satisfactory context for the analysis of social inequality and disadvantage than has been traditional in the literature.

In what follows, these themes are explored in a variety of ways, but in a single empirical context: that of Wales and its particular position within British society. The reasons for this empirical focus are both theoretical and contingent. As Nairn (1977) has put it: 'In the Welsh knot the usual forces of uneven development have been tied together unusually closely and graphically' (p.211). Quite simply, then, Wales provides an exceptionally good example through which to develop our theoretical understanding. It has been for some two hundred years a major locus of capitalist development. The growth of the coal and metal industries in the southern counties of Glamorganshire and Monmouthshire (and, although to a much less significant extent, in North East Wales) during the eighteenth and nineteenth centuries made Wales what has been described as 'a great secondary centre of the European industrial revolution'.

Certainly, by the final quarter of the last century, Industrial South Wales had become a major urban conglomeration: a complex system of industrial towns and villages in the coalfield, closely interacting with the more substantial settlements of the coast. The disastrous decline of the traditional industries during the middle decades of this century has been balanced to a significant extent by the emergence – particularly during the 1960s and 1970s – of new industries in the secondary and tertiary sectors, predominantly, though by no means exclusively, in South Wales. In brief, the economy in Wales has reflected very noticeably the ebb and flow of the wider economic tide.

Clearly, these fundamental economic changes have also given rise to shifting patterns of social inequality and disadvantage. However, these latter shifts are both highly complex and, it must be admitted, poorly understood. Certainly, a number of commentators have attempted to delineate the class consequences of the changing nature of Wales's specific insertion into the British (and, indeed, world) economy. Hence, for example, Hobsbawm (1968) has suggested that the critical consequence of the opening up of the coal industry in Wales was the creation of an urban/industrial proletariat in the south, marked off from the peasantry of the rural areas: the former, he suggests, were dominated by a tiny group of English or at least Anglicised entrepreneurs; the latter by a similarly orientated, land-owning gentry. More recently, Lovering (1978a) has argued that, as a result of the large-scale penetration of Wales by multi-national and multi-regional firms which have created large numbers of semi- and unskilled jobs in their Welsh establishments, it is possible to speak in terms of a changing pattern of 'marginalisation' within the class structure of Wales (see also Chapters 8, 9 and 10 below). Again, Rees and Lambert (1979) have talked in terms of the 'embourgeoisement' of particular areas, in consequence of the restructuring of the economy in South Wales during the post-war period. These arguments are suggestive, but no more than that. Certainly, they give no more than hints at the general framework within which a more precise analysis of the anatomy of inequality and deprivation can be situated.

In what follows, we hope that we succeed in laying some of the founda-
tions of this latter task.

Much clearer has been the shifting pattern of spatial inequality,
particularly as this is measured in the conventional terms of regional
economics (the simple availability of appropriate data is not insignifi-
cant here). Hence, it is possible to trace with a degree of accuracy
Wales's changing situation *vis-à-vis* other parts of Britain in respect of
unemployment, average weekly earnings, net migration and so forth
(see, for example, Keeble, 1976). As Day remarks (Chapter 12, below),
what emerges from such an analysis is a pretty unequivocal picture of
Wales as a 'problem region'; although it is by no means clear that this
'problem region' status is attributable to an unchanging set of underlying causes.

Equally significant are the major inequalities that exist between the
different areas within Wales. This is a theme which recurs at many
points in the current volume and can be traced historically to precisely
the bifurcation in Welsh society which, as we have seen, Hobsbawm
(1968) attributes to the Industrial Revolution (see also Lovering, 1978a).
Hence, important distinctions are to be drawn between the relative
prosperity of Industrial South Wales and the poverty of the rural
hinterland of 'inner Wales'. Moreover, even these categories would
appear to require further elaboration in order to capture the full complexity of distributional inequality in Wales (see, for example, Chapters
9 and 10, below).

It is against this multifaceted background that state policies purport-
ing to ameliorate social inequalities must be judged. Given the conditions which we have outlined, it is not surprising that state intervention
should be of particular significance in Wales. The state is not only a
major employer — there is also a large proportion of individuals and
families dependent upon the state for their means of livelihood. Hence,
Lovering (1978a) suggests that more is spent by the state in Wales than
is raised in taxes and other revenues; he gives figures for 1972 as follows
— Welsh Gross Domestic Product 838 units; Gross Domestic Expenditure 936 units. However, what are much less clear are the precise
effects of this extensive state intervention, especially in the light of the
circumstances which we outlined earlier. Again, in what follows, we
can only hope to begin the task of tracing out these effects.

However, the state can be said to have performed one function in
Wales quite unambiguously. In face of manifold internal divisions, the
state has contributed in a major way to the idea of Wales as a coherent
entity. The fact that the state has treated Wales as an administrative unit

in many aspects of policy making not only reflects Wales's perceived identity in political and ideological terms, but also contributes to and strengthens that identity. In short, it contributes to what we could term Welsh nationalism – with a small 'n'; the state has made possible the political debate which has been one of the central themes of this chapter.

This of course, brings us to the contingent reason for our empirical focus on Wales. In spite of the significance of the recent debates over 'regionalist' reform, it seems to us that they were characterised by a remarkable deficiency of empirical analysis, as well as an almost total absence of theoretical understanding. Obviously, we are not so naive as to believe that research and analysis are translated in some automatic way into political initiative. However, it is possible that such research and analysis will set limits upon legitimate political action. It is hoped that this collection of essays will contribute towards the setting of these limits.

The Structure of the Volume

As we have tried to emphasise, the purpose of this volume is exploratory: if it lays a foundation for further research, then we shall have succeeded in fulfilling our intentions. Accordingly, the essays which follow are divided between two parts, each of which is intended to fulfil a rather different function. Part One comprises a collection of review essays: they set out to do no more than evaluate the contemporary situation in Wales, both empirically and theoretically, and to pose some of the questions which need to be addressed in future work. Each chapter focuses upon what may be considered a fundamental dimension of social inequality, beginning with the distribution of income and wealth generated by the specific context of the economy in Wales and proceeding with analyses of key sectors of the state's intervention – housing provision, education, health care and the currently fashionable area of 'urban deprivation'. In this way, then, we hope to give an answer (albeit a partial one) to the question: what is the nature of social inequality and poverty in Wales?

In Part Two, the focus shifts from review to the development of particular approaches to the explanation of social disadvantage. Hence, Chapter 7 is firmly rooted in what could be called 'radical Keynesianism': the problems of low pay and unemployment are the result of inadequate government policy; the support of the trade union movement is the way to rectify the situation. The theory of 'segmented labour markets', presented in Chapter 8, leads to a rather greater scepticism. The poor are poor because of the very structure of employment opportunities which they face — a structure, furthermore, which is highly functional to capitalism. Conventional, Keynesian regional policy has paid scant attention to these problems. Chapter 9 shifts the empirical focus to rural Wales. Rejecting the emphasis upon 'culture' as an explanation of the disadvantages experienced by such areas which is characteristic of 'diffusionist' theory, an analysis is presented which stresses the 'dependency' of rural Wales upon an externally controlled capital. The resulting 'enclaves' of relative prosperity are contrasted with the progressive 'marginalisation' (i.e. impoverishment) of other groups in the rural population. Similar themes are pursued in Chapter 10, albeit in the very different empirical context of Industrial South Wales. However, here basic questions are raised about the role of the state in actually generating new patterns of inequality and poverty. This line of analysis is pursued more explicitly in Chapter 10. What is emphasised, in a difficult argument, is the necessity of a coherent theory of the state in which to root any analysis of the effects of state intervention on inequality. Certainly, the analysis of urban development policies in Cardiff is such as to undermine any simplistic notions of the state operating in the interests of the 'community as a whole'. Throughout these essays, of course, the attempt is made to understand social inequalities in the specific, 'regional' context of Wales (the combination, in our terms, of class and regional inequalities). This is made explicit in Chapter 12, which draws together the preceding themes, whilst emphasising the changes in the nature of poverty in Wales that have occurred as the economic fabric has itself reorganised. In short, then, we hope that the essays in Part Two will begin to answer the question: in what way can we best understand the nature of social inequality and poverty in Wales?

Concluding Remarks

In preparing this collection of essays, we have been struck more forcibly than previously by how little is known about the structure of Welsh society. In part, this is attributable to the simple absence of research and analysis by social scientists in Wales: there is a clear sense in which the theorisation of 'things Welsh' is not highly rewarded within the social scientific community at large. Moreover, even where work has been carried out, it tends to have framed research problems in highly particular and traditional ways (see Day, 1979; also Chapters 10, 11 and 12, below). It is also remarkable that a very high proportion of the analysis (and especially economic analysis) conducted on Wales has been sponsored directly by departments of government. These comments are especially significant in light of the general arguments that have been made to the effect that the research process is organised in such a way as to generate only certain kinds of 'sanctioned' knowledge (see, for example, Moore, 1978).

Certainly, it seems to us that this research process has in fact operated in a way that makes it possible to identify a further dimension of Wales's poverty: a 'poverty of knowledge'. In suggesting new perspectives from which to view Welsh society, we hope that this collection of essays will contribute to the eradication of at least this dimension of poverty. Who knows — others may follow in consequence.

Note

1. As Westergaard (1978) points out, this is not to say that the distributional principles of a capitalist economy are thereby undermined.

2 INCOME AND WEALTH IN WALES[1]

Paul Wilding

All those with scholarly pretensions and professional reputations to safeguard are bound to begin any discussion of income and wealth by bewailing the limited nature of the available statistics. For those concerned with the national scene in the United Kingdom, such bewailings are now part of an academic ritual, but have much less validity than they had only a few years ago. The Reports of the Royal Commission, for example, and the work it has generated both directly and indirectly, have provided a rich quarry of information which has yet to be fully absorbed in the secondary writings (Royal Commission on the Distribution of Income and Wealth, 1975). For those concerned, however, with the regional distribution of wealth and income the information available is still limited.

The Royal Commission genuflects at ritual intervals in the direction of gathering more and better regional data (Royal Commission on the Distribution of Income and Wealth, 1978, Chapter 2) but for those concerned with the regional issue the fare provided by the Commission is extremely frugal and it is also distributed inequitably. In the Commission's first report, for example, separate figures for the distribution of wealth are supplied for Scotland, but Wales has to suffer the indignity of being lumped with England. Other work has been done on the distribution of wealth in Scotland and in Northern Ireland but very little has been done on Wales, so this conflating of the English and Welsh data is particularly unfortunate.

The absence of the data he would like to have is, of course, a fact of life for the social scientist and there is little point in labouring the problem. Equally, there is little point in labouring the rather dubious nature of some of the information which one has to use when sketching the pattern of distribution of income and wealth in a small country such as Wales. The data are to be regarded as suggestive rather than definitive and the reader should bear this in mind.

This chapter falls into five sections. It begins with a discussion of certain relevant features of the Welsh economy. It then looks in turn at the pattern of distribution of the three crucial resources of earnings, income and wealth. It concludes with a few brief reflections on why things are as they seem to be.

The Welsh Economy

Any discussion of income and wealth in Wales must start from an
examination of certain aspects of the Welsh economy. Perhaps the key
fact from which to begin is the level of the Gross Domestic Product
(GDP) in Wales per head of population. In 1976 it was £1,712 — just
89 per cent of the United Kingdom average. Of the regions of the
United Kingdom only Northern Ireland has a lower figure. If we look at
the figures for the last ten years, then GDP in Wales is consistently
between 83 per cent and 89 per cent of the average for the United
Kingdom. Till the late 1960s the Northern region was Wales's rival for
the position at the bottom of the United Kingdom league table, but
since the early 1970s the North has pulled ahead. Between 1971 and
1975, on the other hand, Wales's performance was undistinguished with
GDP falling fractionally, though less than in several other regions. In
1975-76 GDP per head in Wales grew more rapidly than in any other
region except Northern Ireland — which accounts for the figure of 89
per cent of the United Kingdom average — a higher figure than at any
time in the last ten years. In 1977, however, GDP in Wales fell by 1.5
per cent compared with a slight increase in the United Kingdom in the
same period (Central Statistical Office, 1978a).

In addition to the low level of GDP *per capita,* two other characteristics distinguish the economic situation in Wales from the situation in
England or the United Kingdom. The first is lower rates of economic
activity. The second is higher rates of unemployment. Put more simply,
in the post-war years the Welsh economy has been able to provide jobs
for a smaller proportion of the population than has been the situation in
England or in the United Kingdom generally.

In 1975 there were 100,000 fewer men in employment in Wales than
there were ten years earlier — a fall of some 13 per cent. Fifty thousand
jobs disappeared from the coal industry as a result of pit closures and
'rationalisations'. Employment in agriculture fell by 30 per cent. These
economic trends underlie the fundamental problem of low rates of
economic activity. Rates of male economic activity declined in the
1960s in both Wales and Britain — though the rate of decline in Wales
was greater than in Britain. The fall in employment in Wales was also
sharper than the 10 per cent fall which was the average in the other less
prosperous, 'assisted' regions of the United Kingdom. On the other
hand, female activity rates increased more rapidly in Wales though still
remaining substantially below the general rate for Britain in 1971.[2]

This has continued to be the trend since 1971. Male employment

had declined by 1975 to 87 per cent of the 1965 level compared with
the United Kingdom figure of 91 per cent. By 1976 the provisional
figure for the male economic activity rate had dropped to 76.9 per cent.
On the other hand, female employment has increased more rapidly in
Wales in the last five years than in the United Kingdom generally (Central Statistical Office, 1977, T.18) and by 1976 the economic activity
rate for women had risen to 39.3 per cent (Parliamentary Debates,
1976/7b). So more households in Wales may now have the benefit of a
second income. Much of the increase in female employment has, however, been in part-time employment.

In an economy where work is scarce, certain groups become particularly vulnerable to rejection by the labour market. Up to the age of
forty there is little difference between male economic activity rates in
Wales and in Britain. Thereafter the divergence increases until there is
an 8 per cent difference in activity rates in the last years before retirement. Table 2.1 shows this trend very clearly.

Table 2.1: Age-specific Activity Rates (Male), 1971 (per cent)

	40-44	45-49	50-54	55-59	60-64
Wales	98.0	97.1	95.5	91.9	78.7
Britain	98.3	98.0	97.2	95.3	86.6

Source: Welsh Office, *Welsh Economic Trends*, no.4 (HMSO, Cardiff, 1977),
Table 14.

Whether the problem is primarily the higher rates of sickness and disability in Wales, or whether it is the more general problem that the
skills of older workers become outdated and so expendable remains unclear.

The same trend and pattern is visible in female activity rates. For
women between the ages of 15 and 44 there is a consistent difference
between Wales and Britain of 6.7 per cent in activity rates. This jumps
to 10 per cent for the age groups 45-49, to 11.5 per cent for the years
between 50 and 54 and to 12.5 per cent between ages 55 and 59. This
difference raises the same questions as the male differences, though
women in Wales have not historically been employed in particularly
strenuous and disabling types of employment.

One important and obvious index of the lower economic activity
rates in Wales is the high rate of unemployment which has persisted in

Wales throughout the post-war years.[3] In the last twenty years unemployment in Wales has remained considerably above the rate in
Britain. The worst year relatively for Wales was 1966 with unemployment of 193 per cent of the British figure, the best 1972 when the
Welsh figure dropped to 127 per cent of the British rate. Since high
unemployment returned Phoenix-like from the ashes of Keynesian
economic management in the 1970s, the Welsh ratio has improved, but
the reason is simply that unemployment is higher in the rest of Britain,
not that it is lower in Wales.

Only the Northern region has as black a record for unemployment
as has Wales. Scotland has frequently been worse hit; Northern Ireland
has always been worse. The latest figures for June 1978 show a season-
ally adjusted unemployment rate for the United Kingdom of 5.7 per
cent. At the same date unemployment was running at 8 per cent in the
Northern region, 7.9 per cent in Wales, 7.6 per cent in Scotland and 11
per cent in Northern Ireland. Of the England regions only the North has
a higher unemployment rate than Wales (Department of Employment,
1978b).

What matters to the worker seeking the opportunity to earn his
living is not national or even regional unemployment figures or wage
rates but the situation in the actual area where he is seeking work. If we
look at the figures for employment offices and travel to work areas
then we see that many areas in Wales have unemployment rates well
over double the regional figure. In March 1977, for example, Tenby had
a male unemployment rate of 26.5 per cent, Cardigan of 22.4 per cent,
Tywyn of 20.6 per cent and Rhyl of 19.9 per cent (Welsh Office, 1977b,
Appendix V). These figures also illustrate a more general point — that
Wales is in some measure a dual economy: a high activity, high employment, high wage economy in the industrial south and north-east and a
low activity, high unemployment, low wage economy in the rural heart-
lands of West, Central and Northern Wales.

What is clear from this discussion of economic activity rates and
unemployment is that a smaller proportion of the Welsh population is
at work, and, as long as earnings from employment constitute the
major element in personal incomes, then the range and extent of
employment opportunities form the key factor in the standard of living
of individuals and of a region. A smaller proportion of earners means two
things. It means, firstly, that earnings have to be shared among a larger
number of dependants. Secondly, it means a greater dependence on
social security benefits which, in comparison with the standard of living
of the rest of the community, means relative poverty. On average, for

example, the unemployed lose 25 per cent of their net weekly income
as a result of being unemployed (Layard *et al.*, 1978, p.79). In June
1978 86,500 people in Wales were in this position.

Why is the Welsh economy characterised by the three elements we
have been considering — low Gross Domestic Product, low rates of
economic activity and higher than average unemployment? Is it that
successive governments have failed to recognise the problems of Wales?
Or is it that, although they have recognised the problems, they have
failed to act effectively to solve them?

Let us be clear first of all that there has been no shortage of activity.
In the last ten years there have been a quite bewildering variety of
agencies and policies pursuing the aim of regional development. Most
recently there has been the rich milch cow of the EEC which by the end
of 1976 had made grants and loans to Wales of well over £210m (Welsh
Office, 1977b, p.47).

Whether Wales has had a 'fair' share of regional aid from the United
Kingdom government is an almost unanswerable question. Moore and
Rhodes (1975) think Wales has done moderately well and the annual
figures for the expenditure of monies on various types and categories of
regional aid generally support this view (Welsh Office, 1977b, T.63).

What is quite clear, however, is that regional policies have come nowhere near solving the central problem of the Welsh economy. If Moore
and Rhodes are right in their calculation that 70,000-80,000 jobs were
created by regional policies between 1960 and 1972 (and such calcula-
tions are, of course, subject to a great many questions and assumptions),
then that is no small achievement, but with the need for new jobs estimated at 200,000-250,000 the outcome remains failure.

While there has been considerable activity in the area of regional
policy there has been no attempt at all in recent years to produce a
regional economic plan for Wales. In June 1976 Dafydd Wigley asked
the Secretary of State for Wales if he would draw up, publish and execute an economic development plan for Wales aimed at reducing unemployment and outward emigration, raising economic activity rates
and personal incomes and providing an economic infrastructure of roads
and services that would facilitate the development of the Welsh economy.
The reply he received was a blunt negative and a statement that 'The
government's economic, regional and related policies, which are well
known, are all aimed at achieving the objectives referred to by the Hon.
Member' (Parliamentary Debates, 1975/6). The following month the
Town and Country Planning Association made a vigorous plea for 'a
sensible regional plan' and pointed out that 'the data base of the 1967

White Paper *(Wales: The Way Ahead)* is now over ten years old . . .
there is no coherent over-view or regional strategy to which decision
making can relate their policies' (Town and Country Planning Association, 1976). Wales still waits for such a plan and in spite of regular
questions in Parliament, central government refuses to commit itself to
such strategy making. Until such a plan is worked out there will continue
to be action but little or no strategy — scarcely the best recipe for
success.

Earnings[4]

Table 2.2 sets out the bare bones of a comparison between earnings in
Wales and earnings in Great Britain. Average earnings for all full-time

Table 2.2: Average Gross Weekly Earnings of Full-time Adult Workers
in Wales as a Percentage of the Average for Great Britain, 1973-77

	Men		
	Manual	Non-manual	All
1973	101.5	93.5	96.9
1974	100.2	95.4	96.9
1975	100.4	94.4	97.0
1976	100.4	95.5	97.2
1977	101.0	94.9	97.3
	Women		
	Manual	Non-manual	All
1973	95.4	98.0	97.0
1974	95.8	95.5	95.5
1975	97.5	95.6	95.8
1976	101.0	98.2	98.5
1977	99.0	99.1	98.4

Sources: Welsh Office, *Welsh Economic Trends*, no.4 (HMSO, Cardiff, 1977),
Table 37; Department of Employment, *New Earnings Survey*, (HMSO, London,
1977), Pt.E.

male workers in Wales in April 1977 were just over £2 per week lower
than the average for Great Britain — 97.3 per cent of the British level.
A glance at Table 2.2 shows that this ratio has remained steady over the
last five years. If we compare the situation in Wales with the situation

in other regions of the United Kingdom, then three English regions have
higher average male earnings and five have lower.

For male manual workers the average in Wales exceeds the average
for Britain, by rather less than a pound per week – £72.2 in Wales, £71.5
in Britain. This again has been a consistent pattern over the last five
years. In only two English regions do full-time male manual workers
have higher average earnings than in Wales – the Northern region and
the South East. This high average in Wales is the product of the traditionally high-wage, capital-intensive, male-intensive industries of Industrial South Wales. As we shall see later, however, this average figure, as
with so many averages, conceals quite striking differences between
different areas within Wales.

Non-manual workers do less well in Wales, earning an average of just
under £4 per week less than the British average. In spite of this gap only
three English regions, the North, the North West and the South East,
have a higher average than Wales. If the South East were excluded from
the calculation Wales would be only slightly below the average for the
other English regions. What Wales lacks, it seems, are significant numbers
of very high earners. In England 10 per cent of male non-manual
workers earned more than £134 per week in April 1977; in Wales the
equivalent figure for the top 10 per cent of earners was £10 per week
less.

On the whole it is better to be a woman working in Wales than to be
a man. Earnings for manual, non-manual and all full-time women
workers in 1977 were all slightly below the average levels in Britain but
the differences were only slight and smaller than those for male workers.
What is interesting, too, is that in recent years women's earnings have
been rising more rapidly in Wales than in Britain generally (Welsh Office,
1977b,T.44).

In 1976 average earnings for women manual workers in Wales
exceeded the average for Britain for the first time for many years, but
in 1977 the figure dropped just below the British average. Yet Wales
remains high up in the English regions' pecking order. While earnings
levels for non-manual workers are relatively lower for men, non-manual
female workers in Wales do relatively well. Only the South East region
has a higher average.

If we leave the magic of averages and look instead at the distribution
of earnings – the percentage of different groups of workers earning more
or less than particular amounts – and compare the Welsh situation with
the situation in Britain, England or the English regions, then nothing
very striking can be wrested from the statistics. The distribution of

earnings is very similar to the general situation in Britain. Wales tends to have a slightly larger proportion of workers in the lower bands of earnings and a slightly smaller proportion in the higher bands but the differences are small. There is in Wales, it seems, no particular problem of very low earnings comparable to the problem of men in East Anglia or the South West or women in East Anglia, the East Midlands or Yorkshire and Humberside. The situation in Wales compares much more favourably with the general position in Britain than does the situation in some of the more disadvantaged English regions. This is not to say that there is no problem of low pay in Wales but that it is roughly similar to the general problem in Britain.[5]

As was pointed out above, what we see in Wales is a dual economy. In industrial Wales in 1976 — that is in Gwent, South, Mid and West Glamorgan and Clwyd East — average gross weekly earnings for men were 99 per cent of the British average; in the rest of Wales — Dyfed, Powys, Gwynedd and Clwyd West — they were 89 per cent of the British figure (Welsh Office, 1977b, T.42).

Given the small numbers involved in the *New Earnings Survey*, and the sampling problems in the less populated parts of Wales, figures for individual counties have to be treated with caution but at the very least they are pointers to considerable inequalities. In April 1977, when average earnings for full-time male manual workers in Wales were £72 per week, the range in the Welsh counties was from £79 in Clwyd East to £63 in Dyfed. Whereas nearly 75 per cent of such workers in Dyfed earned under £70 per week, in Clwyd East the proportion was only 40 per cent.

If we look at the earnings of all full-time male workers in Wales, the disparities are just as striking, with Dyfed and Clwyd East at the bottom and top of the prosperity ladder with a difference of £12 per week per worker in their averages.

How then can we sum up the available information on levels of earnings in Wales? In general average earnings are slightly lower than the British average but not strikingly so. The only group with significantly lower earnings consists of male non-manual workers. If we look at the distribution of earnings rather than concentrating on averages, again the Welsh figures are close to the general British picture. Figures for Wales do, however, conceal sharp disparities between areas. Differences in earning and employment opportunities between industrial and rural Wales are striking.

While levels of average earnings and the distribution of earnings are important pointers to the standard of living of a region, they are not the whole story. The key factor is not earnings but incomes. Levels of earnings on their own tell nothing about the resources coming into particular households, nor do they indicate how many people are dependent upon them. So the next stage of our investigation of income and wealth in Wales must be to move on from earnings to look at incomes.

Income

A study of the pattern of earnings in Wales suggests no particular problem of deprivation relative to earnings levels in Britain. A study of incomes, on the other hand, shows that Wales is an area of very considerable deprivation relative to England, the United Kingdom or any of the English regions.

This deprivation emerges clearly and sharply from a number of indices. If we look at a rather crude index such as average weekly household income, then in 1975 and 1976 only Northern Ireland of the regions of the United Kingdom had a lower average household income than Wales. The average for the United Kingdom was £77.59. The average for Wales was £71.39 − significantly lower than for any English region (Central Statistical Office, 1977, T.13.1).

The situation is in fact rather worse than it immediately sounds because average household size in Wales is larger than the United Kingdom average. So a smaller household income has to be divided up among more people. The predictable result is that average weekly household income per person in Wales in 1975 and 1976 was nearly £2 per week below the level of the poorest English region and some £3.50 per week below the United Kingdom average. Only Northern Ireland − as far behind Wales as Wales is behind the United Kingdom − had a lower *per capita* household income than Wales (Central Statistical Office, 1977, T.13.2).

On the other hand, if we look more closely at the distribution of household income and examine the percentage of households in different income bands, Wales does not, on the basis of these figures, stand out as a region with a large proportion of households with strikingly low incomes − i.e. below £20 or £30 per week. The fact seems to be that average household incomes in Wales are low. Although without a large proportion of households with very low incomes, only Northern Ireland has a larger proportion of households with incomes below the average for the United Kingdom.

The data we have used so far on household and *per capita* incomes

are drawn largely from the *Family Expenditure Surveys*. Given the un-
reliability of that source for regional purposes it is useful to check its
findings against data on income from other sources. Data from the
Central Statistical Office's *Regional Statistics* help to substantiate the
picture sketched above. If we look at personal incomes per head of population in 1975 then such incomes were again lower in Wales than in any
other part of the United Kingdom except for Northern Ireland. The
English region returning the lowest figure was East Anglia with just
under 93 per cent of the average — 5 per cent more than Wales. The
South East, in contrast, had personal incomes averaging 113 per cent of
the United Kingdom figure (Central Statistical Office, 1977, T.15.8).

Figures for personal disposable income (that is, personal income
minus taxes on income, national insurance contributions, transfers
abroad and taxes paid abroad) show the same picture. Wales has improved its relative position just slightly and incomes have struggled up
to just under 90 per cent of the United Kingdom figure but it remains
securely at the bottom of the regional league table apart from long-
suffering Northern Ireland (Central Statistical Office, 1977, T.15.8 and
15.9). In the early 1970s the Northern region had the dubious honour
of occupying the position which Wales now occupies. In 1974, however, Wales dropped below the North and for the first time for some
years personal disposable incomes in Wales fell below 90 per cent of the
United Kingdom average. If we compare the position in Wales with
figures of personal disposable incomes in the 'assisted regions', those
regions granted various forms of special regional assistance, of which
Wales is one, then incomes in Wales are some 5 per cent below the
average for these other disadvantaged areas (Welsh Office, 1977b,p.6).

The *Inland Revenue Survey* of taxable incomes is helpful on two
further aspects of income distribution in Wales. Firstly, it shows the
very large differences between the Welsh counties in 1974/75 with a
range of average income from £971 per head in South Glamorgan to
£784 in Gwynedd, £819 in Dyfed and £841 in Powys (Parliamentary
Debates, 1976/7a)[6]. Secondly, it helps to confirm the small number of
large or very large incomes in Wales. Where income from employment
was the principal source of income, just over 3 per cent of tax cases in
Wales had incomes of £4,000 per annum or more, in comparison with
just over 5 per cent in England and just under 5 per cent in Scotland
(Central Statistical Office, 1978b,T.89). Another suggestive index is to
examine the contribution which incomes of £6,000 per annum or more
make to total net income. In Wales they made up 4.7 per cent of total
income compared to 7.3 per cent in the United Kingdom and 7.7 per

cent in England. Only the Northern region produced a lower figure —
4.4 per cent. If we look at profits and professional earnings taxed under
schedule D, then in Wales earnings of this kind of £8,000 a year or more
made up 16.8 per cent of the total, the lowest proportion in any region
of the United Kingdom, the average being 25.4 per cent with only one
region — Yorkshire and Humberside — falling below 20 per cent (Central
Statistical Office, 1978b,T.65-77). The thrust of the evidence is plain —
Wales is short of people with large incomes.

Why are family and individual incomes in Wales so far below those
in the rest of Britain? We can begin to answer this question if we compare the sources of household incomes (per head) in Wales and the
United Kingdom. In 1974/75 *per capita* household income was over 12
per cent below the United Kingdom average. Average income *per capita*
from wages and salaries was some 15 per cent lower than in the United
Kingdom, whereas income from social security benefits was more than
12 per cent higher. Investment income, although relatively small in
amount, was some 20 per cent below the national average (Welsh Office,
1977b,p.36). The two most significant disparities are the contributions
from wages and salaries and from the social security system. The figures
for *per capita* income from wages and salaries illustrate yet again the
lower economic activity rates in Wales. *Per capita* incomes from earnings are lower for the simple reason that earnings have to be divided
between more people because fewer people are earning.

The other factor which distinguishes incomes in Wales — the greater
contribution of social security benefits — is an important reason for
relatively low average incomes. Given the way in which we use the level
of basic social security benefits as a yardstick of poverty, it also helps
explain the extent of poverty in Wales.

Why is there greater dependence on social security benefits in Wales?
Table 2.3 sets out the facts. Over-all expenditure per head on social
security is 16 per cent higher in Wales than in the United Kingdom, 18
per cent higher than in England, 13 per cent higher than in Scotland,
8 per cent higher even than in Northern Ireland. It is unambiguously
higher than in any English region. On most important benefits *per
capita* expenditure in Wales is higher, on some it is strikingly, even
disturbingly, higher.

Per capita expenditure on supplementary benefit in Wales is exceeded in two English regions, the North and the North West, and in
Scotland and Northern Ireland. In expenditure on unemployment
benefit the same two English regions are ahead of Wales. Expenditure
on family income supplement is, however, strikingly higher in Wales

Table 2.3: Estimated Expenditure Per Head on Certain Social Security Benefits in 1974/75 in Certain Regions of the UK (UK = 100)

	Suppl. benefit	Unemploy. benefit	Family income suppl.	Attend. allowance	Sickness and invalidity benefit	Disabl. benefit	Injury benefit	Total
Wales	115.0	122.5	145.0	184.5	171.2	196.9	169.1	116.1
England	95.7	93.3	86.1	94.9	89.0	94.4	93.7	98.4
North	126.1	167.0	127.7	108.4	143.3	200.2	198.7	111.6
Yorkshire and Humberside	103.1	—	81.6	86.6	122.6	127.9	158.7	103.4
North West	123.6	129.8	121.3	115.8	125.1	126.7	117.9	108.7
South East	88.5	67.0	70.7	85.0	62.3	61.5	55.0	93.4
Scotland	117.8	116.3	76.6	65.0	138.1	104.1	119.2	103.4
Northern Ireland	142.2	207.2	516.7	219.2	170.9	81.0	100.5	108.4

Source: Central Statistical Office, *Regional Statistics*, no.13 (HMSO, London, 1977), Table 4.2.

than in any region except Northern Ireland.

Per capita expenditure on attendance allowances in Wales is less than in Northern Ireland but 70 per cent more than in any English region. No English region approaches the figure for expenditure on sickness and invalidity benefit in Wales. Northern Ireland is only just behind Wales but the next English region is 30 per cent below the Welsh figure. In 1974/75 *per capita* expenditure on disablement benefit was greater in the Northern region than in Wales – for the first time for some years. The North, too, was well ahead on expenditure on injury benefit.

The extra expenditure on social security in Wales is in part a product of the country's industrial structure and history. It is a comment on the physically destructive nature of the industries which have dominated, and continue to dominate, the Welsh economy. The general shortage of employment opportunities, particularly for older workers and in lighter work, may also be a factor in the higher expenditure on sickness and invalidity benefit (Wilding, 1977, p.19). What is quite clear, though the reasons for it are not, is that the average male worker in Wales has twice as many days off work per year because of illness or incapacity as his counterpart in England. In no other region of the United Kingdom does the number of days of certified incapacity for work approach the Welsh total (Central Statistical Office, 1977, T.4.5).

While the reasons for the higher *per capita* expenditure on social security in Wales – £30 per head more than in the United Kingdom, £33 per head more than in England, £25 per head more than in Scotland in 1974/75 – remain obscure, the meaning of such higher expenditure is all too plain. It means lower individual and household incomes because whatever the media and the myth makers may believe – or wish other people to believe – the levels of social security benefit rarely equal the level of earnings of even the lowest-paid members of society.

While earnings in Wales are not very different from the national average, incomes in Wales are significantly lower. Wales emerges from the jungle of statistics as a region distinguished by a level of *per capita* incomes strikingly below the average for the United Kingdom or any English region.

Wealth

It is in relation to an examination of the distribution of wealth in Wales that information is particularly short. Apart from the study by Revell and Tomkins (1974) little or no work seems to have been done and at the moment, as we have seen, it does not seem as if the situation will be very different when the Royal Commission on the Distribution of Income and Wealth has finished its labours.

Revell and Tomkins estimate that in 1970 Wales had personal wealth per head of 72 per cent of the figure for the United Kingdom (Revell and Tomkins, 1974, p.35). With just under 5 per cent of the adult population of the United Kingdom, Wales has 4 per cent of the United Kingdom's physical assets, 3.4 per cent of its financial assets and 3.6 per cent of all assets (Revell and Tomkins, 1974, pp.33-4).

There are various ways of investigating the wealth of a region or a country, all of them beset by methodological difficulties of varying enormity. One approach is to look at investment income as an index of one particular kind of wealth. In 1974/75 investment income in Wales amounted to 5 per cent of total net income compared with 6 per cent in the United Kingdom and 6.2 per cent in England. If we look at investment income per head of population, then, of the English regions, only the Northern region (£39) has a lower figure than Wales (£44). With a United Kingdom average of £62 and an English average of £65 — and a figure for the South West region of £89 — the evidence clearly shows that Wales has less of the capital which generates investment income (Central Statistical Office, 1978b,T.65-77).

Revell and Tomkins also try to approach the distribution of wealth in Wales through an examination of the number and value of dutiable estates in Wales and Great Britain in 1966/67 and 1967/68. The estate multiplier method — which uses the estates of people who die during a given year as a representative sample of the wealth of the living — is widely used as a method of estimating the distribution of personal wealth but is not without its problems (Royal Commission on the Distribution of Income and Wealth, 1977, Appendix C). What Revell and Tomkins found was that, firstly, a smaller proportion of the population in Wales have estates large enough to be liable for estate duty. Secondly, they found that, when they examined the size of dutiable estates, Wales was producing a smaller proportion of estates of substantial size than was Great Britain generally (1974, pp.18-19).

Personal wealth is also less concentrated in Wales than in Britain. Whereas Revell and Tomkins calculate that in 1966 5 per cent of the population owned 32 per cent of personal wealth in Britain, they had to rub along with a mere 25 per cent in Wales. Ten per cent of the population owned 40 per cent of wealth in Britain, 34 per cent in Wales (1974, p.22).

One important kind of asset is, however, more commonly held in

Wales — the owner-occupied house. In 1975, 58.3 per cent of dwellings in Wales were owner-occupied compared with 52.8 per cent in
Great Britain (Welsh Office, 1977a,T.86). Also, a much larger proportion of owner-occupied dwellings in Wales are owned outright. In 1970/
71 nearly one-third of all dwellings in Wales were owned outright compared with just over a fifth in Great Britain (Revell and Tomkins, 1974,
p.27). It needs to be emphasised, however, that the Welsh housing stock
is older and more of it is unfit and lacking basic amenities than the
British stock; and many owner-occupied houses will suffer from these
disadvantages.[7]

Does the absence of the very wealthy matter? Does it really affect
the welfare of the rest of the population of the region? The effect of
low personal incomes is clear and obvious. Is the fact that personal
wealth in Wales is 72 per cent of the United Kingdom average important to any but the envious and the obsessive egalitarian? Revell and
Tomkins are emphatic that it is. The welfare of a region, they argue,
'depends on the accumulated wealth of its inhabitants as much as on
their current incomes' (1974, p.1). A region with a poor share of
national personal wealth will benefit from a smaller inflow of interest
and dividends and so will lack this increment to regional living standards.

Conclusion

As far then as income and wealth are concerned, Wales is one of the
poorest and most deprived regions of the United Kingdom. Only
Northern Ireland consistently emerges as worse off on most of the
indices we have examined. Why are incomes in Wales so low?

At the end of the day the crucial factor seems to be the low rates of
economic activity which mean, quite simply, that fewer households
have the benefit of a second income and more people in Wales depend
for their standard of living on the level of social security benefits — and
so live in relative poverty.

What is the explanation for the low rates of economic activity? The
most obvious one lies in the processes of economic and industrial
change — which have led to the loss of so many jobs in Wales in the
last twenty years — and the failure of regional policies to make good
more than a portion of this loss. Two other factors need to be mentioned in this connection. The first is that the development of a European economy has emphasised Wales's geographically peripheral position. As the focus of economic activity has become European rather

than British or Imperial, Wales has emerged even more clearly as a peripheral region a long way from where the action really is.

The second factor is the nationalisation of wage levels in recent years. The erosion of regional wage differentials as a result of trade union pressure has deprived the peripheral, disadvantaged regions of the one possible advantage which they possessed in the past – cheaper labour. There can be no doubt that this nationalisation of wage levels has benefited those with jobs, but it may well have made a contribution to low economic activity rates by destroying what to the entrepreneur were tangible advantages to set against the disadvantages of geography (Clark, 1966).

Deprived regions can improve their position. We saw earlier how personal incomes in the Northern region have improved relatively in recent years. Davies and Thomas stress the improvement in the Scottish economy in the 1950s and 1960s well before North Sea oil began to flow. Scotland's position, they argue, was improved by positive use of regional policies. '"Scottish" oil has simply lubricated the new economic structure and speeded up her rate of advance' (1976, p.151).

Not everyone would agree with the judgement that regional policies have been responsible for the rejuvenation of the Scottish economy and can do the same in other regions. Certainly, the economic climate is harsher now than it was in the 1950s and 1960s. There is more competition for regional aid and positive discrimination. There are fewer new jobs seeking homes. However, even if one is sceptical about the ability of regional policies to solve the problems of the depressed regions, clearly regional planning can make a contribution in the attraction of new industry and the provision of employment opportunities. While providing some increase in jobs, however, such policies can increase inequalities within a region, helping the less badly off areas and leaving untouched the most unattractive areas. Such policies may also increase individual income inequalities within areas by providing new opportunities for some, but not for all.

Regional policies are not, on their own, going to provide an answer to the economic problems of Wales. The first prerequisite of an effective attack on the problems of low economic activity rates, high unemployment and low incomes is an economic plan for Wales. 'Demand for such a plan', wrote Davies and Thomas in 1976, 'is growing within Wales to such an extent that it appears incredible that a positive and affirmative answer can be much longer denied' (p.201). They underestimated the resilience of central government in the face of regional pressure. There is now little sign of such a plan but an effort to organise ideas and develop a strategy must surely be a prerequisite of any serious attack on the economic problems of Wales.

The value of planning lies not in the plan which emerges at the end, with its assumptions to be instantly savaged by its critics and its projections soon to be falsified by events. The value lies in the process of thought and consultation, and the examination of existing and past policies which goes into planning. A plan requires a strategy, albeit tentative and sketchy. This would be the first step to an attack on the central problems of the Welsh economy − the establishing of the facts, the examination of alternative policies, the stating of preferences and a commitment to considered action. All these remain to be achieved.

Notes

1. The material in this chapter draws heavily on the work I did for *Poverty: The Facts in Wales* published by the Child Poverty Action Group in 1977.
2. See Ch. 8 (eds).
3. See Ch. 7 (eds).
4. The basic source for regional comparisons of earnings is, of course, the most recent *New Earnings Survey Pt.E, Analyses by Region and Age Group,* an annual publication of the Department of Employment. This section draws continuously on the 1977 Survey and references for particular sets of figures are therefore omitted.
5. See Ch. 7 (eds).
6. The range of taxable incomes is, of course, only part of the story of the distribution of income. Clearly we need to know more about the over-all pattern of inequalities of income (and wealth) within Wales, particularly in view of the widespread notion that Wales is an example of that fantasy of the bourgeois imagination, a classless society.
7. See Ch. 3 (eds).

3 POVERTY AND HOUSING IN WALES: AN ACCOUNT OF CURRENT PROBLEMS

Malcolm Fisk

Issues of housing are central to any discussion of inequality and poverty. Adequate shelter is an essential requirement for all and constitutes a key dimension of real income or 'quality of life'. Access to housing is, however, unequally distributed within society, opportunity being restricted particularly for those lacking wealth or with low incomes. In addition, aspirations and opportunities are restricted by non-market criteria such as ethnic status, gender or life style, embodied in the 'housing class' model developed by Rex and Moore (1967).

The importance of housing explains the level of state intervention in its provision through Councils, development corporations and housing associations. In addition, the state exercises some control over the private sector (regulating the provision of land, specifying minimum standards of quality, influencing the availability of finance, regulating rent levels, security of tenure, etc.). Whatever the intentions of this intervention, it is clear that the state has itself become a critical factor in the generation of housing inequalities, for example by controlling access to local authority housing (see Welsh Consumer Council, 1976). Hence, any discussion of poverty in housing must devote a great deal of attention to the state and its institutions.

However, in spite of this centrality to issues of poverty and inequality, remarkably little research has been carried out on housing in Wales. This chapter sets out to provide an account of the current Welsh situation, by in turn examining the nature of the housing stock and its origins in the economic development of Wales, by focusing on the issues of housing need and demand, emphasising the inequalities, both spatial and social, in these, and, finally, by examining the nature, extent and effectiveness of state intervention in Wales's housing problems.

The Housing Stock

Historical Background

The character and evolution of housing in rural Wales is admirably described by Peate (1940) in his study *The Welsh House*. Much of the

51

housing of this period has, however, disappeared, the properties falling into ruin as local people left the land for the new opportunities in the industrial areas and as the basis of the Welsh economy shifted rapidly away from agriculture.

Standards were sacrificed in the scramble for land and profits as the iron and coalfields were opened up in South and North East Wales and as a consequence conditions were appalling. The following description is of Maesteg in the 1840s:

The houses are all overcrowded. They are commonly of two storeys and comprise of four or five rooms; the fifth room, however (where there is one), is seldom more than a pantry. The average of inhabitants is said to be nearly twelve to each house. (Report of the Royal Commissioners of Inquiry into the State of Education in Wales, 1847, p.119)

Conditions were just as bad in North East Wales; the same source describes Rhosllanerchrugog in the same period as follows:

Some (cottages) consist of a single room from nine to twelve feet square; others have in addition a sort of lean-to forming a separate place to sleep in . . . Each of these hovels contains on an average a family of six children with their parents. (p.530)

Those who stayed in the rural areas frequently suffered from similar deprivations, but at least were spared the risk to health through the poor or non-existent sanitation which was instrumental in the spread of illness and disease that continued prior to the implementation of the 1875 Public Health Act.

The rate of housebuilding in the valleys, though rapid, fluctuated considerably, peak periods being in the late 1850s, the mid-1870s and in the 1890s (Richards and Lewis, 1969; and Jones, 1969). The major agencies of housebuilding were the building clubs, private speculators and employers, though the employers in later years found it more expedient to grant 99-year leases to the building clubs and speculators rather than to build houses themselves. Hence, the Ebbw Vale Company abandoned its policy of providing cottages and wash-houses for its workers in 1852 (Gray-Jones, 1970) and other coal and iron companies adopted similar policies.

Building clubs consisted of groups of potential owner-occupiers who financed their work by monthly paid-up shares. The deeds of the

properties were only distributed after shares had been fully paid, often
after a period of ten or more years. Private speculators included both
investors who engaged builders to provide housing for letting and builders themselves who built for sale. Subsequent decline in the valleys and
in much of rural Wales has resulted in populations living in an increasingly obsolete housing stock, insufficiently supported by jobs, newer
houses, roads, railways, public utilities, community facilities and services which are the necessary prerequisites for community health and
vitality.

Age, Condition and Quality

Housing in Wales is older than in all other regions of Britain, the oldest
of the stock being found throughout most rural areas and the valleys.
This fact has substantial implications for Welsh housing policies and the
level of necessary housing investment. Within rural Wales there are
certain concentrations of older housing in former slate-quarrying
communities and their ports, for instance Blaenau Ffestiniog and Porthmadog respectively. Older properties outside the towns frequently date
from before the nineteenth century. In Industrial South Wales the
greatest concentration of older housing, almost all built in the latter
half of the nineteenth century and before 1914, are to be found in the
Central and Eastern valleys, notably in the Rhondda, Cynon and
Merthyr Valleys. Some parts of inner Cardiff, Newport and Swansea
are similarly characterised, though in many cases the dwellings concerned are larger properties that are multiply occupied.

Closely linked to the age of the housing stock is the proportion of
dwellings lacking in the essential amenities of indoor toilet, fixed bath/
shower and hot water. Wales is the worst region with regard to this
aspect of housing quality if comparison is made with other parts of
Britain, some 21 per cent of dwellings lacking one or more essential
amenity in 1973. In the absence of objective measures at a local level of
condition and fitness, the presence or absence of such amenities is
frequently taken as the most convenient proxy. Analyses earmark the
areas where amenities are frequently absent as those in which the highest proportion of substandard housing is present. Hence, in 1961, the
areas of worst housing were identified as Rhondda, Mountain Ash,
Blaenavon, Abertillery and Ffestiniog where the percentages of houses
lacking one or more of these amenities – indoor toilet, fixed bath or
shower, or exclusive use of hot and cold water – were over two standard deviations above the mean (Drakakis-Smith, 1970). The position
in Rhondda is particularly acute – in 1971 some 50 per cent of

dwellings were without the exclusive use of an indoor toilet (see Table 3.1).

Of dwellings deemed unfit, there is a higher proportion in Wales than in all other regions of Britain (Welsh Housing Associations Committee, 1978). The *Welsh House Condition Survey* of 1976 identifies 100, 200 dwellings as unfit and an additional 31,300 dwellings as fit but out of repair. The latter figure embraces dwellings that would have been classified as unfit in the 1973 survey and in fact should come within the definition of unfitness used in both studies. This suggests a small (11 per cent) reduction in unfitness over the three-year period (Welsh Office, 1973 and 1976b). The statistics, however, need to be viewed with caution, being based on the subjective judgements of many public health inspectors. Indeed, a survey undertaken in Rhymney Valley suggests that the 1973 figures of unfitness were underestimates (Mid Glamorgan County Council, 1977b).

Tenure

In Industrial South and North East Wales, the role of private entrepreneurs and building clubs helped the emergence of a higher proportion of owner-occupiers than are to be found in most other parts of Britain. This is complemented in the rural areas where high levels of owner-occupation have emerged, possibly following greater pressure being placed upon tenants to purchase farm small-holdings from distant landowners than was the case in other areas of rural Britain (Howell, 1978).

A small but significant number of properties, however, which are of leasehold tenure are reverting to the ownership of the ground landlords or remain on short leases. This presents particular difficulties for the elderly owner-occupier who may not in any case be able to afford normal maintenance costs and for the private tenant whose landlord retains no interest in the property in question.

The pattern of tenures is still largely a reflection of the past. Nowhere is this more marked than in the valleys where owner-occupation is still at the high level of 53.5 per cent despite the almost continuous economic decline of the past fifty years (Ty Toronto Socio-Economic Research Group, 1977). Most remarkable is the 67.8 per cent level of owner-occupation in Rhondda which has seen both the peak of prosperity and the depths of suffering during the Depression, and is today enduring the consequences of decline probably more intensely than all other parts of the South Wales coalfield (Fisk, 1978). Outside the valleys the most notable high levels of owner-occupation are reached in several

Table 3.1: A Summary of Welsh Housing Statistics

	Total[a] dwellings (000's) (1971)	% households[a] with exclusive use of all 3 amenities (1971)	New dwellings[b] completed (000's) 1974-7		Length of[c] council waiting list (1977)	% council[a] tenure (1971)	% private[a] rented (1971)	% owner[a] occupied (1971)	% unfit[d] or out of repair (1976)
			Public	Private					
Alyn and Deeside	21.2	88.2	0.4	1.2	1,081	27.4	12.2	60.3	
Colwyn	16.8	89.1	0.5	0.7	1,269	15.3	21.9	62.7	
Delyn	18.9	83.2	0.8	1.1	1,100	29.3	14.1	56.4	Clwyd = 8.2
Glyndwr	13.0	81.3	0.2	0.6	525	28.5	24.2	47.2	
Rhuddlan	17.7	91.8	0.1	1.0	1,005	16.3	18.5	64.8	
Wrexham Maelor	35.6	85.3	1.0	2.0	1,809	45.9	14.0	40.0	
Carmarthen	16.5	77.0	0.7	0.4	1,509	21.1	20.0	58.6	
Ceredigion	20.0	76.4	0.5	1.0	1,739	17.3	24.4	58.1	
Dinefwr	12.8	73.7	0.3	0.2	500	21.2	17.7	60.8	Dyfed = 12.8
Llanelli	26.5	77.7	0.7	0.7	1,100	33.0	11.1	55.8	
Preseli	20.9	87.0	0.6	1.1	2,000	32.5	16.1	51.2	
South Pembrokeshire	12.8	82.4	0.4	0.7	1,172	25.4	21.5	52.9	
Blaenau Gwent	28.7	73.2	1.0	0.5	2,381	33.9	9.8	56.2	
Islwyn	21.8	73.4	0.4	0.6	1,142	37.7	15.5	46.7	Gwent = 7.4
Monmouth	20.6	86.9	0.6	1.1	2,000	31.6	17.5	50.7	
Newport	44.0	82.4	1.8	1.0	4,080	31.1	15.1	53.6	
Torfaen	29.3	82.9	1.0	0.6	1,405	53.9	9.1	36.9	

Table 3.1 (continued)

	Total[a] dwellings (000's) (1971)	% households[a] with exclusive use of all 3 amenities (1971)	New dwellings[b] completed (000's) 1974-7		Length of[c] council waiting list (1977)	% council[a] tenure (1971)	% private[a] rented (1971)	% owner-[a] occupied (1971)	% unfit[d] or out of repair (1976)
			Public	Private					
Aberconwy	18.1	86.6	0.3	0.6	1,314	20.6	22.1	57.2	Gwynedd =
Arfon	18.1	75.3	0.4	0.6	994	31.2	17.7	50.9	14.3
Dwyfor	10.4	74.1	0.0	0.5	510	16.5	27.7	55.5	
Meirionydd	12.0	78.7	0.3	0.4	650	20.4	22.3	57.1	
Ynys Mon	20.5	81.3	0.5	1.4	1,700	28.4	23.3	48.1	
Cynon Valley	23.9	59.5	0.4	0.2	800	23.8	15.9	60.1	
Merthyr Tydfil	21.3	61.3	0.9	0.4	909	32.5	14.7	52.6	Mid
Ogwr	39.8	80.5	1.4	1.8	1,994	28.2	13.7	57.9	Glamorgan=
Rhondda	30.2	49.3	0.2	0.1	783	15.8	16.3	67.8	25.2
Rhymney Valley	32.4	72.0	1.2	1.6	1 600	31.4	19.0	49.4	
Taff Ely	27.5	77.0	0.8	1.7	2,015	33.9	12.3	53.7	
Brecknock	12.7	78.8	0.8	0.6	831	25.5	22.2	52.2	Powys =
Montgomery	15.2	72.9	0.4	0.6	797	26.0	25.3	48.7	16.5
Radnor	6.3	76.5	0.3	0.5	651	18.0	28.5	53.5	

Table 3.1 (continued)

Cardiff	90.7	77.0	2.0	2.2	3,279	27.1	20.8	51.7	South Glamorgan=
Vale of Glamorgan	32.3	85.4	1.3	1.3	2,354	22.7	20.2	56.9	8.3
Afan	18.9	80.4	0.1	0.6	904	46.5	8.4	44.9	West
Lliw Valley	19.4	71.9	0.5	0.6	1,016	26.2	11.6	62.0	Glamorgan=
Neath	22.7	72.7	0.4	0.6	1,084	29.1	13.3	57.5	9.5
Swansea	62.5	79.5	1.9	1.2	2,500	28.4	15.1	56.3	
Wales	911.8	77.7	26.9	31.7	52,502	29.3	16.8	53.9	12.9

Note: Figures do not always add up to Wales total because of rounding.

Sources:
a. 1971 Census.
b. Welsh Office/Department of the Environment, *Local Housing Statistics* (HMSO, 1975, 1976, 1977).
c. F. Kelly and J. Wintour, *The Housing Crisis Nationwide* (Shelter, London, 1977).
d. Welsh Office, *Welsh House Condition Survey 1976* (HMSO, Cardiff, 1976).

coastal areas and in the Ffestiniog and Buckley/Connah's Quay areas
(see Table 3.1).

The relative attractiveness of different forms of tenure has been
drastically affected by the nature of new housebuilding in recent
decades. In Industrial South Wales private developments have essentially been confined to the more prosperous areas of industrial development and diversification rather than to the declining upper valleys. In
rural Wales the rate of development has, perforce, been slow, reflecting the lower level of absolute demand for housing, but has, with the
exception of some coastal towns where there is an additional demand
for second houses, been relatively well balanced (see Table 3.1).

In the areas of decline there is ironically a high demand for housing
which it has fallen largely to the local authorities to try to satisfy.
However, there being high levels of owner-occupancy, much of the
demand is for private rather than public housing; hence continuing out-
migration takes place in search of the desired tenure. The lack of suitable housing is cited as the second most important factor (behind jobs)
leading to out-migration from at least one valley area (Rees, 1977)
and a plethora of studies reveals the strong desire to stay in the local
community (see, for instance, Ty Toronto Socio-Economic Research
Group, 1977 and Glyncorrwg Community Development Project, 1973).

The private rented sector accounts for 50 per cent of unfit housing
in Wales, despite being only 15 per cent of the total housing stock
(Welsh Office, 1976b), a substantial element of which is accounted for
by unimproved National Coal Board properties in the valleys. Higher
proportions of tenanted properties are to be found in the rural areas,
with significant concentrations (much of which is furnished) in the
coastal resorts and university towns. Multiply occupied furnished
accommodation in Swansea is characterised by shared amenities and a
transient population (Swansea City Council, 1975) and in some of the
coastal resorts such housing has led to the concentration of elderly
people.

The declining profitability to the landlord (resulting from progressive rent controls and increased security of tenure to the tenant)
of providing accommodation to rent has been a major factor in the
shrinkage of this sector. This, together with the lack of opportunity to
become an owner-occupier, has led to an increasing proportion of
young people seeking local authority housing.

Council housing predominates in several districts in Wales, notably
in Torfaen (incorporating Cwmbran New Town), Afan and Wrexham
Maelor. On the other hand, council housing forms only a small

proportion of the housing stock in Colwyn, Rhondda, Rhuddlan and Dwyfor and in many coastal resorts and other areas where there are high levels of owner-occupation.[1] This housing varies considerably between authorities but generally lacks quality and character. Nearly forty years ago, Peate (1940) commented of council housing:

> The new houses, however, seem too often to conform to a standard-ised pattern adopted indiscriminately by local authorities without thought for the particular requirements of their own areas. There are notable exceptions, but it is unfortunately true that in many areas, the new housing schemes have no regard for 'decency' in architecture nor is any serious attention paid to the relationship of houses to their environment.

And more recently a Department of the Environment (1976) report stated that the rigid adherence by local authorities to design standards has frequently stifled imagination in estate design and imposed 'environments based on narrow professional preconceptions'.

Housing Demand and Housing Need

Discussion of housing demand tends to emphasise 'manifest' demand exhibited by private buyers in the open housing market and fails to acknowledge a huge 'latent' demand attributable to those who are unable to compete in this market, including vast numbers of single people and families on low incomes who are in substandard and insecure accommodation, in hostels or institutions or actually homeless. Such emphasis tends to be reinforced by the patterns of private house building and the *laissez-faire* attitude to planning that could otherwise seek to produce a better distribution of private housing investment. Thus, private house building tends to concentrate in those areas of relative prosperity to the detriment of areas of decline, and in so doing has helped perpetuate the out-migration of those very elements of the population who have most to contribute to the local economy of declining areas.

Part of the latent demand has to be satisfied by the local authority and thus further imbalances in housing tenure are reinforced, council housing accounting for most of the newer housing stock in declining areas. Some indication of the latent demand is given by the length of the council waiting lists, though the numbers of applicants fall far

short of the total in need of housing and in any case must be viewed
with caution owing to different rules of eligibility and a number of
other factors (Welsh Consumer Council, 1976). Notable are the lengths
of lists in Newport (4,080), Cardiff (3,279), Swansea (2,500), Vale of
Glamorgan (2,354) and Blaenau Gwent (2,381) (see Table 3.1). Per
head of population the relative lengths of the waiting lists are greatest
in Radnor, South Pembrokeshire, Preseli and Newport (Kelly and Wintour, 1977). Clearly, the length of waiting lists has a substantial bearing
on the time an applicant is waiting, and this varies considerably between
authorities. The mean waiting period, for instance, of respondents to a
Welsh Consumer Council survey was over five years in Swansea and
less than six months in Wrexham Maelor (Welsh Consumer Council,
1976).

Two aspects of the problem of latent demand warrant special
attention in Wales: homelessness and second homes.

The Homelessness Problem

Precious little information is available on the problems of the homeless
in Wales. In 1969, however, the Department of Health and Social
Security commissioned a research team to study homelessness in South
Wales and the West of England which involved the investigation of over
500 case histories of families entering temporary accommodation
(Glastonbury, 1971). Some disturbing facts were unearthed; it was
found that decisions made concerning homelessness were arbitrarily
made, that local authorities had failed to adopt recommendations
embodied in the earlier Seebohm Report, and that the figures for
families in temporary accommodation represented no more than a
sixth of all homeless families. A working party set up to examine the
findings of the Glastonbury study later concluded that 'there are
grounds for assuming that the problem in the areas of South Wales
covered by the Glastonbury Survey is as large today as it was in the
whole survey area in 1968' and acknowledged that there is a particular pressure on Cardiff (Welsh Office *et al.*, 1972).

Despite the attention given to the problems of the homeless in
South Wales examined by Glastonbury and mulled over by the working party, things have changed very little. More recently the 1977
Housing (Homeless Persons) Act vested greater responsibility with the
housing authorities and again the problem of the homeless has attracted
a certain amount of public attention. Since April 1978, Welsh housing
authorities have been required to make returns, and the first quarter
reveals that 1,146 cases of homelessness were accepted and dealt with

in Wales. It would be premature to state the extent to which these figures can give an indication of the magnitude of the problem but, in view of the continuing need for hostel and institutional accommodation and the persistence of squatting, it is likely to represent only the tip of the iceberg.

Second Homes

The growth of second home ownership has emerged as an important phenomenon in the last two decades, and has been localised in areas of excessive decline and in some coastal resorts. The confusion of information about second homes precludes any rigorous estimate of the numbers in Wales being made (see, for instance, De Vane, 1975; Bollom, 1978; and Davies and O'Farrell, 1978). Nevertheless, it is clear that most second homes are to be found in Gwynedd, with significant concentrations in the Lleyn Peninsula, the Towyn/Llangelynin and Trearddur Bay/Rhosneigr areas, all within the heartland of Welsh culture, where the language not only survives but thrives. Other concentrations are to be found throughout most other parts of rural Wales, embracing most of Dyfed, western Clwyd, Powys, the Gower Peninsula and the Wye Valley.

The implication of concentrations developing in Welsh-speaking areas is that the increasing numbers of English-speaking monoglots pose a real threat to the future of the Welsh language. A survey undertaken in a community in Cardigan reveals that the proportion of Welsh speakers in the holiday homes was nil, whereas three-quarters of the permanent residents spoke the language (Cymdeithas yr Iaith Cymraeg, no date). As a consequence, unfavourable attitudes have frequently been engendered.

The second major factor that has brought about the unfavourable attitude to second homes is the fact that the number of available homes for local people is reduced. The extent to which this reduction does in fact take place depends, firstly, on the extent to which second home owners seek properties that would otherwise remain unoccupied and, secondly, on the extent to which new houses are built by private developers specifically for second home purchasers and would otherwise not have been built. Clearly, there is much local variation. Generally speaking, however, in house availability terms, potential competition between locals and outsiders is minimised where new developments take place (e.g. marina developments at coastal resorts such as Porthmadog and Port Dinorwic), in areas of substantial decline (e.g. in former slate-quarrying areas such as Blaenau Ffestiniog), or in remote areas, distant from local villages and towns.

Local planning authorities tend to look at the second home pheno-menon in purely the latter terms, recognising that demand factors will have implications on house prices and hence ability to purchase by local people, but tend to take little or no account of the potential effects on language and culture (see, for instance, Tuck, 1973 and Jacobs, 1972). Some assessment clearly has to be made of the financial and employment benefits that are brought about and the extent to which alternative investment can be made available to provide similar benefits without adversely affecting community life and exacerbating the already difficult position of the Welsh language.

The impact on house prices has been drastic. In Denbighshire prices rose, over a ten-year period to 1972, by 40 per cent more than in the rest of Britain (Jacobs, 1972) and anomalously high price increases are noted in at least two other studies (Tuck, 1973; and Carr and Morrison, 1972). Competition for such houses clearly affects the extent to which the local authority will need to provide municipal housing for local people and it is notable that in the Gwynedd area in 1977 there were over 6,000 second homes whilst 4,500 families waited for council accommodation (Cymdeithas yr Iaith Cymraeg, 1977).

Housing Policy

New Housing

Wales is adding to the permanent housing stock at a slower rate than the rest of Britain and the pattern is such that, between 1974 and 1977, 54 per cent of the houses built were in the private sector. There was much variation between authorities, a mere 30 council houses being built in Dwyfor compared with over 2,000 in Cardiff, and for private developments there were a little over 100 houses built in Rhondda, compared with some 2,150 in Cardiff. Regional variations were such that private developments predominated in all of North and most of Mid Wales. The low levels of completions in both public and private sectors, in relation to population, are particularly apparent for the valleys authorities. The lowest by far is in Rhondda, and the low levels in other valley authorities clearly indicate that, as long as present trends continue, the proportion of older properties in the valleys will increase, and hence the relative availability of new housing will diminish (see Table 3.1).

The desire to own a home is clearly very great in Wales, 83 per cent preferring owner-occupation to other forms of tenure − a higher

percentage than in any other region of Britain, according to a 1967
survey (Opinion Research Centre, 1967). This has substantial repercussions as regards the extent to which the legitimate aspirations of
potential householders are satisfied. The lack of new private developments in some areas and the fact that this has been identified as a
major factor in leading to out-migration suggest that numerous people
are either living in the kind of accommodation they like but in the
wrong area, or have chosen to stay in the area of their choice despite
unsatisfactory housing. It is notable that, despite demand for owner-
occupation in areas where availability of such accommodation is low,
few Welsh authorities seek to sell houses in their ownership.

Area Improvement

It has already been pointed out that Wales has a disproportionately
high number of dwellings that are old, in poor condition and lacking
essential amenities. Few authorities, however, have produced strategies
to deal with areas of older housing or embarked upon comprehensive
programmes to ensure the upgrading of such areas. Perhaps the best
example of a comprehensive strategy being effectively implemented is
that of Newport (see Newport Borough Council, 1976). A few other
authorities have worked out similar strategies but have failed to deploy
the resources to ensure their success. The statutory requirement to
produce 'Local Housing Strategies' and 'Housing Investment Programmes' appears to have made little difference in this respect.

The impetus that many authorities are placing behind the General
Improvement Areas (GIAs) and Housing Action Areas (HAAs) for which
they are responsible is open to doubt. There are some 50,000 dwellings
within General Improvement Areas, and 4,000 dwellings within Housing
Action Areas. The failure of GIAs (with grant levels having been reduced
to 60 per cent) to stimulate the required improvement of dwellings is
perhaps evidenced by the few declarations of such areas since the 1974
Act gave birth to Housing Action Areas (where 75 per cent grants or
higher are available). On the other hand, declaring an HAA is not going
to stimulate the required improvement unless positive support is forthcoming from the local authority concerned. The first HAA in Wales,
for instance, consisting of 266 dwellings, was declared by Blaenau
Gwent District Council at Six Bells, Abertillery and should in many
ways have been a showpiece for the rest of Wales, but in the first two
and a half years of its operation only one house out of the eligible
dwellings had been improved!

The present distribution of GIAs and HAAs bears little relationship to the areas of greatest housing need.[2] Of particular note is the fact that Rhondda and Cynon Valleys, which rank worst in Wales (and Britain) for lack of essential amenities, rank only 30th and 31st of the 37 Welsh districts for the proportion of dwellings in GIAs and HAAs. It must further be noted that GIAs and HAAs are essentially directed at overcoming the problems of housing in need of repair and without essential amenities in urban areas and hence, despite the considerable needs in rural areas, their usage is not always appropriate.

Clearly there is a major role that may be played by housing associations to assist in the rehabilitation of vacant and tenanted properties in areas of poor housing. However, few authorities have taken steps to encourage such housing associations despite the magnitude of their housing problems. Worthy of note is the Secondary Housing Association for Wales which has responsibility for setting up local autonomous associations and is buying and improving property in the valleys.

Area improvement problems do not accrue only to the areas of older housing, lacking amenities. Many council estates, though of modern construction, provide very poor living environments. Such environments are to be found to a greater or lesser degree in most parts of Wales and the number of people on the transfer lists from such estates is testimony to their undesirability as places to live. Maintenance problems often abound on such estates; a survey in Rhondda revealed that two-thirds of tenants were dissatisfied with the service (Fisk, 1978) and considerable variability in attitude is evidenced in a study recently undertaken by the Welsh Consumer Council (Welsh Consumer Council, 1979a).

Clearly, it is difficult to identify the reasons why some estates become unattractive living environments. There may be faults in the original design that cannot be easily remedied; the layout, size and location of estates may give rise to feelings of isolation, anonymity and insecurity; and past allocations policies may have led to concentrations of individuals and families deemed 'problematic' by the local authority concerned. Undoubtedly, mistakes of the past are hard to rectify, but little attempt appears to have been made to improve such living environments, or indeed to avoid similar mistakes being made in the future. It is sad but true that the politics of housing requires waiting lists to be reduced in length as rapidly as possible with only the scantiest regard being paid to the quality of the living environment being created.

Homelessness Policy

Despite the widespread incidence of homelessness, the resources devoted to combating the problem have been limited. The coming of the
1977 Act has brought some hope, but there remains little conformity in
the attitude of local authorities to the Act and the accompanying 'Code
of Guidance'. It must be pointed out that all Welsh housing authorities
have had ample time to prepare for the new responsibility for housing
the homeless that is now vested on them. At least four Welsh authorities, however — Cardiff, Blaenau Gwent, Merthyr Tydfil and Taff Ely
— appear largely to have ignored the recommendations of the appropriate government circular (Tai Nos, 1978).

Most debate surrounds the question of defining 'intentional homelessness'. Some authorities have sought to define those evicted for rent
arrears as 'intentionally homeless' and are reluctant to provide assistance, guidance and temporary accommodation. It is interesting to note
that the 'Code of Guidance' specifically excludes certain groups from
being classed as intentionally homeless — namely, battered and preg-
nant women, those becoming homeless through domestic disputes, and
those in accommodation which has become intolerably unsafe or in-
sanitary. Nevertheless, over 10 per cent of cases dealt with by local
authorities in the second quarter of 1978 were deemed 'intentionally
homeless'. A clearer picture will emerge in due course as to the extent
to which Welsh authorities are failing in their responsibilities for the
homeless. Meanwhile, those without or with totally inadequate
accommodation must continue to suffer.

Allocation of Finance

In view of Wales's exceptional housing problems, it is to be expected
that Wales's share of resources for housing would be relatively higher
than for other regions of Britain. In fact, despite possessing over 5 per
cent of Britain's housing stock, Wales's expenditure on housing has
been consistently below this level (Welsh Housing Associations Committee, 1978).

As regards Section 105 — allocations to local authorities for
improvement grants, mortgages and the acquisition and improvements
of older properties — Wales requires almost as large an allocation as
London, but in practice receives only a small fraction of this. The
needs of both urban and rural parts of Wales are largely ignored — 19
of the 37 authorities in 1977 needed more than six times the expenditure the government has allowed. Over ten times the expenditure
appeared necessary in Arfon, Dwyfor and the Cynon, Merthyr and

Rhondda Valleys (Kelly and Wintour, 1977).

The manner in which housing allocations are spent has been dictated largely by the Welsh Office, until 1976/77 when block allocations were given so that the local authorities could, at least in part, determine how resources could be divided between improvement grants, mortgages and the acquisition and improvement of older properties. The way in which such resources have been divided between different categories and different geographical areas has, however, been largely *ad hoc* and no attempt has been made to allocate extra resources in areas where significant private investment is absent.

The efficiency of housing authorities in spending the money allocated to them must also be called into question. In 1976/77 Welsh authorities underspent to the tune of £25 million, mostly attributable to inadequate new housebuilding, a low take-up of improvement grants and a limited take-up of mortgages. Eleven Councils did not seek additional Section 105 allocations and 14 did not seek additional mortgage moneys. Montgomery, Neath, Preseli and Radnor featured on both lists. The underspending stimulated a Welsh Office inquiry that recommended that authorities should risk committing more of the resources available to them in anticipation of slippage taking place, and maintain more schemes 'on the shelf' which might be brought into a building programme at short notice (Welsh Office, 1977c and 1978a).

In addition, despite the fact that a major part of Wales's housing problems accrues to older housing, no attempt has been made to reinstate the 75 per cent improvement grant level, as has taken place in Scotland. Meanwhile, the take-up of grants in Wales continues to slump.

Conclusion

It has been shown that inadequate housing can take a number of forms and clearly relates differently to the particular circumstances of individuals and families. Thus, the disadvantaged may be found on a modern council estate or in a remote cottage or terraced property that is falling into disrepair. The occupant may be young or old, a tenant or an owner-occupier. Particular housing types are, however, clearly associated with certain social and economic characteristics and the distribution of these gives a clearer indication of how the nature of disadvantage varies geographically. The areas of problem housing are evidenced in a recent study undertaken for Shelter (Fisk, Radford and Roberts, 1979). Three contexts of problem housing are identified:

(i)   Older housing in rural areas – where twice the national average
number of dwellings lack exclusive use of basic amenities, where twice
the national average are privately rented (unfurnished), and where
there is a high proportion of elderly people. Three per cent of Wales's
population (87,000 people) lives in areas of this housing type which is
well distributed throughout rural Wales and is clearly associated with
low incomes and low levels of newer housing development. Hence,
many occupants have difficulty in financing repairs and improvements
to their houses and have only restricted access to housing alternatives,
especially in certain areas where house prices are artificially inflated
through a demand for second homes. Statutory policies are, generally
speaking, unable to bring about, to any substantial extent, greater
accessibility to more satisfactory housing alternatives and area improvement policies are clearly inapplicable.

(ii)   Older housing in urban areas – which comes in two types.
   Type 1. The major characteristic of this type is the absence of
exclusive use of essential amenities in areas where owner-occupation
and private (unfurnished) rentals predominate. Twenty-two per cent of
Wales's population (600,000 people) lives in areas of this housing type.
It is characteristic of the South Wales coalfield and inner Cardiff,
Swansea and Newport. The sheer concentration of this housing type
over very wide areas is itself a reflection of the lack of local housing
alternatives, adjoining areas often manifesting the same characteristics.
A severe lack of newer development, particularly in the private sector,
in many such areas exacerbates the situation and is shown to be a factor
leading to continuing net out-migration of the younger, mobile element,
often leaving the elderly and others on low incomes, who are unable to
take advantage of any area improvement policies that are being applied.
   Type 2. Often three-storey, of which the essential characteristic is
multiple-occupancy composed of unfurnished and furnished private
rentals (often for students). One per cent of Wales's population (27,000
people) lives in areas of this housing type, which is almost exclusively
confined to areas of multiply occupied rented accommodation in
Cardiff, Barry, Swansea, Newport and Aberystwyth. The transient
population therein includes a large number of students who in many
cases, by virtue of their transience, are prepared to tolerate what
might be regarded in other circumstances as inadequate accommodation.
However, many other people occupy such accommodation on a more

permanent basis, including the elderly and many single people of all ages. The available alternatives open to these people are few and their present accommodation is threatened by the continuing shrinkage of the private rented sector. Local authority housing policy tends to discriminate in favour of families and building programmes are thus geared to larger units. Private developments, on the other hand, in similar city or town centre locations, although often incorporating smaller flats, tend to be very highly priced.

(iii) High-risk council estates — housing in which there is characteristically over twice the national average proportion of unskilled workers and unemployed, and in which there are larger, younger families. Seven per cent of Wales's population (200,000 people) lives in areas of this housing type. It is found in all the areas of population concentration. Acceptance of a tenancy on such estates will frequently result from the acute housing need of the applicant, who is in a weak position to exercise any choice. High levels of unemployment, low levels of skills and unbalanced family structures are frequently found, resulting in a high number of 'insecure' families, often with intermittent or permanent financial problems. The policies of housing authorities could clearly be better geared to the dispersal of 'insecure' families throughout the public housing stock.

The manner in which such housing types are distributed is shown in Map 3.1. It is clear that, for the poor, choice of housing is severely limited, and hence the kind of accommodation obtained tends to reflect that disadvantaged position. The absence of statutory policies effectively to widen the choice of housing alternatives tends to allow the perpetuation of local geographical concentrations of the disadvantaged within a context of clear sub-regional concentrations. Local differences in the quality of housing and the extent of social deprivation are exemplified in many valleys areas where modern council estates juxtapose settled communities in often substandard terraced housing that is largely owner-occupied.

Access to council housing for private tenants and owner-occupiers (particularly the latter) who live in unsatisfactory housing conditions is somewhat limited under the allocations systems currently adopted by the housing authorities (Welsh Consumer Council, 1976). In addition, the single homeless are frequently ignored by the statutory authorities, squatters are frequently perceived as lawbreakers, and both are forced to tolerate insecure or non-existent accommodation. Those in institutions are frequently deemed as satisfactorily housed, despite their

Map 3.1: Areas of Problem Housing in Wales

× Older Housing in Rural Areas
● ● Older Housing in Urban Areas (type 1)
■ Older Housing in Urban Areas (type 2)
○ ○ High Risk Council Estates

Note: Larger Symbols represent over 1000 people in area of particular housing type.

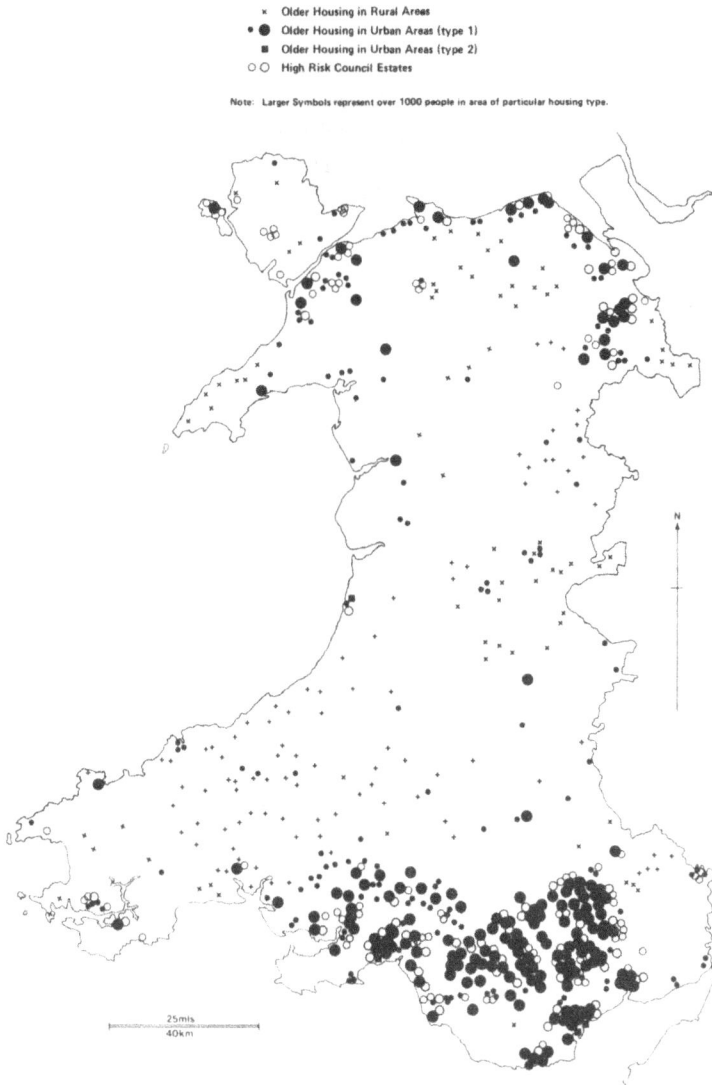

presence all too often reflecting the inadequacy of housing alternatives.

The picture is thus one in which about a third of the population of Wales is either without accommodation at all or lives in accommodation that is clearly inadequate. It is a picture of geographical concentrations of particular kinds of housing problems, exacerbated by the growing problem of the increasing physical obsolescence of the housing stock and by the failure of statutory authorities to devise and execute effective counter-measures. Most disturbing of all is the fact that poor housing circumstances are intricately bound up with a plethora of other social and economic deprivations that serve to perpetuate those circumstances with which this chapter is concerned.

Notes

1. The size of estates tends to be largest in the most populous areas and the age of the dwellings is such that those built prior to 1945 form only a tenth of the council stock in at least six districts (Carmarthen, Ceredigion, Newport, Ogwr, Rhondda and Vale of Glamorgan). This has particularly important repercussions for these authorities in that they are in many cases saddled with substantial debt burdens, to the detriment of their over-all housing service.

2. See Ch. 6 (eds).

4 EDUCATIONAL INEQUALITY IN WALES: SOME PROBLEMS AND PARADOXES[1]

Gareth Rees and Teresa L. Rees

The relationship between performance in the educational system and subsequent life-chance is, of course, a highly complex one: there is a good deal of often conflicting evidence, set within widely diverging theoretical frameworks (for a useful general account, see Tyler, 1977). However, what is much clearer is that there is a widely held belief that education provides the potential of upward occupational mobility (and all that this entails in terms of improved standards of living) to the children of working-class and other disadvantaged parents. It was exactly this sort of belief that was translated into pressure to extend and improve state education during the nineteenth and early twentieth centuries, perhaps culminating in the 1944 Butler Education Act, which established the principle of free secondary education for all (Barker, 1972; Simon, 1960). It is also this sort of belief, albeit in a somewhat more complex form, that has underpinned much of the more contemporary debate about 'equality of educational opportunity'.

In its earlier phases, this debate was essentially liberal and merito-cratic in character: children from different social classes, ethnic groups and geographical areas — all categories apparently independent of educa-tion — were demonstrated to vary systematically in their levels of educa-tional performance. Educational performance, in turn, was viewed as closely implicated in the perpetuation, between generations, of member-ship of disadvantaged groups. Accordingly, educational reforms to over-come the injustices of differential educational opportunity were advo-cated as a means of breaking down the rigidities of class and race. As the then Minister of Education, Sir Edward (later Lord) Boyle, put it in his Preface to the Newsom Report (Central Advisory Council for Education (England), 1963): 'The essential point is that all children should have an equal opportunity of acquiring intelligence, and of developing their talents and abilities to the full' (p.iv). The inadequacies of this approach subsequently led many to call for the substitution for the objective of equality of access to educational opportunity that of equality of educa-tional achievement. It was this sort of objective that was most closely associated with the post-Plowden Report (Central Advisory Council for Education (England), 1967) call for 'compensatory' programmes of 'positive discrimination' in favour of socially disadvantaged areas and their inhabitants. However, as Halsey (1972) makes clear, even this highly developed conception of educational equality was grounded in the belief that the educational system could (and should) function to improve the situation of the disadvantaged child via upward occupational mobility.

This view of the interrelatedness of education and life-chances has a particular significance in Wales. It has frequently been used as an explanation of what is held to be the especially high esteem in which education is held in Wales. The Gittins Report (Central Advisory Council for Education (Wales), 1967) suggests a more complex picture, however.

> There can be no doubt that in Wales education is very highly regarded and a high status is accorded to those who practise it professionally. At its best, education has earned high respect as a purveyor of literary, religious and social values. But the Welsh . . . also see education as an insurance policy, or as a gateway to financial security and possible affluence. (p.9)

In its historical dimension, there is considerable evidence that is at least consistent with this sort of analysis. Hence, it has frequently been reported that one of the effects of Nonconformism, which was pervasive in its influence in Wales, was the inculcation of particular educational aspirations amongst chapel members.

Undoubtedly, the massive presence of the Nonconformist chapels did exert a powerful influence upon the development of Welsh education. In its emphasis upon education as a vehicle for the furtherance of religion and, more generally, for the engendering of acceptable cultural values, Nonconformism did serve to shape a specific definition of appropriate educational achievement.[2]

However, we should not ignore the much more secular influence exerted upon the educational system in Wales by the Labour movement. In this context, the celebrated dispute between O.M. Edwards, the Chief Inspector for the Welsh Department of the Board of Education, and the local School Board over the curriculum of the Higher Elementary School opened at Tonypandy (in the Rhondda Fawr Valley) in January 1915 is highly instructive (Davies, 1974a).[3] The intended nature of the school was clearly specified by Edwards himself: 'The Headmaster had to prepare the boys with continual reference to the industrial needs of the area and to the future probable occupations of the boys' (quoted in Davies, 1974a, p.170). However, this was clearly unacceptable to the residents of the area and, more significantly, to the local politicians represented on the School Board. They were determined that the school should provide their children with the opportunity to escape from 'the industrial needs of the area' — that is to say, from mining. As Edwards again put it:

> The Labour men who have the whole power insist upon Latin and French. They object to the school which is a 'blind alley'. They think that a Higher Elementary School is intended to keep the working man's son down and they want to find ways for their children to rise above coal-mining. They think that Latin and French are the two doors. (quoted in Davies, 1974a, p.171)

Interestingly, the School Board appears to have been successful in achieving the sort of school that it wanted.

The crucial question that we have not yet attempted to answer is that of the extent to which the historical attitudes with which we have been concerned are reflected in the contemporary Welsh situation. As we have seen, this is clearly held to be the case (Central Advisory Council for Education (Wales), 1967; Welsh Education Office, 1979). It is argued that not only is a particular significance attached to educational achievement in Wales, but also this exerts a significant influence upon the nature of the current educational system and its products. Certainly, as we have seen, the general issue of the relationship between educational performance and subsequent life-chances has continued to be a central concern of educationists and policy makers. However, the question remains: is there anything special about Wales? It is to this question that we shall try to give an answer in the remainder of the chapter.[4]

The Welsh Education System: its Current Performance

Clearly, we need to begin by evaluating the relative performance of the educational system in Wales. One approach to this task is to examine the outputs of the system: that is, the individuals who are leaving full-time education. This is what we shall be doing here. We would argue, moreover, that, given our immediate concern with the relationship between education and life-chances, it is appropriate that we should focus upon what Byrne, Williamson and Fletcher (1975) have termed 'socially significant attainment': those educational qualifications which, *prima facie*, are directly related to opportunities in the job market. Unfortunately, even this limited exercise is hampered by the quite remarkable paucity of serious research studies of these aspects of the educational institutions of Wales.[5]

Perhaps the most direct measure of such qualifications is the rate of success achieved by school leavers in the public examinations held at secondary school level: that is, in the Certificate of Secondary Education (CSE) and in the General Certificate of Education (GCE) Ordinary and Advanced level examinations. It is the credentials acquired at this stage of their career that many pupils will carry with them directly into the labour market.

Traditionally, schools in Wales have performed very well in these terms; a fact which has been held to reflect the esteem in which such attainment is maintained. Hence, for example, if we take a period before large-scale comprehensivisation and before local government reorganisation, say, 1965-66, the proportion of Welsh school leavers attaining a 'high level of achievement' (at least five passes at Ordinary level and/or one at Advanced level GCE) was considerably higher than the average score for the English regions. More recently (1975-76), although Wales's relative position has deteriorated, it remains the case that only two English regions (the South East — excepting Greater London — and the South West) have a larger proportion of 'high-level achievers' (see Table 4.1).

This picture is confirmed by related indices. Hence, success in public examinations is clearly closely connected with the number of years pupils stay at school, particularly past the minimum leaving age. As Table 4.2 shows, the proportion remaining at school beyond this minimum leaving age in Wales is far in excess of that in England. Only the South East, of the English regions, has figures comparable to the Welsh ones.

Here again, however, Wales's situation is much less favourable than it was. For example, if we look at the mid-1960s (1966), 17 per cent of 17-year-olds and 7 per cent of 18-year-olds were still at school in Wales: in England, the comparable statistics were only 12 per cent and 4 per cent. Indeed, even in the South East, the most favoured of the English regions, only 15 per cent of 17-year-olds and 5 per cent of 18-year-olds remained at school. What this means, of course, is that the rate of expansion of post-compulsory secondary schooling in England has been massively greater during the past ten years or so than it has in Wales. Even though Wales began from a much higher base point, the discrepancy is striking. Hence, in England as a whole, the proportion of

Table 4.1: School Leaver Achievements in England and Wales, by Region, 1975-76

	% of leavers with at least 5 'O' levels and/or 1 'A' level	% of leavers with no formal qualifications
North	21.1	16.8
Yorkshire and Humberside	22.1	18.9
North West	23.5	16.9
East Midlands	20.5	17.9
West Midlands	22.2	19.1
East Anglia	22.8	16.5
Greater London	24.7	19.0
South East	29.0	11.5
South West	27.6	13.3
England	24.4	16.3
Wales	24.8	26.0
England and Wales	24.5	16.8

Source: Welsh Office, *Statistics of Education in Wales* (HMSO, Cardiff, 1978), Table 6.05.

Table 4.2: Percentage of Pupils in Public Sector Schools Remaining Beyond the Statutory Leaving Age, January 1977[a]

	Aged 16	Aged 17	Aged 18
North	19.3	15.8	5.4
Yorkshire and Humberside	22.5	17.6	5.9
East Midlands	21.0	16.9	5.9
East Anglia	19.6	14.8	5.0
South East	33.8	23.9	7.7
South West	23.8	17.3	5.6
West Midlands	22.9	17.5	5.9
North West	18.9	15.1	4.9
England	25.6	19.0	6.3
Wales	28.5	21.7	7.5
England and Wales	25.7	19.2	6.4

Note: a. All figures give the numbers of pupils aged 16, 17 and 18 expressed as a percentage of the 13-year-old pupils 3, 4, and 5 years previously, except those for England and Wales which give pupils aged 16, 17 and 18 and whose birthdays fall between 1 January and 31 August as a percentage of 14-year-old pupils 2, 3 and 4 years previously.

Sources: Central Statistical Office, *Regional Statistics,* no.15 (HMSO, London, 1979), Table 7.2; Welsh Office, *Statistics of Education in Wales* (HMSO, Cardiff, 1978), Table 1.03.

17-year-old pupils has grown by some 57 per cent between 1966 and 1977 and that of 18-year-olds by about 58 per cent. In Wales, this expansion was by only 21 per cent and 12 per cent respectively. Clearly, then, the sluggish growth of Wales's sixth forms is a matter of some concern.

Nevertheless, it remains the case that a large proportion of Welsh school leavers go on to full-time further education of some kind. In 1975-76, 24 per cent of these school leavers were able to continue their education; in England, only 22 per cent were able to do so. In fact, only two of the English regions recorded significantly higher scores (the South East and the South West). Once again, however, Wales's relative position is not as good as it has been: for example, ten years previously, in 1965-66, Wales had a higher proportion of pupils proceeding to further education than any of the English regions and, as we shall see later, the record of a number of the individual education authorities in this respect was truly exceptional (see Byrne, Williamson and Fletcher, 1975). It is also worth noting here that there has been a consistent pattern in Wales of large numbers of school leavers entering the more 'academic' sectors of post-school education (in particular, the universities and colleges of education) — a fact which is in line with what is said about the traditional emphases of Welsh education.

The tenor of this evidence is, then, broadly consistent with those analyses which have stressed the high quality of the Welsh educational system. Academic attainment is highly valued in Welsh society and this esteem is reflected in the performance of Welsh schools and their pupils. It is true that Wales's relative position is not pre-eminent, as it once was, but this can reasonably be attributed to improvements elsewhere, rather than to any real deterioration in Wales. However, if we turn to the other end of the qualifications spectrum — as measured by the proportion of school leavers with *no* passes at either CSE or GCE — this sort of straightforward account appears much more dubious.

As Table 4.1 shows, the schools of Wales produce a massively higher proportion of leavers who have no formal qualifications at all than do any of the English regions: twice as many, for instance, as the South East and the South West.[6] Although the proportions of wholly unqualified school leavers in both Wales and the English regions have been declining in recent years, what emerges very clearly is that the gap between the two countries has been widening considerably. As we shall see later, at a time at which opportunities in the labour market are so severely limited, this trend can only be viewed with considerable anxiety.

It is this large proportion of unqualified school leavers which presents perhaps the central problem to the Welsh educational system. It
also presents the central paradox for analysis. How are we to account
for the fact that, whilst relatively large numbers of Welsh school leavers
are highly qualified and thereby enjoy the opportunity of acquiring
extra credentials in further education, by far the most distinctive feature of the educational system in Wales is its ability to turn out over a
quarter of its pupils with no tangible benefit from their five or so years
of secondary schooling? As one commentator (Wilding, 1977) has concluded:

> The picture we are left with after this statistical foray is of an educa-
> tion system which does very well by the abler young people and very
> poorly by the less able so perpetuating and exacerbating broader
> deprivations. An education system which, at the same time, produces
> far and away the largest proportion of young people who leave with-
> out any academic qualifications at all and is a leader in the produc-
> tion of O and A-level passes and entrants to full-time further educa-
> tion demands further examination. (p.31)

One way in which to begin this 'further examination' is to look at the
pattern of educational performance within Wales. Table 4.3 accordingly
gives the distribution of examination successes for boys and girls leaving
school in 1976-77 for each of the local education authorities. Although
detailed analysis is precluded because of the size and internal heterogeneity of these authorities, some important points do emerge quite
clearly. Hence, a distinction can be drawn between the predominantly
rural counties — most clearly exemplified by Dyfed and Gwynedd —
and the predominantly urban/industrial ones — such as Gwent and Mid
Glamorgan: the former have relatively high proportions of both boys
and girls achieving at least five Ordinary level passes and/or one Advanced level pass at GCE and relatively low levels of unqualified school
leavers; in the latter, very high proportions of young people leave school
without any sort of qualification. Clearly, this division is not exact: for
example, Powys, in many respects somewhat similar in character to
Dyfed and Gwynedd, occupies an intermediate position in terms of
educational achievement. Although comparable with the other rural
counties in most respects, it does not produce high levels of achievement amongst its boys. Similarly, West Glamorgan, although clearly one
of the urban/industrial group, attains quite high standards of 'output'
amongst its boys. Only South Glamorgan is wholly outside the urban/

Table 4.3: Examination Achievements of School Leavers, by Authority, 1976-77

	% of leavers with at least 5 'O' levels and/or 1 'A' level		% of leavers with no formal qualifications	
	Boys	Girls	Boys	Girls
Clwyd	19.3	22.4	23.0	17.3
Dyfed	26.3	27.3	23.6	19.1
Gwent	19.3	22.9	30.6	25.3
Gwynedd	27.6	26.2	22.6	23.9
Mid Glamorgan	18.5	21.9	38.4	37.6
Powys	19.3	25.0	22.5	14.1
South Glamorgan	26.7	24.1	22.1	17.1
West Glamorgan	23.5	22.1	24.1	33.8

Source: Welsh Office, *Statistics of Education in Wales* (HMSO, Cardiff, 1978), Table 6.04.

industrial pattern, in spite of being dominated by Cardiff. It may be, of course, that this very dominance in some way accounts for the county's aberrant profile.

This admittedly rather crude distinction between rural and urban/ industrial areas is given some support in the data on entry to full-time further education (see Table 4.4). As can be seen, the former group of authorities has much higher proportions of school leavers who continue their education in some way. It is also worth drawing attention to the fact that South Glamorgan's high levels of attainment are not translated

Table 4.4: Percentage of School Leavers Entering Full-time Further Education, by Authority, 1976-77

	Boys	Girls
Clwyd	21.1	34.1
Dyfed	21.0	36.3
Gwent	15.7	25.0
Gwynedd	20.9	43.4
Mid Glamorgan	10.7	22.3
Powys	36.3	50.6
South Glamorgan	18.5	19.7
West Glamorgan	17.4	18.6

Source: Welsh Office, *Welsh Social Trends* (HMSO, Cardiff, 1978), Table 47(b).

into high levels of entry to further education, which perhaps reflects the sorts of job opportunities open to qualified school leavers in a major service centre such as Cardiff. Similarly, Powys records the highest scores on this measure, in spite of its relatively low attainment levels amongst boys – again, possibly reflecting the nature of the local labour market. More generally, the far higher proportions of girls entering further education for each of the local authorities are remarkable and are not obviously a function of differential levels of attainment (compare Table 4.3). Again, we can only suggest that the choice between entering the labour market directly and undertaking further education is subject to different constraints as between boys and girls.

The very limited nature of this analysis makes major conclusions difficult to draw. However, the general distinction that emerges between the rural and the urban/industrial areas is instructive, even though it is by no means a perfect one. Certainly, the exceptionally high levels of achievement attained by pupils in rural Wales have been recognised in previous studies. For example, Byrne, Williamson and Fletcher (1975) in their cluster analysis of the local education authorities in England and Wales (as they existed in 1970) allocated the Welsh rural counties to their own specific cluster.[7] This is not to suggest, however, that the 'dualistic' nature of educational achievement in Wales can be accounted for simply by reference to a rural-urban/industrial distinction. The data are too complex to support such an account. Neither, of course, would such an account actually explain the observed patterns of achievement.

Some Determinants of Educational Attainment

In spite of the massive research effort that has been directed at discovering the determinants of educational attainment, very few entirely unambiguous conclusions have been produced (for an especially sceptical summary, see Tyler, 1977). Now, it is clearly not the function of this review to attempt to resolve the ambiguities of the general debate. Our intention is much more limited: we shall be concerned to assess the relevance of various of the general explanations that have been advanced to the understanding of the pattern of performance in Wales that we described in the previous section. Of course, given the preliminary nature of these general explanations, as well as the limited empirical data available to us, we cannot expect to provide a wholly conclusive discussion. However, we do hope to highlight some avenues of fruitful future research.

As we have seen, perhaps the most frequently used explanation of
the pattern of attainment in Wales has been the supposed high esteem
in which academic achievement is held. This type of argument parallels
the more general concern in the educational literature with the effects
of values with respect to education: more specifically, it has been
argued that the aspirations of children and their parents with respect to
the children's education and future careers exert a key influence over
likely educational performance.

Much more contentious, however, is the question of what sorts of
families create the home background in which the aspirations conducive
to high levels of achievement are inculcated. Many studies have drawn a
straightforward distinction between middle-class families (high aspirations) and working-class families (low aspirations) (Floud, Halsey and
Martin, 1956; Douglas, 1964; Douglas, Ross and Simpson, 1968).
Whilst not wishing to deny completely the value of this distinction, it
seems unlikely to contain the whole truth. As Keller and Zavalloni
(1964), for example, have pointed out, there are simply too many
deviant cases among both middle- and working-class families to be
ignored. There are clearly many working-class children who place a high
value on education as a vehicle for upward occupational mobility and,
equally, many middle-class children who do not.

Given this rather confused picture, it is perhaps strange that there
has not been more investigation of regional variations in these factors.
As we have emphasised, historically there is some reason to believe that
the particular character of the social structure in Wales was reflected in
attitudes towards educational provision and the value of academic
achievement. It certainly seems to us worth asking the question whether,
in the contemporary period, there are significant differences in value
orientations between, say, unskilled manual workers and their children
in Industrial South Wales and those in inner London.

Not surprisingly, of course, only very limited data are available to us
in respect of this question (and there is a clear need for further research). However, the Gittins Committee (Central Advisory Council for
Education (Wales), 1967), as part of its investigation of primary education in Wales, did conduct a survey of 1,222 families with one or more
children at a primary school; moreover, limited comparisons are
possible with the equivalent data collected for England by the Plowden
Committee (Central Advisory Council for Education (England), 1967).
The central conclusion of both Committees was that parental attitudes
toward education varied in the expected way according to social class.
However, the Gittins Report suggests that these social class differences

were '. . . perhaps not as marked (in Wales) as they appear to be in England'. The tentativeness of this suggestion is understandable: for example, in England, 61 per cent of parents in social classes I and II (professional and managerial) wanted their children to continue their education until age 18 and over, compared with 25 per cent in social class V (unskilled manual); in Wales, the figures were broadly comparable – 56 per cent in classes I and II and 22 per cent in class V. However, it is true that 15 per cent of class V in England wanted their children to leave school as soon as possible, whilst only 7 per cent did in Wales; for classes I and II, the figure was about 1 per cent in both countries. Also in Wales, 14 per cent of parents in class V and 13 per cent in classes I and II wished their children to continue their education for as long as possible (unfortunately, equivalent data are not available for England).

In addition, there were quite marked differences between the Welsh and English parents with regard to their preferred type of secondary school. Hence, a total of 59 per cent of the Welsh sample wanted their children to go to a grammar school, compared with only 51 per cent of the English parents. More strikingly, even amongst unskilled manual workers in Wales, the figure was 56 per cent, almost double the 30 per cent recorded for England. It may be, of course, that this difference is explicable in terms of the much more generous provision of grammar school places in many parts of Wales than in England. However, it is clear that the Welsh respondents based their choices upon their estimation of the quality of education offered in the secondary schools and the effect of such education on the future prospects of their children (admittedly, somewhat similar results were obtained in the English survey). The Gittins Committee itself was able to conclude: 'This confirms the longstanding tradition of commitment toward education in Wales, which appears to be as strong now as ever, if not stronger' (p.16).

The theoretical implications of this evidence on aspirations are by no means clear. In part, of course, this is simply because of the very partial nature of the evidence itself. However, within their limitations, the data do give some support to the notion that at least parents in Wales are committed to the importance of educational achievement for their children; they appear to value staying at school beyond minimum leaving age and they opt for the more 'academic' grammar schools over other types of secondary education. Moreover, there is a suggestion that in Wales the differences between social classes in these respects are less than they are in England. Instructive though these findings are, they do not, however, offer any very clear insight into the causes of the observed pattern of educational performance in Wales; whilst the evidence of high levels of aspiration may be taken to be consistent with the relatively large proportion of 'high-level achievers', it does not help us account for the very large proportion of school leavers with no qualifications at all.

It should not be thought, however, that the only possible manifestation of high esteem for educational attainment lies in the values and aspirations of individual families. It may also be reflected in the sort of educational provision made by the community for its children (as, indeed, we saw in the example from the Rhondda which we gave earlier). Moreover, numerous commentators have argued that the nature of educational provision is a major determinant of the sort of performance achieved by the recipients of that provision (for example, Eggleston, 1967; Byrne, Williamson and Fletcher, 1975). Perhaps the most controversial issue here has been that of the effects of different types of school on the educational attainment of their pupils. More specifically, of course, the debate has centred upon the relative merits of comprehensive and selective secondary schools.

Compared with other parts of Britain, Welsh education authorities responded with some alacrity to central government requirements to switch to a comprehensive system. By January 1974, 85 per cent of secondary school children were in comprehensive schools and, by January 1977, the figure had risen to about 92 per cent. Indeed, within Wales, only Dyfed, Gwent and Mid Glamorgan retained any selective schools at all.

However, the effects of this reorganisation are rather more difficult to disentangle. At a general level, it has been argued that comprehensive schools benefit the children from working-class and other disadvantaged backgrounds by removing the eleven-plus hurdle and ensuring greater flexibility in the secondary school (for example, Tuck, 1974; Neave, 1975). Other commentators, however, have argued that the change to comprehensives makes little positive difference and does little more than underline existing class differentials in educational opportunity (Ford, 1969). In Wales, the situation is further complicated by the fact that in many areas reorganisation has itself been minimal. Partly, we suppose, because of difficulties in coping with a very sparse population, many of the old grammar schools in the rural counties were admitting as much as 60-70 per cent of eleven-year-olds (Bell and Grant, 1977); whilst the average for Wales during the late 1960s was 33 per cent (Central Advisory Council for Education (Wales), 1967).

In other respects, as well, the change in secondary education in Wales appears to have had rather limited impact on the nature of the educational opportunities offered to secondary school pupils. In short, there is some considerable evidence to suggest that an academically elitist ethos, more conventionally associated with the grammar schools, pervades the comprehensives in Wales. Hence, for example, Benn and Simon (1970) singled out the Welsh comprehensives as 'narrowly meritocratic' and pointed to the 'near bilateral divisions inside the schools'. The Welsh schools streamed their pupils earlier than in England and were strictly limited in the extent to which they band or group pupils other than on the basis of measured performance. Similarly, entry to the sixth form was limited strictly in terms of Ordinary level GCE qualifications: in consequence, a low proportion of pupils in comprehensives stayed on beyond the minimum school leaving age compared with the maintained sector as a whole. Moreover, conditions of entry to sixth forms appear to have changed very little since the Benn and Simon survey (Welsh Committee of the National Union of Teachers, 1975). This fact may account in part for the slow growth of sixth forms in Wales which we noted above. All this is, of course, quite the opposite of the situation in the English comprehensives, in which sixth-form entrance tends to be 'open' with pupils being allowed to 'catch up' on missing Ordinary levels (a point to which Neave (1975) attached considerable importance in his study of university entrants from comprehensive schools).

What evidence we have suggests also that substantially less curriculum change has taken place in Welsh comprehensives than in their English counterparts, where such changes have often been specifically concerned with the modification of the content and presentation of syllabuses to adapt to the needs of the less able. Hence, for example, 90 per cent of Welsh candidates sit the CSE Mode 1 examinations (in which the syllabus is specified, the questions set and marked by the examining board) compared with only 73 per cent in England. Conversely, almost 25 per cent of CSE candidates in England in 1976 took Mode 3 (which allows for continuous assessment of pupils and the preparation of a syllabus by the school in which the course is to be followed) compared with only 10 per cent in Wales. It has been suggested that the sort of preparation possible under the Mode 3 scheme may be of some considerable benefit to weaker pupils (for example, Welsh Education Office, 1979).

This same formalism would appear to extend even to the pattern of entry of pupils for public examinations, a factor that is obviously directly related to subsequent success rates. Most significantly, of the 26 per cent of Welsh school leavers in 1976-77 with no formal qualifications, no less than 24 per cent had not been entered for any examinations: and this latter figure is, of course, substantially higher than those recorded in all of the English regions.

Clearly, these examples are inconclusive in themselves. However, taken together, they do provide a not inconsiderable foundation for the claim that the educational system in Wales maintains a highly traditional and narrow 'academic' orientation. In apparent contrast with what happens in English schools, their Welsh counterparts have clung to a form of organisation which prizes the highest levels of formal examination achievement at the expense of the development of the less intellectually gifted; and this is so irrespective of the reforms that have taken place in secondary education. As we have seen, there is some evidence to suggest that in this respect the schools do little more than reflect the wishes and attitudes of parents — the Welsh community at large. Nevertheless, this line of argument would appear to take us some way toward accounting for an educational 'output' in Wales which can scarcely be described as other than unsatisfactory.

In addition to the internal organisation of schools, however, it is important to examine the level of provision made for Welsh children, if we are to attain a proper understanding of the functioning of the educational system. This is so not only in terms of the determination of levels of attainment, where this type of argument is especially well suited to the explanation of average attainment for aggregate units (of the kind with which we are concerned here), but also in view of the universalistic principles upon which the state education system is presumed to operate.[8]

It is, in fact, well established that on almost every conceivable indicator there are major differences between the regions of Britain and, indeed, between the local education authorities which comprise them (for example, Boaden, 1971, Taylor and Ayres, 1969). Conventionally, of course, it has been argued that educational provision in Wales has been very generous. Indeed, as Table 4.5 shows, it *is* the case that total expenditure per pupil in Wales is relatively high in both primary and secondary sectors when compared with those parts of England outside the somewhat exceptional Inner London Education Authority area.

However, again as can be seen from Table 4.5, a major part of this superiority is attributable to greater expenditure on staff. This does not necessarily indicate better levels of actual provision, as it may simply be the result of longer average length of service of teachers, extra payments for teaching in areas of high 'social deprivation' and so on. In fact, for other specified types of expenditure, Wales is worse off than any part of

Table 4.5: Expenditure per Full-time Equivalent Pupil, by Area, 1978-79 (estimates, £)

	Primary				Secondary			
	Teaching staff	Premises	Books etc.	Total	Teaching staff	Premises	Books etc.	Total
Wales	249	49	12	310	341	62	20	423
English Non-metropolitan Counties	227	42	12	281	327	61	23	411
English Metropolitan Counties	229	45	12	286	336	66	23	425
Inner London Education Authority	331	62	17	410	430	83	33	546
Powys	293	56	17	366	362	77	27	466
Gwynedd	263	36	10	309	340	55	18	413
Dyfed	268	40	15	323	333	53	20	406
West Glamorgan	253	68	18	339	362	82	31	475
Clwyd	241	40	13	294	341	58	22	421
South Glamorgan	228	45	12	285	337	64	22	423
Gwent	241	49	7	297	339	53	12	404
Mid Glamorgan	227	54	10	291	331	64	19	414

Source: CIPFA, *Education Estimates* (1978-79).

England: for example, books and other essential materials are significantly less well provided for in secondary schools in Wales than they are
in England. Moreover, the difference in levels of provision is actually
widening: the relative position of Welsh schoolchildren in these terms is
deteriorating (see also Wilding, 1977).

Within Wales, as well, there are significant disparities in educational
spending by the various local education authorities. Contrast, for
example, Gwent's total expenditure (both primary and secondary) per
pupil on books and so forth of £19 with West Glamorgan's equivalent of
£49! However, although we can highlight these differences, without a
much more sophisticated analysis than we were able to carry out, it is
much more difficult to distinguish any pattern of expenditure. This is
true both in respect of the characteristics of the areas concerned (rural/
urban, social class, political complexion, etc.) and in respect of the levels
of achievement recorded. It is simply not the case, for example, that
high expenditure yields high levels of academic success or *vice versa*.

Clearly, it is more realistic in many ways to take as our measure
actual provision, rather than levels of educational expenditure: the
effect of different amounts of spending will in part depend upon the
nature of what is already provided. At least one pressure group has
expressed considerable concern over this actual provision, in spite of
the relatively high level of total expenditure. Hence, the Welsh Committee of the National Union of Teachers (no date) has commented:

> the problems created by the inadequacy of educational equipment
> and materials, staff provision and of school buildings, has had an
> effect on the quality of education in secondary schools in Wales and
> the solution of such problems (will) only be achieved by the deter-
> mined efforts of society to improve the standard of provision in its
> schools. (p.9)

There is, of course, no reason to believe that this assessment is in any
way a disinterested one. Nevertheless, the evidence would appear to
bear out the assertion that educational provision in Wales is not of a
high standard.

Hence, the staff/pupil ratios in primary and secondary schools in
Wales have changed remarkably little during the 25 years or so up until
1977-78, in spite of the massive changes that have taken place in the
size of the school-age population: in 1950-51, the primary school ratio
was 25:1 and the secondary 19:1; by 1977-78, the equivalent figures
were 22:1 and 17:1. Moreover, the staff/pupil ratio for secondary

schools in Wales is worse than that of five out of the eight English regions. Indeed, only Dyfed of the Welsh counties enjoys a ratio comparable to that of the most favoured English regions (East Anglia and the South West). Similarly, there would seem to be considerable justification for the Welsh Committee of the National Union of Teachers' assessment of the state of school buildings in Wales. Primary schools are in a particularly poor condition: some 29 per cent of permanent primary school buildings were built before 1903, 40 per cent before 1918 and 48 per cent before 1945. Neither should it be thought that Welsh secondary schools are without problems: 5 per cent of buildings date from before 1903, 10 per cent from before 1918 and 19 per cent from before 1945 (in Mid Glamorgan, however, this latter figure rises to 39 per cent!).

It emerges quite clearly, then, that the high levels of total expenditure on education by Welsh local authorities are not matched by comparably high levels of actual provision. It is therefore to be expected, perhaps, that there is little evidence of special provision for disadvantaged (in whatever way) children in Wales. Hence, for example, the Gittins Report (Central Advisory Council for Education (Wales), 1967) pointed out that the proportion of children receiving special education in Wales was lower than in any of the English regions; and Wilding (1977) has argued that the situation has changed very little during the period since the publication of the Report. Equally, it is instructive to examine the provision of nursery education by Welsh education authorities. Following the analysis presented in the Plowden Report (Central Advisory Council for Education (England), 1967) nursery education came to be seen as critical in 'compensating' for children's 'poor home backgrounds' (see, for example, the 1972 White Paper, *Education: a framework for expansion,* Cmnd. 5174). It is true that in Wales a higher proportion of children under five years of age attend school than in England. However, this is not because of superior nursery provision, but rather because, traditionally, Welsh children have begun in infants' schools in the first term after their fourth birthday. In fact, the Gittins Report (Central Advisory Council for Education (Wales), 1967) was critical of the sort of teaching received by these children, in that much of it was inappropriate to their stage of development and certainly did not fulfil the objectives set out in the Plowden Report. Whilst there has been some expansion of *bona fide* nursery provision during the past ten years, this has been concentrated to a considerable extent in the urban areas and acute problems remain in the other parts of Wales (Welsh Education Office, 1978).[9]

This relative lack of educational provision for the less able and otherwise disadvantaged is entirely consistent with what we have already said about the Welsh educational system. As we have seen, there is at least limited evidence to the effect that educational achievement is disproportionately highly prized by parents in Wales. Moreover, total expenditure on education is relatively generous, particularly in view of the comparative poverty of many of the Welsh local authorities. However, whether as a simple consequence of community values or not, the Welsh educational system appears to have adopted a very restricted view of its legitimate functions: it seems geared to producing traditional 'academic' success, at the expense of new developments to assist the less intellectually able and other disadvantaged groups. In addition, educational expenditure, in spite of its high level, is neither sufficient to preserve a parity of many kinds of provision between Wales and other parts of Britain, nor directed in any systematic way toward the 'compensation' of less favoured pupils. Indeed, in at least some instances, the opposite may be the case: for example, Byrne, Williamson and Fletcher (1975) remarked upon the generosity of the provision of grants for further education made by many of the Welsh education authorities.

All this would appear to offer some sort of account of the pattern of educational attainment which we described in an earlier section. The 'dualistic' nature of this pattern may be explained in terms of the fact that familial support and community provision in Wales are based upon a particular view of the nature and role of education: in short, schools are in the business of producing high-level, 'academic' performance. This works quite well for those pupils who aspire toward and are capable of 'success' defined in these terms. For other sorts of pupils, schools in Wales provide a much less happy and rewarding experience.

However, this argument, derived ultimately from the values which obtain toward education in Wales, can be satisfactory only at one level. Clearly, it cannot account for the origins of the values themselves. Indeed, Byrne, Williamson and Fletcher (1975) put the point succinctly:

> There is no doubt, however, that simple explanations of the pressure of Welsh culture are inadequate. Welsh traditions are a product of, and integral with, the social and economic structure of Wales itself, and the pattern of its social and political development. (p.109)

Therefore, in the concluding section of the chapter, we shall explore some of the interrelationships between education and the wider issues of Wales's economic and social development.

Concluding Remarks

Inevitably, such an exploration brings us back to the question with which we began this review: that of the links between performance in the educational system and subsequent life-chances. Clearly, at a surface level, these links are very close. Indeed, one commentator has concluded of the Welsh educational system:

> At one and the same time, the country is contriving to perpetuate an unqualified work force at a time when paper qualifications are all — or nearly all — and to prepare a large proportion of its young people for further and higher education which will in due course lead large numbers of them to leave Wales for employment in England. The education system is, it can be argued, too clearly reflecting the image of the Welsh economy and perpetuating its problems rather than providing an impetus to economic development. (Wilding, 1977, p.32)

Certainly, there is a sense in which much of what we have said about Welsh education is made comprehensible by reference to the nature of the economic structure of Wales and the latter's relationship with the wider framework of the British and, indeed, world economy. Hence, for example, the underdevelopment of much of rural Wales, with consequently severely limited chances of employment, may well exert a considerable pressure on parents to look for income opportunities for their children away from home. Educational qualifications can only be seen as an aid in this quest for social (and geographical) mobility; and hence the tradition of generous expenditure on certain kinds of educational provision in these areas (Byrne, Williamson and Fletcher, 1975). Ironically, of course, the out-migration of young, well-qualified people from rural Wales is itself one of the conditions of its continued underdevelopment.

Similarly, in the more densely populated urban/industrial parts of Wales, although employment opportunities are not by any means as limited, they are restricted in their range: until very recently, at least, the labour market has been dominated by manual occupations in extractive and heavy manufacturing industry. Moreover, even in these areas, unemployment has been a more or less persistent phenomenon. Again, it is not difficult to understand that families should respond to these structural conditions by emphasising the escape-route of education.

More specifically, the opportunities awaiting the school leaver are especially limited at the present time. Hence, in Wales as elsewhere, there has been a dramatic growth in unemployment amongst school leavers and young people generally since the early 1970s. Although this growth has been less than that which has occurred in Britain as a whole, the recent indications are that the gap between the rates is closing (Rees and Smith, 1979). More seriously, there appears to have been a major increase in long-term unemployment amongst young people (and especially young women) in Wales (Davies, 1978).

It would also appear to be the case that the nature of Wales's economic base is reflected in the sorts of opportunity that are available to those who do enter employment. Wilding (1977) reports,that, in 1974 in Wales, rather more than one in three boys getting jobs for the first time gained apprenticeships to skilled occupations. The figures for other industrial areas — for example, the North, North West, Yorkshire and Humberside — were close to one in two. At the other end of the employment spectrum, around half the new male entrants to employment in Wales went into jobs with no planned training at all. In comparable areas, and in Britain as a whole, the proportion was about a third. For girls, the story was equally dismal: very large proportions going into unskilled, dead-end jobs (see also Wales TUC, 1977). Of course, it is not the better-qualified male school leaver who suffers in Wales. He has as good a chance of obtaining an apprenticeship as those in other areas. Rather, it is the less well qualified who tend to miss out (Manpower Services Commission, 1975). Given these circumstances, it may well be an entirely rational decision for those pupils who find themselves not achieving 'success' in the terms set by the school to minimise their effort, thereby reinforcing their non-achievement.

There is, however, a paradox here. Although it may be true that education is highly esteemed as an avenue of escape from the very limited opportunities made available in the nature of the economy in Wales, it is only a minority of individuals who are actually able to benefit by their academic endeavours. Although it is in the interest of each individual to acquire the maximum educational credentials, there is no reason to believe that the structures of material inequality are very much affected by education. This remains true in spite of the apparent increase in demand from prospective employers for 'qualifications' and the manifold educational reforms that have taken place since 1944. Tyler (1977) puts the point thus:

Education has been given the job of breaking down the inequalities between ethnic groups, classes and regions. It is supposed to be an agent not only of modernisation, but also the legitimator of the inequalities of advanced industrialism. This is far too much to expect of any 'secular religion'. Despite the huge amount of public money that the educational system eats up, the mechanism of selection, allocation and rewards is still not working according to any model of social engineering and probably never will. (p.131)

Given this, of course, it may well be that, as Wilby (1977) has suggested, 'we should see education, not as a means of redistributing the national cake, but as part of the cake itself' (p.360).

It remains, however, to ask the question as to why the beliefs about the educational system that we have depicted persist. Certainly, it can be argued that they are highly functional to the smooth working of the existing order of things. As Bourdieu (1974) has commented:

It is probably cultural inertia which still makes us see education in terms of the ideology of the school as a liberating force ('l'école libératrice') and as a means of increasing social mobility, even when the indications tend to be that it is in fact one of the most effective means of perpetuating the existing social pattern, as it both provides an apparent justification for social inequalities and gives recognition to the cultural heritage, that is, to a *social* gift treated as a *natural* one. (p.32)

Indeed, it may well be that this sort of analysis is particularly relevant to the Welsh situation. Not only is Welsh society characterised by severe internal and external inequalities, but also there is the vexed question (which we have not touched on here) of its language and culture (Rawkins, 1979). The function of the educational system (and beliefs about it) are critical to both problems. It is certainly impossible to divorce the examination of the internal workings of Welsh schools from the theoretical interrelationships between education and the wider context of class, region and ethnicity (Roberts, 1979).

Notes

1. We should like to thank Sara Delamont and David Reynolds for their comments on earlier drafts of this chapter.

2. However, it should be remembered that, for at least the first part of the nineteenth century, Nonconformism saw the appropriate vehicle of this education as the Sunday school, rather than the day school of the British pattern. It is arguable that this hindered the development of education in Wales (Evans, 1971). We should also be careful not to suggest that the relationship between Nonconformity and education was specific to the Welsh: for example, Moore (1974) has described comparable attitudes (admittedly at a later period) amongst Methodist mining families in County Durham.

3. We are grateful to David Reynolds for drawing our attention to this material.

4. For many commentators, the single most distinctive aspect of education in Wales is the Welsh language. Whilst in no way wishing to deny its significance, conventional treatments of this issue have served to divert attention from other, equally important features of education in Wales. It is with these latter questions that we shall be concerned here. However, we recognise that perhaps the most fruitful avenues of future research will have to encompass the interrelationships between the educational inequalities and the wider aspects of Welsh society, including, of course, language and ethnicity.

5. We are grateful to Sara Delamont for access to her survey of contemporary educational research on Wales, which helped us to come to this conclusion. In this respect, research on education seems to be in the same situation as that on most other aspects of state intervention in Wales (see Ch. 1 above).

6. Interestingly, only Scotland and Northern Ireland are comparable to Wales in this respect.

7. The cluster comprised Breconshire, Caernarvonshire, Cardiganshire, Carmarthenshire, Merioneth, Montgomeryshire, Pembrokeshire and Radnorshire (as well as the Isle of Wight).

8. This sort of consideration is especially pertinent at a time of cuts in public expenditure. The Welsh total of expenditure on education for 1978-79 of £379 million represents a cut of 3 per cent from the previous year. Further cuts are, of course, planned in accordance with the policies of the current central administration.

9. We refer here only to nursery education provided by local education authorities. The Welsh Nursery School Movement (Mudiad Ysgolion Feithrin) has provided large numbers of nursery school places, especially in the rural areas.

5 HEALTH, THE DISTRIBUTION OF HEALTH SERVICES AND POVERTY IN WALES [1]

Gareth Rees
(with the assistance of John Parkinson and Ellie Scrivens)

State intervention in the provision of health care in Britain is by no means simply the product of the National Health Service Act of 1946; on the contrary, the development of public health legislation is one of the central features of nineteenth-century urban history (see, for example, Briggs, 1963), whilst national health insurance was first introduced in 1911. However, what is significant about the 1946 Act is that it was based upon a principle quite distinct from previous legislation — namely, that access to adequate medical care should be available to all, independent of ability to pay for it. As Aneurin Bevan himself put it:

> No society can legitimately call itself civilised if a sick person is denied medical aid because of lack of means . . . Society becomes more wholesome, more serene, and spiritually healthier, if it knows that its citizens have at the back of their consciousness the knowledge that not only themselves, but all their fellows, have access, when ill, to the best that medical skill can provide. *(In Place of Fear,* p.74; quoted in Foot, 1975, p.103)

What this has meant is that, given the state's commitment to provide proper health services, inadequate access to health care has itself come to be seen as a dimension of social disadvantage. Again in Bevan's words, health has been seen as the 'birthright' of the whole population.

Moreover, in quite another sense, the National Health Service (NHS) has been one of the key instruments of the Welfare State's attempt to ameliorate conditions of poverty and inequality. It is a commonplace that for much of the population sickness and disability have material consequences in terms of under- and unemployment, reduced incomes and resultant individual and family hardship (see, for example, Abel-Smith and Townsend, 1965). Quite simply, by providing adequate access to health care facilities (preventative as well as curative), it has been hoped to raise general standards of health amongst the population, thereby lessening these social consequences. As we shall see, of course, the NHS has achieved its objectives to only a very partial extent.

Given these considerations, then, in examining health and poverty in Wales, we can distinguish a number of key dimensions, which will provide a framework for this chapter. Firstly, it is important to assess the nature and extent of health problems amongst the Welsh population. Secondly, we need to examine the actual provision of health services in Wales and the resources devoted to this provision. Thirdly, we should evaluate the extent to which the provision of services is 'adequate' to the health characteristics of the Welsh population.

In performing these tasks, we shall for the most part be dependent upon the official health statistics. The difficulties of using data of this kind are well known (for example, Hindess, 1973). The first problem is that of the definition of 'health' itself. Clearly, we shall be concerned only with states of health that are actually recorded by the health service; for example, we can say nothing about sickness that is never reported to some part of the NHS. Yet even here, there are many variations in definition. In between the obviously 'well' and the obviously 'ill' there is a vast grey area, in which no rigorous and objective criteria operate. For the most part, we are dependent on 'professional judgement'.

However, by far the most serious difficulties arise over the fundamental distinctions between 'need' and 'demand' and 'use' (see, for example, Culyer, 1976). In assessing the adequacy of health service provision, we are presumably concerned with the extent to which health 'needs' are being met. Much of the available data, however, measures the extent to which health services are demanded or used. High levels of demand or use *may* give an indication of greater need, but they may equally reflect nothing more than particular cultural norms with respect to the health service. Equally, higher levels of use may simply reflect greater availability of health services in a particular geographical area. Again, higher levels of use may be interpreted as indicating more ill health or simply disproportionate benefit drawn by high users from the NHS. These are points to which we shall return later.

In spite of these difficulties, however, the distribution of health problems and that of health services do provide useful points of access to the subject of this chapter. As we shall see, the gross inequalities that exist even in these crude terms make the pursuit of ever more sophisticated measures of 'need' and so forth somewhat superfluous.

The State of Health in Wales

Health in Wales has been worse than in other parts of Britain for at least the past hundred years. Of course, Wales, in common with Britain as a whole, has improved enormously during this period in terms of the average life expectancies and mortality rates of its population. Nevertheless, as Table 5.1 shows, in the early 1930s Wales had a death rate eleven

Table 5.1: Ratio of Locally Adjusted Death Rates to England and Wales Rates 1931-73[a]

	Wales	Industrial South Wales	South East England
1931-35[b]	1.11	1.12	0.87
1936-39	1.14	1.17	0.86
1940-47[c]	n.a.	n.a.	n.a.
1948-50	1.08	1.11	0.90
1951-55	1.09	1.12	0.88
1956-60	1.13	1.17	0.92
1961-65	1.13	1.17	0.92
1966-70	1.12	1.17	0.88
1971-73	1.10	1.14	0.87

Notes:
a. England and Wales rate = 1.00.
b. No figure available for 1933.
c. No figures available for 1940-47.

Sources: Registrar General's Annual Commentary, 1932; Registrar General's Annual Tables, 1934-73.

points above that of England and Wales combined; forty years later, in the early 1970s, that disparity was almost exactly the same. Even more instructive, perhaps, is the massive and persistent difference between the death rates for the South East of England and those for Industrial South Wales (Table 5.1). Certainly, there is no indication in these statistics that the inception of the NHS has had much effect in reducing inequalities in life expectancies.

In only one respect has the Welsh situation improved dramatically: the infant mortality rate. During the 1970s, for the first time in many generations, the infant mortality rate in Wales fell below that for England and Wales together. More specifically, the rate for the industrial valleys of South Wales fell from a level that had been consistently 25 per cent or more in excess of that for England and Wales to a figure that was actually below the England and Wales average. Significantly, Hart (1976) comments that these changes are unlikely to be the effect of any dramatic change in obstetric practice, but rather the result 'of efficient contraception and termination of pregnancy . . . with a shift into the non-reproductive age group of the women who experienced childhood malnutrition as a mass phenomenon' (p.890). Again, the efficacy of the NHS appears limited.

A distinctive pattern of health in Wales emerges equally clearly if we examine mortality rates from particular causes; again, there are striking differences between the experience of Wales and that of England. This can be inferred quite readily from the comparisons between Wales, and England and Wales presented in Table 5.2.

Hence, death rates from tuberculosis are strikingly higher for men in Wales, although much lower for women. Similarly, for certain types of cancer (apart from lung and breast cancer) the Welsh death rates are very much higher than in England; for example, death from stomach cancer is some 13 per cent higher than in England and Wales for men and 21 per cent higher for women. The same pattern is revealed for heart disease, death rates for both men and women being considerably higher than the combined figures. Again, the death rate for men from bronchitis is higher in Wales, but lower for women. However, these average figures conceal an even more striking picture; hence, the death rates among particular age groups in particular areas are massively different from those for England and Wales. For example, male mortality from coronary heart disease for the age group 35-44 years in the valleys of Glamorgan is approximately 75 per cent above the rate for England and Wales and treble the rate for East Anglia. Similarly, Howe (1972) shows that death rates from bronchitis in many parts of South Wales are as much as 50 per cent above the United Kingdom average, the worst areas being Swansea, Merthyr Tydfil and the valley towns of Glamorganshire and Monmouthshire.

Finally, the standard mortality rates from accidents — and especially for those other than motor vehicle accidents — are generally higher in Wales. More specifically, the rates from accidents at work reveal an extremely poor safety record in Wales. Hence, although Wales has only some 4 per cent of the total labour force of the United Kingdom, it has consistently produced about 8 per cent of industrial accidents (in factory and construction processes) and 10 per cent of the fatal ones. More detailed breakdown (by industry, for example) is not available, thereby precluding more specific analysis. However, it appears quite clear that these excessively high accident rates are to a considerable extent

Table 5.2: Deaths and Standard Mortality Ratios for Selected Causes in Wales, by Sex, 1975

	Males		Females	
Cause of death	Numbers of deaths	Standard[a] mortality ratio	Numbers of deaths	Standard[a] mortality ratio
All causes	18,478	109	17,132	105
Tuberculosis of respiratory system[b]	52	122	9	69
Malignant neoplasm oesophagus	108	99	120	141
Malignant neoplasm stomach	460	113	345	121
Malignant neoplasm lung, bronchus	1,429	94	313	80
Malignant neoplasm intestine	475	108	542	103
Malignant neoplasm breast	4	84	639	96
Malignant neoplasm uterus	⌐	—	103	123
Leukaemia	94	93	77	94
Chronic rheumatic heart disease	140	110	266	122
Hypertensive heart disease	260	123	342	135
Ischaemic heart disease	6,030	117	4,194	112
Cerebro-vascular disease	2,003	116	3,014	112
Pneumonia	1,044	87	1,330	87
Bronchitis and emphysema	1,237	114	334	95
Cirrhosis of liver	75	142	64	122
Motor vehicle accidents	233	102	93	92
All other accidents	344	139	432	150
Suicide and self-inflicted injuries	111	90	78	91

Notes:
a. England and Wales = 100.
b. 1972 figures.

Source: Report of the Chief Medical Officer, *Health Services Wales 1976* (Welsh Office, Cardiff), p.49.

explicable in terms of the disproportionate employment share of recognisably dangerous industries, such as metal manufacturing, in the Welsh economy. It is also of some significance that the data given above *exclude* notoriously dangerous sectors such as mining and quarrying, and forestry and fishing (see Liddell, 1973a and 1973b, for an analysis of mining). Equally, these data for Wales are at least consistent with Steele's (1974) finding that there was a significant inverse relationship between observed accidents (adjusted to take account of regional industrial mix) and labour scarcity (ratio of unfilled vacancies to number of unemployed) — that, in other words, economic activity is a key issue in the incidence of industrial accidents.

If we turn from a consideration of mortality rates to look at patterns of sickness and disability, again a remarkably consistent picture emerges, although a strict interpretation of the data is more difficult. Firstly, we know that expenditure on sickness benefit, injury benefit, invalidity benefit and disablement benefit is strikingly higher in Wales than in any of the English regions.[2] Not surprisingly, then, Welsh workers have many more days, on average, of certified incapacity than do their English counterparts (irrespective of the region in which they live); hence, the days of certified incapacity per man at risk for 1974-75 in Wales was 31.8 whilst the equivalent figure for England was 15.2 (Central Statistical Office, 1979). Hart (1976) has pointed out that between 1953/54 and 1972/73 there was a 30 per cent rise in certified incapacity to work from illness in Great Britain. The increase in Wales during the same period was 59 per cent, nearly double the British average and a greater increase than in any other region. Hart suggests that the explanation of this disparity lies in the general economic conditions of Wales, where high morbidity and mortality are combined with high rates of long-term unemployment, particularly in areas without alternative work after pit closures and lacking protected light employment for those disabled by heavy industry. In these circumstances, there is 'a large . . . concealment of unemployment as long-term sickness absence' (p.889); that is, men (particularly older ones) register sick, rather than unemployed, an action which 'is neither illegal nor immoral'. It is unfortunately more difficult, of course, to obtain adequate data on the standards of health of the general population, as opposed to those registered for employment.[3]

We are on much firmer ground in considering the extent of physical disability in Wales as a result of the study *Handicapped and Impaired in Great Britain* (OPCS, 1971). The data presented mark Wales as a country with a major problem of physical disability. Hence, the rates of reported impairment[4] in Wales are markedly higher than those for England; for men and women (over 16 years of age) in Wales the figure is 88.7 per thousand population; the equivalent for England is 77.9 per thousand population. Only two of the English regions — the South West (95.1 per thousand population) and Yorkshire and Humberside (89.3 per thousand population) — have higher rates than Wales. Similarly, only two English regions have a higher proportion of people reporting limited mobility; whilst only one English region has a larger proportion of the population housebound, chairfast or bedfast.

However, in terms of the proportion of the population very severely, severely or appreciably handicapped, Wales has a slightly smaller proportion than England. This situation, however, is reversed for men, only the South West region having a higher rate than Wales. The explanation of these statistics would seem to lie in two central features of Wales's economic and demographic development (although we would require a much more detailed analysis to be categorical). Firstly, as we have seen, relatively large numbers of workers in Wales are (and have been) employed in industries which are known to be dangerous. Secondly, patterns of population change — and, in particular, age-selective net out-migration — have produced a population structure in which old people are over-represented. It is also important to bear in mind that the clear relationship between physical disability and financial poverty is well established (for example, Maclean and Jefferys, 1974).

These latter points, however, suggest certain limitations of our discussion so far. The analysis that we have presented has taken the form of comparisons between the state of health in Wales and that in other parts of Britain. Whilst this is useful, it ignores the very major differences that exist *within* Wales (to some of which we have already referred in passing). It is clearly the case that the generally adverse conditions of health exhibited in Wales are not distributed evenly, either between social groups or between geographical areas. Hence, for example, it is well known that differential mortality rates are experienced by different social classes, with those in higher social classes enjoying lower mortality rates. Table 5.3 shows that these class differences in mortality rates have actually been greater since the Second World War than before it; whilst absolute rates have fallen, at least in infancy and childhood, the gap between social classes has increased. Hence, age-standardised mortality rates for unskilled manual workers were only 23 per cent higher than those for professional men in 1931, but 88 per cent higher in 1961. (See also Brotherston, 1976; Blaxter, 1976) . Table 5.4 shows the same trend for sickness rates, but with even greater clarity. Unskilled manual workers reported suffering more than two-and-a-half times as much limiting, long-standing illness as professional men, and their wives more than three times as much. Even for

Table 5.3: Standardised Mortality Ratios, by Social Class, Men Aged 15-64 Years, 1930-72[a]

Years	Social classes[b]				
	I	II	III	IV	V
1930-32	90	94	97	102	111
1949-53	86	92	101	104	118
1959-63	76	81	100	103	143
1970-72	77	83	103	114	137[c]

Notes: a. Mortality rate for all classes = 100.
b. I — professional occupations; II — intermediate occupations; III — skilled occupations; IV — partly skilled occupations; V — unskilled occupations.
c. Estimated from Central Statistical Office, *Social Trends,* 9 (HMSO, London, 1979), Chart 8.6, p.134.

Sources: Registrar General's Decennial Supplements on Occupational Mortality; Central Statistical Office, *Social Trends,* 9 (HMSO, London, 1979).

Table 5.4: Persons Reporting Limiting, Long-standing Illness, by Sex, Age and Socio-economic Class, 1976: Rates per Thousand Population

Social class[a]	Males		Females	
	All ages	15-44	All ages	15-44
I	80	50	86	66
II	121	76	131	77
III	149	85	163	84
IV	160	95	143	83
V	178	105	213	98
VI	234	104	299	120
All classes	153	90	170	88

Notes: a. I — professional occupations; II — employers and managers; III — intermediate and junior non-manual occupations; IV — skilled manual and own account non-professional; V — semi-skilled manual and personal service; VI — unskilled manual.

Source: OPCS, *General Household Survey 1976* (HMSO, London, 1978).

those aged 15-44 years, unskilled manual workers had twice as much chronic illness, and their wives almost twice as much, as professional men and their wives.

These established relationships between class and indices of poor health are presumably reflected in the state of health of the Welsh population; although no separate analyses are available for Wales, there is no reason to believe that the basic relationships do not hold. To what extent, then, are the aggregate differences that we highlighted earlier simply reflections of these relationships? Whilst it is by no means straightforward to give an answer to this question, it is the case that semi-skilled and unskilled occupations (as recorded in the 1971 Census) were over-represented in Wales relative to Great Britain. Correspondingly professional, upper managerial and intermediate occupations were relatively under-represented. Yet these aggregate differences in occupational structure are not enormous and, on the face of it, seem insufficient to provide a wholly convincing explanation.

The situation is significantly altered, however, if we examine particular areas within Wales. Hence, the coalfield areas exhibit not only somewhat atypical occupational structures, but also markedly deviant health characteristics. Hence, for example, the weighted mean-adjusted mortality rate for the Glamorgan valleys in the mid-1960s was 29 per cent above the rate for England and Wales. In the valleys of Monmouthshire, it was 19 per cent above the England and Wales figure (Hart, 1970). These rates were much worse than for other parts of Wales. What appears to have happened is that mortality rates generally in England and Wales have improved considerably in recent decades. In some areas and for some occupational groups, however, improvements have been very much slower. Hence, Hart's researches (for example, 1971b) have shown that, on a whole range of indices, the relative state of health of mining communities in South Wales was worse in the 1950s and 1960s than it was thirty or forty years before. In the Glamorgan and Monmouthshire valleys, in the years 1939-43, the standard mortality rate was 28 per cent higher than the rate for England and Wales; during the years 1964-68, it was 31 per cent higher (a finding that is broadly consistent with those reported earlier for class differences). The significance of this evidence is that it suggests an analysis of the state of health amongst a given population that is situated firmly in the context of the latter's 'total environment'. Welsh economic development has been such as to imply for major sections of the population, concentrated for the most part in quite specific geographical localities, employment in unhealthy and dangerous conditions, interspersed with periods of under- and unemployment. Critically, many areas were destitute from the 1920s until the Second World War, with lasting effects on the health of children and young adults. These circumstances, in turn, have implied lower-than-average family incomes and older and damper houses than in most other parts of Britain. In addition, the economic development of the coalfields has generated appalling general environmental conditions (Howe, 1972).

It is in the specifics of these conditions that we should locate the explanations of the mortality and morbidity rates which we have outlined in this section. More specifically, as the industrial structure and wider environmental conditions in Wales change, we should expect health problems to change as well. Indeed, Lowe (1978) has already suggested that in Wales 'the young are as healthy as, if not healthier than the English population'. In other words, the current rates of mortality and morbidity are very much 'a legacy of the past'. Similarly, Dowie (1978) has commented:

If these trends (i.e. the decline in employment in terms of metal manufacture and mining and quarrying) continue over the next decade, it can be anticipated that not only will improved technology contribute to a reduction in the prevalence of some industrially-induced mortality causes, but also the diminution in employment numbers in the 'heavy' industries will be reflected in a decline in the overall incidence of these causes of death plus other morbidity conditions thought to be pronounced among such workers. (p.58)

The question of whether there will be a significant improvement in the state of health of the Welsh population remains to be answered definitely. However, there can be little doubt as to the central relationship between health and economic and environmental conditions. Nevertheless, we do not suggest that this relationship provides a sufficient account of Welsh health or lack of it. We must also consider the nature of health care provision; and this we shall do in the next section.

Health Services in Wales

As we have already seen, since the establishment of the NHS the state has undertaken to provide adequate health care facilities for the whole of the population, irrespective of ability to pay. In practice, this means that the health service should allocate resources and facilities in a way which responds 'equitably' to differing levels of 'need'. In the previous section, we sought to establish some measure of these health 'needs' in Wales (whatever the imperfections of the available data). A partial explanation of Wales's state of health was given in terms of the nature of economic and other development in Wales. However, it is also presumably the case that the extent and quality of health care available in Wales have an effect upon the general health of the population. Hence, the question of 'equitable' responses to health 'needs' is a complex one, given this interaction between health care provision and health itself. Nevertheless, given the generally poor state of health of the Welsh population (and, more especially, particular groups within it), we are led to general expectations as to an adequate provision of health facilities.

The 1977 Public Expenditure White Paper (Cmnd. 6721-II) set the targets for expenditure on health and personal social services in Wales at £331 million for 1976/77, £332 million for 1977/78, and £335 million for 1978/79 (at 1976 survey prices). In comparative terms, the 1977/78 figure represented an estimated *per capita* expenditure in Wales of £119, in England of £117 and in Scotland of £141. On the basis of these admittedly crude statistics, there would appear to be a clear disparity between the relative severity of Welsh health 'needs' and the resources allocated to meet them: what Dowie (1978) has referred to as 'a relative "need" inequity in the *per capita* financial allocations to health in Wales' (p.77). However, the analysis is somewhat complicated if we look at the actual services provided in Wales. Table 5.5 compares service provision in Wales with the average for England and Wales.

As can be seen, for the vast majority of headings, provision in Wales seems somewhat superior to that in England and Wales. However, this face-value assessment ignores the significantly different health problems that, as we have seen, exist in Wales. It also ignores the fact that the pattern of economic development in Wales has generated an uneven demographic structure and an uneven pattern of communications within Wales. What this implies is that the health service required to achieve the same level of provision is likely to vary both within Wales and between Wales and other parts of Britain. Therefore, we must look beyond the gross measures of relative provision provided in Table 5.5.

Hospital Services

The hospital service, despite the planned integration of NHS reorganisation in 1974, remains a largely independent and very expensive part of the health service. Typically, some 75 per cent of revenue expenditure, 95 per cent of capital and 85 per cent of personnel resources are devoted to the provision of hospitals. Moreover, since the decision to decentralise acute hospital facilities to medium-sized district hospitals (the third policy change since the NHS started) there has been a rapid escalation in the costs of building and running such hospitals. These

Table 5.5: Distribution of Health Services, Wales, and England and Wales, 1975

	Number	Rate per 100,000 population	
	Wales	Wales	England and Wales
Manpower			
Medical staff			
Community health care	193	7.0	5.6
Hospital service	1,528	55.3	57.8
Family practitioner service (number)	1,369	49.5	47.0
Dental staff			
Community health care	117	4.2	3.2
Hospital service	49	1.8	1.8
Family practitioner service (number)	531	19.2	23.8
Ophthalmic and dispensing opticians	431	15.6	12.7
Nursing and midwifery staff	21,000	759.5	718.0
Non-psychiatric hospitals 1973	13,922	506.4	456.0
Psychiatric hospitals 1973	3,466	126.1	121.0
Health visitors 1974	425.6	15.4	14.3
Home nurses 1974	855.3	31.0	23.7
Midwives (domiciliary) 1974	298.8	10.8	7.5
Professional and technical staff	2,879	104.1	101.0
Chiropodists	83.3	3.0	2.7
Dental surgery assistants	181.7	6.6	4.8
Dietitians	21.7	0.8	1.0
Occupational therapists	92.5	3.3	4.1
Orthoptists	16.0	0.6	0.7
Pharmacists	157.9	5.7	4.5
Physiotherapists	255.7	9.2	10.8
Radiographers	373.8	13.5	11.9
Local authority social services			
Senior social service staff	399	14.4	14.4
Social workers	913	33.0	35.4
Home helps	2,790	100.9	95.4
Facilities			
Allocated beds available daily, (000's)			
Medical	3.7	133.8	117.2
Surgical	5.2	188.1	173.1
Obstetrics and GP maternity	1.3	47.0	45.3
Geriatrics/units for younger disabled	3.9	141.0	123.7
Total non-psychiatric	15.8	571.4	507.5
Mental illness	6.0	217.0	213.3

Table 5.5 (continued)

Mental handicap	2.5	90.4	114.8
Total psychiatric	8.5	307.4	330.2

Source: R. Dowie, 'Demographic and Socio-economic Indices and Sickness Absence Statistics: their relevance as morbidity indicators', in J. Brotherston (ed.), *Morbidity and its Relationship to Resource Allocation* (Welsh Office, Cardiff, 1978), p.83.

problems are not, of course, specific to Wales. However, they have combined in Wales in an environment where many of the existing hospitals are old, unsuited for the district hospital concept and expensive to maintain in usable condition. Hence, given that a generous estimate of the life-in-use of most hospital designs is fifty years, the NHS would need to build a new hospital in Wales every two or three years to maintain the capital stock in 'modern' condition and should have built 10-15 units in Wales since the NHS was set up. Needless to say, this has hardly been the case. It is also important to note that the rise in the costs of running the hospital service in Wales has been greater than the rise in the costs of the health service as a whole (170 per cent compared with some 150 per cent for the period 1970-76). Hence, not only is the cost of the hospital service rising in real terms, it is also consuming a greater proportion of the available financial resources. Consequently, relatively less is being spent on other aspects of health care — a point of some significance given the peculiarities of the Welsh situation.

Over about the same period (1971-75), the number of available beds in hospitals per 100,000 population declined from 951 to 876; yet the number of annual cases per available bed rose slightly (by 0.7). Attendances at out-patients' clinics remained remarkably stable over the period, in terms of both total and new attendances (Welsh Office, 1977a, Table 51). What emerges most clearly, however, is that increased resources have not succeeded in tackling the central problem of poor access to hospital facilities. Hence, the number of people on in-patient waiting lists in Wales rose from some 27,500 in 1967 to about 37,500 in 1976; whilst the out-patient waiting list grew from just over 25,000 to some 55,000 during the same period (Report of the Chief Medical Officer, no date). Unfortunately, it is not possible to say whether particular population groups are over-represented on the waiting lists (except in so far as the well-known high use of medical services by the elderly is reflected in the waiting lists).

Outside the acute sector, the picture is even less encouraging. The development of facilities for the mentally ill, the mentally or physically handicapped, the chronically sick and the very old has taken a distinct second place in any division of resources within the hospital service in Wales. Some measure of this is given by the fact that, of the 24,000 beds available in Wales, 16 per cent are dedicated to geriatric use, 34 per cent to psychiatric use (24 per cent mental illness; 10 per cent mental handicap) and the remaining 50 per cent to acute and GP use. It is also important to note that the through-put of patients per bed in these categories varies widely, largely as a result of the kind and intensity of medicine practised: hence, in the acute sector, through-put per bed is 20-30 patients per year; for geriatric beds it is under five and for psychiatric beds under three.

Once again, however, the situation that we have described in the hospital service is not uniform over the whole of Wales. As can be seen from Map 5.1, hospital provision is heavily concentrated in the most populous parts of Wales. Even more dramatically, compare the 11.4 hospital staff per 100,000 population in Powys or the 36.6 in Gwynedd with the massive 132.5 per 100,000 population in South Glamorgan or 55.9 in West Glamorgan. Whilst this has an obvious logic, it does pose particular problems for those living in the less highly populated areas; they are inevitably disadvantaged in terms of the accessibility of hospital care and have to spend more time and money travelling the longer distances to hospital facilities. This has, in fact, been recently recognised in a recommendation that Powys should receive special resource allocation to ameliorate some of the problems caused by the area's scattered population (Welsh Office, 1978b).

Community Services

Community medical services in general, and the role of GPs in particular, have undergone major changes of emphasis over the past twenty years. Most significant, perhaps, is the growing separation of the hospital and community services, in spite of the attempt to reverse this trend in the 1974 NHS reorganisation. The growing demand for 'social' rather than medical help has left GPs with little opportunity to practise anything but the most rudimentary diagnostic and therapeutic skills. Hence, for example, a recent study by the Welsh Consumer Council (1979b) indicates that, amongst their samples of parents of children under ten years old and of people over 60 years old in the Merthyr and Cynon Valley Health District, there was a significant dissatisfaction with the time and attention given by their GPs. In parallel with the changes outlined above, there has been a significant reorganisation of general

Map 5.1: Major Hospitals

with 150 or more staffed beds allocated
DECEMBER 1976

Hospitals

Acute   ●

Psychiatric   ■

Health Authority Boundaries

Area   ——

District   ----

Llandudno General

●Royal Alexandra

●Bryn-y-Neuadd
●Caernarvonshire
St. David's ● and Anglesey General

Lluesty General ●
H.M Stanley ●

North Wales ■

●Llangwyfan

Wrexham and East
Denbighshire War Memorial ●

Maelor General ●

N

●Bronglais General

Bronllys ●
Mid Wales ■

St. David's ■ ● West Wales General

Nevill Hall ● ■ Pen-y-fai

St. Tydfil's ●

Pembroke County
War Memorial

Llanelli ●

● Morriston

Cefn Coed ■ ● Neath General

Singleton ● ● Mount Pleasant

● Llwynypia

County Griffithstown
Mount Pleasant ●
● St. Lawrence

Caerphilly District Miners ●
Llanfrechfa Grange

● St. Cadoc's
● Royal Gwent

Pen-y-fal ■ East Glamorgan ● General
Glanrhyd ■ ■ Parc

St. Woolos ●

Whitchurch ■ ● University Hospital of Wales

Bridgend General

Hensol ■
Prince of Wales ● ● ● Cardiff Royal Infirmary

Ely ■ St. David's

Llandough ●

Sully ●

25mls
40km

practice into group practices and, to a lesser extent, health centres. On the one hand, this reorganisation holds the promise of better-quality primary health care (for example, in terms of facilities and equipment, availability of specialist medical care, etc.). On the other hand, however, the centralisation of services that has inevitably accompanied this re-organisation may have the effect of decreasing the accessibility of these services, particularly to the less mobile groups in the population. It may well be the case that the major beneficiaries are the health professionals rather than the patients.

In one field, however, there can be no dispute about the short-comings of health services in Wales; this is in the provision of dental services. There are fewer dentists in Wales today than there were twenty years ago. In 1951, there were 519 dentists and an average of 4,985 people per dentist; in 1974, there were 505 dentists and an average of 5,453 people per dentist. In spite of the improvement in this situation over the past few years, the Chief Medical Officer for Wales has acknowledged that significant change is unlikely; even if there were 1,000 dentists in Wales, it would only provide a ratio of one dentist per 2,729 people, which remains unsatisfactory. In fact, the average annual increase in the number of dentists in Wales is currently only 26; therefore, dental care will remain highly unsatisfactory for many, many years. Moreover, what makes the Welsh situation particularly serious is the gross maldistribution of dental services.

Quite apart from general and dental practices, community services encompass a wide range of other facilities: home nurses, health visitors, midwives, opticians, pharmacists and chiropodists, as well as blood donor, mobile X-ray and immunisation services. As can be seen from Table 5.5, provision in Wales appears rather better than that in England under most of these headings. However, it is not clear that this level of provision adequately reflects Welsh needs. Similarly, the changes in patterns of provision and their effects have yet to be systematically analysed. Nevertheless, it is worth noting that the Welsh Consumer Council (1979b) has drawn attention to the problems created by the relative under-provision of chiropodists in Wales and by the closure of local chemist shops.

The effects of changes in community services provision are clearest in the rural, sparsely populated parts of Wales. Whilst no detailed studies have been carried out in Wales, it is instructive that a recent survey (Standing Conference of Rural Community Councils, 1978) reports that one-fifth of Cornish villages have lost their doctors' surgeries. These effects are not, however, reflected either in numbers of

GPs per 100,000 population or in sizes of patient lists. In fact, as can be seen in Table 5.6, it is rather the more densely populated industrialised areas that have adverse patient:GP ratios.

However, these statistics ignore the consequences of geographical area. The areas covered by practices outside the industrial south and north-east are considerably in excess of the Welsh average of 3,460 hectares. Hence, as with hospital services, accessibility to GPs may be more difficult, especially for those without adequate means of transport.

We can also identify particular groups in the population which, independent of geographical location, are being especially badly affected by changes in community care. Hence, Wales has a relatively high proportion of its population over 65 years of age (14.4 per cent as compared with 13.9 per cent in England). Moreover, there is a considerable variation within Wales; 18 per cent of the population of Gwynedd is over 65 years old, compared with only 12.7 per cent in Gwent. These proportions are likely to rise considerably over the years to come as a straightforward function of general demographic trends (Buxton and Craven, 1976; Welsh Office, 1976a). It seems clear that service provision for the elderly in Wales is being adversely affected by current changes in the methods of health care: in general terms, they form a less mobile group and, in consequence, are being particularly hard-hit by the trend towards centralisation of community health facilities. More specifically, for example, the elderly are less likely to have telephones and are therefore disadvantaged in negotiating modern appointments systems. It should be noted, however, that the Welsh Consumer Council study (1979b) of the Merthyr and Cynon Valley Health District suggests that in most respects the quality of treatment received by their sample of people over 60 years old was better than that received by their sample of parents. Unfortunately, this tells us little about the changes brought about by the reorganisation of general practice.

In evaluating the consequences of changes in the nature of community health services in Wales, it is clearly important, then, to keep in mind the different effects that will bear upon diverse groups within the total population. We have drawn particular attention to the disadvantages suffered by those who live in sparsely populated, rural areas and the elderly. We have suggested (albeit tentatively) that the changes which are currently taking place do not appear to be working to their advantage. We should, however, be careful not to over-stress the homogeneity of these groups. Clearly, there will be variations in

Table 5.6: Distribution of GPs: Number of GPs per 100,000 Population; Number of Patients per GP, 1975

	Clwyd	Dyfed	Gwent	Gwynedd	Mid Glamorgan	Powys	South Glamorgan	West Glamorgan	Wales
GPs per 100,000 population	45.1	51.3	45.2	56.7	46.5	66.5	54.1	48.2	49.5
Number of patients per GP	2,328	1,986	2,316	1,838	2,298	1,626	2,019	2,266	2,143

Source: Welsh Office, *Welsh Social Trends*, no. 1 (1977); Economic Services Division, Welsh Office, HMSO, Cardiff.

their actual access to health (and other) services; more significantly, there will be major variations in their abilities to overcome difficulties of access, largely as a consequence of their income and wealth. We must not lose sight of the fact that the problems associated with old age, etc., can be significantly less (at least in terms of access to health care) for those with adequate financial resources. This point raises, of course, the whole question of the adequacy of current provision; it is to this that we turn in the next section.

How Adequate a Health Service in Wales?

As we have already noted, there are considerable difficulties in assessing the adequacy of health service provision. We have seen that there is some considerable evidence to suggest that health problems are more severe in Wales (and particularly in certain areas of Wales) than in other parts of Britain. We have also suggested that, in spite of the somewhat higher level of resource provision for health services in Wales, numerous problems remain for particular population groups; quite apart from the fact that in a service designed to provide treatment according to need one would expect service provision to reflect the greater incidence of health problems. One way in which we can extend our analysis of the health service in Wales is to examine the actual use made of the medical facilities available. In what follows, we examine a number of aspects of the use of medical services; the overwhelming impression which emerges is that levels of use are higher in Wales than in other parts of Britain.

If we begin with the hospital sector, Wales has higher rates (per thousand population) both of beds available and of use of those beds than the average for England; this is true of all the major specialities (acute, geriatric, medical, obstetrics and GP maternity and surgical) with the exception of psychiatric. The same is in general true if we compare Wales with the English regions individually (although not, it should be noted, if the comparison is with Scotland or Northern Ireland) (Central Statistical Office, 1979). With regard to out-patient attendances, however, the rates for Wales are generally slightly lower than those for England as a whole (Central Statistical Office, 1979). These statistics should, of course, be read in conjunction with the analysis of waiting lists which we presented earlier.

The position with respect to the use made of GP services is more difficult to present. *Morbidity Statistics from General Practice: Second National Study* (OPCS, 1974), completed during 1970-72, reports consultation rates for 115 practices in England and Wales. The study reveals consultation rates for men in Wales only slightly higher than in England; whilst those for women were slightly lower. This latter point is to some extent supported by Dowie's (1978) contention that Welsh mothers and their children are under-users of primary health care facilities — a fact which she attributes to cultural attitudes! However, as Hart (1976) has argued, these data do need to be treated with caution. In surveys of this kind, dependent upon the voluntary co-operation of GPs, it is extremely likely that those practices with the heaviest workloads will be severely under-represented.[5]

Certainly, much higher consultation rates are recorded in the *General Household Survey 1972* (OPCS, 1975). The data here consist of the number of people who report consulting an NHS GP during a particular two-week period. The data reveal that consultation rates for Wales are very much higher than for England and Wales combined. Of the English regions, Yorkshire and Humberside has the highest over-all rate (125 per 1,000) some twelve points below the Welsh figure (137.5 per 1,000). It is also significant that the greatest difference between the Welsh figures and those for England and Wales is in the 15-44 age group, the most economically active group; these results are consistent, of course, with those for reported restricted activity. The *General Household Survey* also reports that in England and Wales the average person has 3.7 consultations per year with his GP. In Wales, the average is 4.7. Again, Yorkshire and Humberside is the English region with the highest figure, 4.2. This suggests, then, that people in Wales are having some 25 per cent more consultations with their doctors than are people in England.

As with sickness rates, there is a very marked class gradient with respect to consultations with GPs: semi- and unskilled workers and their wives make more use of their doctors (see Cartwright and O'Brien, 1976). Yet, again as we have seen previously, the difference in class structure between Wales and other parts of Britain is insufficient to provide a wholly convincing account of the wide differences in consultation rates. Further insight is given, however, by the limited studies that have been carried out in specific parts of Wales. Hence, Hart (1976) reports a mean rate of 5.3 consultations per patient per year for his Glyncorrwg practice for the period 1964-72. Moreover, 'there was no excess of consultations per episode of illness; the whole of the excess lay in an increased rate of episodes of sickness, rather than revisits and follow-up' (p.885). This picture is confirmed in Williams's (1970) study of 76 general practices in various parts of South Wales, which reveals an average consultation rate of 5.4 per patient per year. In the eleven practices in mining areas, the rate rose to 6.4 consultations per patient per year. This evidence suggests, therefore, that the explanation of higher consultation rates in Wales lies in the over-representation of specific occupational groups within the working-class population.

In the very nature of the data that we have presented so far in this section, our conclusions can only be tentative. As we stressed earlier, the interpretation of use rates is highly complex. A pattern does emerge, however, of consistently greater demand on health services in Wales than in other parts of Britain. Taken together with the evidence presented in earlier sections on the nature of health problems in Wales and on the problems of health service provision, there can be little doubt that Wales is badly off relative to other parts of Britain in terms both of health and of health care. Health services provision per head of population may be slightly greater in Wales than in Britain as a whole, and staff-patient ratios may seem favourable. However, these statistics must be set against the massive evidence of the greater health problems and needs of Wales.

Conclusion: the 'Inverse Care Law'

Manson (1979) has recently presented an account of the problems of resource allocation to geographical areas with different levels of health needs and provision within the NHS. The health service inherited, on its initiation in 1948, a situation characterised by marked degrees of inequality. The operation of a private market in many aspects of health care provision had ensured that most working-class areas had few GPs per head of population, whilst prosperous middle-class districts were 'over doctored'. Similarly, there were major differences in the quality of facilities between areas. Hospital provision was dominated by the vastly favourable situation in London (and, somewhat surprisingly, Liverpool) compared with other parts of Britain. Moreover, during the 1950s and 1960s, remarkably little was done to eradicate these inequalities because the system of resource allocation simply added a percentage increase to each of the regions' previous year's budgets (see Cartwright and O'Brien, 1976). The reorganisation of the NHS in 1974 was aimed partly at overcoming some of the problems generated by this 'incrementalist' system; in particular, it aimed to improve the 'efficiency' with which resources are spent. However, the 1974 Labour Government also determined to change the basis upon which resources were allocated to different regions, establishing in England the Resource Allocation Working Party (RAWP) and in Wales the Steering Committee on Resource Allocation in Wales (SCRAW). Although operating on somewhat different bases, in general terms the effect of both working parties has been the implementation (or, in the case of SCRAW, recommendation) of 'scientific' assessment as a basis for the fair allocation of resources. Whatever the doubts about the specific assumptions involved, this new basis of allocation has resulted in actual cuts in the expenditure of some 'rich' regions and the pegging of levels in others. However, as Manson (1979) argues, these changes have not resulted in significant reallocation of resources to 'poorer' regions, given the parallel cuts in the over-all NHS budget following the IMF-induced public expenditure cuts. This is to say that 'the actual result of RAWP has been not so much an improvement in the poor areas, but a worsening of the standards of health care in the "rich regions", many of which have pockets of social deprivation' (Manson, 1979, p.43).

In spite of these recent changes, then, the general nature of resource allocation has been summarised by Hart (1971a) in his 'inverse care law'. He says:

> In areas with most sickness and death, general practitioners have more work, larger lists, less hospital support, and inherit more clinically ineffective traditions of consultation, than in the healthiest areas; and hospital doctors shoulder heavier case-loads with less staff and equipment, more obsolete buildings, and suffer recurrent crises in the availability of beds and replacement staff. These trends can be summed up as the inverse care law: that the availability of good medical care tends to vary inversely with the need of the population served. (p.412)

Moreover, those areas with the highest rates of sickness and death are also those that suffered most from unemployment, low family incomes, poor housing and other environmental conditions. Hart himself has recognised that, given the current dearth of information on health needs and health services, a rigorous testing of his law is well-nigh impossible. Nevertheless, the weight of the admittedly imperfect evidence on the situation in Wales does provide significant general support for the thesis.

The patterns of industrialisation and urbanisation in Wales have yielded a 'total environment' which accounts for a major part of the excess of morbidity and mortality in Wales. More specifically, particular types of working-class communities have been created (especially in the coal-mining areas) which are significantly disadvantaged in terms of their health. State provision of health services, whilst marginally favourable in certain senses, is clearly insufficient to meet these special requirements – especially given the uneven distribution of population and poor communications in Wales. This is to say that health services provision is insufficient to fulfil the basic objectives of the NHS. This failure, in turn, may itself contribute to the high levels of illness and death in Wales.

In conclusion, therefore, our brief consideration of health and health care in Wales raised fundamental questions about the operation of the NHS. At the very least, we can only be sceptical about what Thane (1978) has described as 'the broad path of social betterment school' account of the development of the institutions of the Welfare State. Whatever the good intentions of those who were responsible for establishing the NHS or, indeed, of those who are currently responsible for it, the health service is manifestly not fulfilling the functions which were set for it in 1948. The task of future research is to provide an adequate explanation of why this should be so.

Notes

1. We would like to acknowledge the enormous help given in the preparation of this chapter by Paul Wilding; we draw heavily on his work for the Child Poverty Action Group (Wilding, 1977) and he also commented on earlier drafts. Helpful comments were also made by Paul Atkinson, Denis Gregory and Colin Rees.
2. See Ch. 2 (eds).
3. Data are available on sickness rates from the *General Household Survey*. However, we have not used this source here, as the method used to obtain the information – self-report survey – seems unlikely to yield adequate data on a topic such as this.
4. Impairment is defined as 'lacking part or all of a limb or having a defective limb, organ or mechanism of the body'.
5. Hart (1976) reports that the Seventh Report of the Review Body on Doctors' and Dentists' Remuneration, based on visits by Regional Medical Officers to over 3,000 GPs in 1964-65, gave an annual equivalent of 5.6 consultations per person per year (p.886).

6 URBAN DEPRIVATION AND URBAN POLICY

David T. Herbert

The pervasive impact of urbanisation and urban growth in Western societies has affected people and settlement in Wales as elsewhere. There are at least two ways, however, in which these processes can be shown to have had a muted, even a truncated effect. First, Wales has a thinner urban tradition than many other parts of the United Kingdom (Carter, 1965) – urbanism has largely been superimposed late from outside. Second, Wales still lacks a city of true metropolitan scale. Urban characteristics and urban problems are often a matter of degree rather than of kind, but the scale of urban places in Wales does not allow either to have full expression. For our present purposes, the fact of a limited urban tradition is of marginal relevance, but the relatively small scale of urban places is of more direct concern. It means, for example, that problems which are specifically urban – that is *of* rather than *in* the city (Herbert and Johnston, 1976) – may be less evident in Wales than in other parts of the United Kingdom. Further, it suggests that national policies designed to cope with the most significant problems of the city may be less appropriate for Wales.

Both urban problems and urban policies form the themes for this chapter. The objective is to assess, through use of selected examples, the areal variation of urban problems – particularly some forms of deprivation – within Wales and to relate these to the impact of urban policies. The policies discussed are area policies which occupy a major role in the state's general anti-poverty programme. Whilst the effectiveness of such area policies have been questioned (Barnes and Lucas, 1974), their reality as an implement of government strategy is undoubted. In tandem with welfare policies aimed at the individual, they provide a main instrument for governmental intervention in a problem-ameliorating context in areas such as Wales. Of the many area policies (Eyles, 1979), two which are primarily concerned with housing and the urban environment will be used as bases for discussing the impact of government policy and its relationship with deprivation. We are concerned, therefore, with obtaining indicators of deprivation and with identifying deprived areas against which to assess the efficacy of related policies. This objective raises a number of basic issues for initial discussion; these are the question of defining deprivation, the concept of territorial justice and the broad issue of scale of analysis.

Deprivation, Territorial Justice and Scales of Analysis

Most attempts to define deprivation, or associated concepts such as poverty and substandardness, stress that any definition must be expressed in relative terms. Deprivation implies a standard of living or quality of life below that of the majority in a particular society, to the extent that it involves hardship, inadequate access to resources and underprivilege. Comparisons are made less to an average than to a threshold or standard which varies both temporally and spatially. For most individuals, feelings of deprivation may involve comparisons with others 'visible' within the same society; Runciman (1966) identified as deprived the individual who lacks a resource which he wants and sees with others.

The concept of territorial justice is concerned with deprivation, or more precisely with need, but specifically with the extent to which measurable need finds a compatible response in the provision of local services. Territorial justice examines the areal variations in need and the record of local authority agencies as decision makers with respect to resource allocation. Davies (1968), in developing the concept, suggested that, if the units of observation are areas which are aggregates of individuals, then territorial justice could be defined as 'An area distribution of services such that each area's standard is proportional to the total needs for services of its population' (p.39). Studies of territorial justice should involve measures both of needs or levels of deprivation and of provision.

> The statistical definition of territorial justice is a high correlation between indices of resource use or standards of provision and an index measuring the relative needs of an area's population for the service . . . Territorial justice is a necessary but not of course a sufficient condition for achieving social justice. (Davies, 1968, p.16)

This early work has proved a significant stimulus and analyses of area variations in local services have become relatively commonplace; rather fewer attempts have been made to relate service provision to need in ways exemplified by Davies's (1968) studies of care of the elderly and of the education service (see, however, Pinch, 1978, 1979). The problem of measurement remains an inherent difficulty with the con-

concept of territorial justice; access to reliable and adequate data is very much part of this problem. Need is a thorny concept to transform into measurable terms and Bradshaw (1972) suggested a typology of need composed of normative, felt, expressed and comparative forms. As Pinch (1979) has stated, however, it is the distinction between need as measured or perceived objectively by the policy maker or researcher and that felt or expressed by the general public which is crucial. It is improbable that data will ever be adequate to measure the nuances of need but recent advances in the measurement of levels of satisfaction (Knox and MacLaran, 1978) have opened up some promising research avenues. Some other key aspects of the concept of territorial justice can be noted but not elaborated here. There is, for example, a central need to understand the processes involved both in the emergence of deprivation and in the procedures used to allocate resources. These are by no means independent. It is likely that the system of priorities and rewards existing in a particular society and the procedures used to allocate these are in themselves initiators and perpetrators of inequality. Study of provision of local services has to account for the substitutability of one service for another and has, centrally, to be concerned with the roles and interrelationships amongst the various tiers of government.

The last concept to discuss in this introduction is that of scale. It is relevant to the chapter as a whole in two respects. First, the problem of reconciling aggregate and individual effects is endemic to territorial justice as it is to all areal variations and areal policies. Area need does not necessarily identify individual need; area policies do not necessarily imply that resources reach the most needy. Whilst both Davies (1968) and Pinch (1978) rest on the assumption that deprived areas probably contain deprived individuals, Barnes and Lucas (1974), in their study of educational deprivation in London, produced contradictory results. Without closely co-ordinated studies at aggregate and individual scales, there is no guarantee that territorial justice does in fact lead to social justice. The second point of relevance of scale to this chapter is more pragmatic. Whilst all of the stages of analysis in this study have been conducted at an aggregate scale, the stages are so arranged that they proceed from larger to smaller units of observation. These are, for the first 'stage' of analysis, the 37 local authorities in Wales; for the second stage, wards and parishes within Industrial South Wales; and for the third stage, enumeration districts within Cardiff. Two of these stages, therefore, employ units of local government, whilst the third adopts an arbitrary territorial census-taking area. In combination they do allow a progression from macro towards micro scale, and in so doing focus progressively onto the precise spatial incidence of need.

Identifying Urban Deprivation in Wales

Housing Indicators

Virtually all studies of the quality of life have given indicators of housing a central place in their measurements; shelter is a basic necessity for mankind and housing indicators are selected here as basic elements of any attempt to measure deprivation. The housing market is a particularly complex institution which continues to attract research from a variety of disciplines and for both central and local government the provision of good housing remains a central priority. Pinch (1978), in his study of patterns of local authority housing allocations in Greater London, identified some of the special characteristics of housing as a topic for study in the context of territorial justice. Housing construction involves an expenditure pattern which is concerned largely with the repayment of long-term loans, a detailed planning procedure and a prolonged construction stage. It is a commodity subject to short-term fluctuations, due to the influence of external market factors, and to significant time lags between identification of need and organisation of provision. A further special consideration in the provision of new housing, or indeed in renewal of old, is that strategic factors are of importance. The geography of housing need may, for good reasons, not correspond with the geography of housing provision. Older residential areas are often, for example, unsuitable for new housing or may be unable to cope with modern space standards.

There are several critical distinctions within housing which correspond with the varying levels of poverty and disadvantage amongst its occupants. Tenure provides one such distinction with owner-occupancy in general the most favoured and private rental the least advantageous form of residence. Rex and Moore's (1967) concept of 'housing classes' has strong links with tenure and has provided one useful typology with which to classify urban housing. These 'classes' are measurable but most studies of housing deprivation have focused upon indices of overcrowding and substandardness. Both of these pose difficult problems of definition and are relative to standards which vary over time and space. Indices of overcrowding relate to the density of occupancy of dwellings, with persons per room as a key variable, and to levels of sharing of dwellings and facilities. Indices of substandardness normally focus upon the presence or absence of household facilities such as inside w.c., fixed bath and hot water. Pinch (1978) developed a housing needs index calculated from ten measures of overcrowding and substandardness.

For the first stage in the measurement of urban deprivation in relation to policy in Wales, a simple index of housing substandardness was used to establish the needs side of the equation. From data in the 1971 Census, the numbers of households without exclusive use of amenities (fixed bath, inside w.c. and hot water) were calculated together with the proportions which these formed of the total number of households for each of the 37 local authority districts in Wales. Map 6.1 shows the areal variation, by Welsh districts, of these measures of housing deprivation, with no distinction being made — at this scale — between urban and rural areas.

In relative terms the three most deprived areas are Rhondda, Cynon and Merthyr, all highly urbanised areas within Industrial South Wales. Blaenau Gwent, Lliw and Neath, all similar urban-industrial areas, are well above average on this deprivation index but some of the large rural districts in North and Central Wales, such as Dinefwr and Montgomery, also have comparable scores. Very low ratios of substandardness are found in the more 'modernised' urban environments of the coastal fringe of South Wales, including the districts of Vale, Ogwr and Swansea, and in other coastal districts from Preseli in the south-west to Alyn Deeside in the north.

If absolute numbers of substandard dwellings rather than proportions are taken, a rather different pattern emerges, one which emphasises the dimensions of the housing problem with which local authorities are faced.[1] This criterion clearly picks out the severe problems of the larger urban areas in Wales. Cardiff, with 21,650 substandard houses, heads the list, followed by Rhondda 15,205, Swansea 13,065, Cynon 9,585, Rhymney 9,035, Merthyr 8,200 and Newport 7,975. All of these districts are within Industrial South Wales, and Wrexham Maelor, 5,250, has the highest number of substandard houses outside this sub-region. On this criterion, therefore, which expresses the dimensions of the housing substandardness problem, the deprivation of the three largest cities becomes apparent and shows a close correlation with the over-all size of urban places. The problems of these 'conventional' cities, however, do not dwarf those of the old mining areas: Rhondda still ranks second in terms of scale of substandardness; Cynon, Rhymney and Merthyr all rank more highly than Newport.

Map 6.1: Urban Deprivation in Wales: Substandard Housing

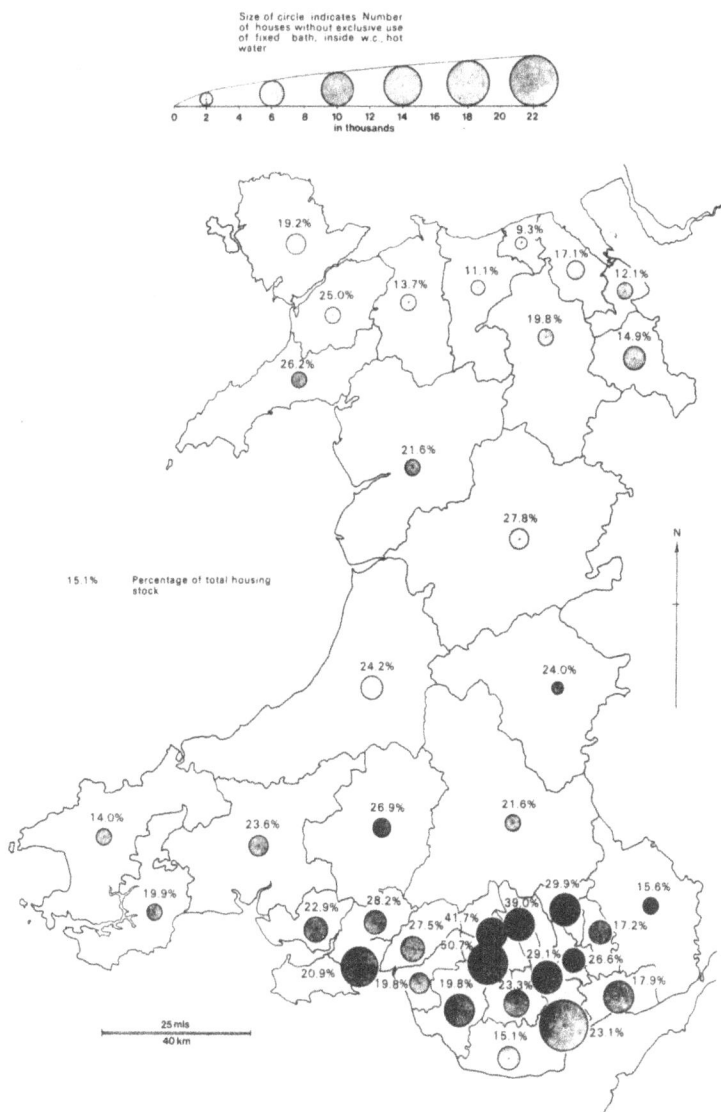

Deprived Residential Areas

Absence of amenities provides one simple index of housing deprivation in Wales; in order to obtain a more comprehensive perspective use was made of the National Classification of Residential Neighbourhoods, based again upon the 1971 Census data. The methodology of this classification has been well documented (Webber, 1977) and will not be detailed here[2] but basically a cluster analysis of 40 variables was used to classify wards and parishes in England and Wales according to their dominant characteristics. From this procedure, a typology which comprised seven 'families' and 36 clusters of residential area types was devised. From this classification eight clusters were selected, falling within families two, four and six, all of which could be described as deprived residential areas. A special extraction from the national tape, to identify which wards and parishes in Wales fell into these selected types, showed that three clusters — all from family six — were not represented in the Principality. Analysis of Welsh districts proceeded, therefore, with the five remaining clusters, the main features of which are summarised in Map 6.2. All of these cluster types can be seen to be characterised by measures of deprivation such as substandardness, overcrowding, form of tenure and low socio-economic status; this part of the analysis, therefore, employs a much wider range of deprivation indicators than housing alone.

In Map 6.2, the percentage of total population in each local authority area living in each of the five cluster types is shown and is taken as another indicator of the incidence of urban deprivation in Wales. Type 11, described on a United Kingdom basis as containing the poorest-quality older terraced housing, is found within the two major cities of Cardiff and Newport and also in the South Wales valley town of Rhymney. Type 12, also composed of terraced housing, but with a more elderly population and rather lower levels of social deprivation, is very common in South Wales, but hardly appears at all outside the sub-region. Residential area type 16 comprises large local authority estates occupied by tenants decanted from slum clearance areas; the deprivation is social rather than environmental. All three major cities of Cardiff, Swansea and Newport possess this type of area; it also appears in Merthyr and Afan, but not elsewhere. Type 19 has substandard housing and an admixture of tenures and is described as typical of old mining areas. It is in fact dominant in districts such as Cynon, Ogwr, Neath and Blaenau Gwent. Finally, type 21, comprehensive redevelopment, is only dominant in one ward in Swansea.

At this scale of analysis the distribution of 'deprived' residential area

Map 6.2: Urban Deprivation in Wales: National Classification of Residential Neighbourhoods

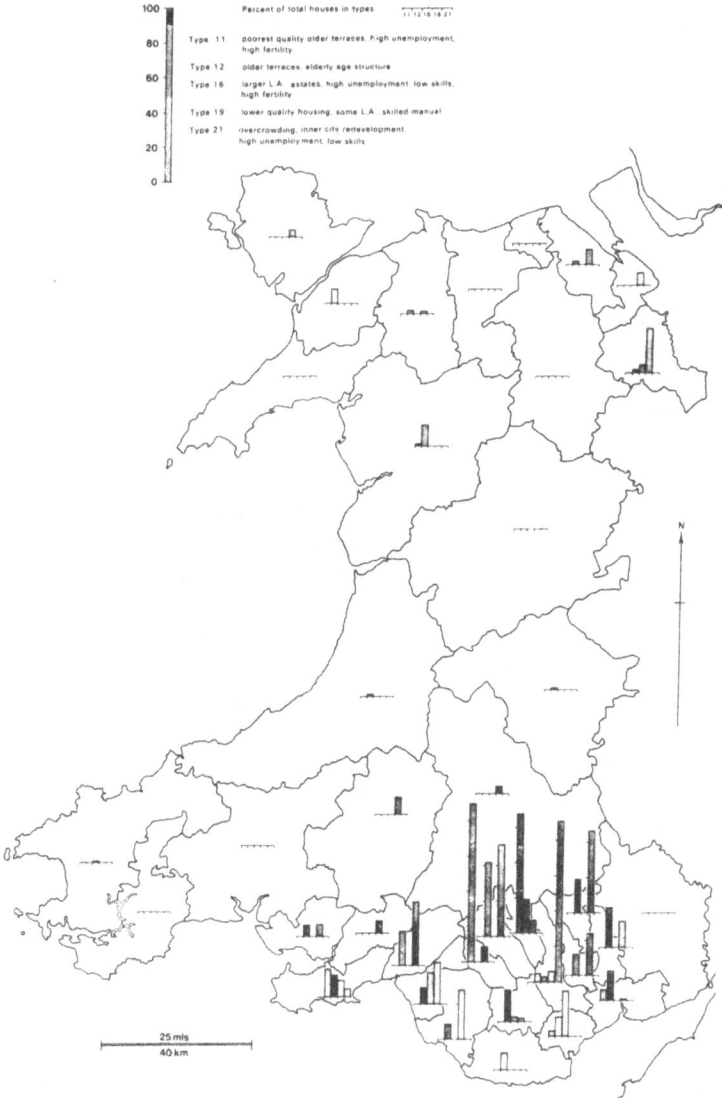

types in Wales confirms the broad pattern of need shown by the simple measures of housing substandardness. Deprivation of any real dimensions in Wales is —simply, as a function of scale — inevitably an urban problem; it is particularly evident in the three largest cities and shows an expected correlation with city size but is also acute in several parts of the highly urbanised sub-region of Industrial South Wales. The valleys districts, though possessing some significant differences in both economic and cultural terms, have more unity than diversity and as a whole have an undeniable claim to be suffering disproportionately high levels of deprivation.

Urban Policies

In his original statement on a classification of standard indices designed to measure the provision of a particular service, Davies (1968) included a range of measures of resource allocation, of intensity and extensiveness of provision, and of the performance and output of the service. Pinch (1978) in his provisions index for housing in Greater London included a range of rates of both house construction and improvement grant allocations. Whereas the former attempts to be comprehensive and faces considerable data problems, the latter compromises with more limited but readily available information. For this study the latter approach was adopted and a measure of provision was sought which held closest correspondence with the type of housing need index already employed to identify levels of substandardness.

Under government legislation, notably the Housing Acts of 1969 and 1974, the emphasis has shifted towards improvement rather than replacement as a medium for dealing with housing problems. Local districts, in their roles as housing authorities, are able to form schemes for General Improvement Areas (GIAs) and Housing Action Areas (HAAs) which, if approved by central government, qualify for substantial grant-aid in terms of the Acts (see Eyles, 1979). In Wales, the Welsh Office acts as the decision-making body in approving schemes and is an intermediary between Whitehall and the local authorities. This role is interesting in relation to one of the original statements on the territorial justice concept. 'Territorial justice and the development of the services would be impossible without a strong regional organization . . . some of the more detailed decisions involving territorial justice now made by central government departments should be made by the provincial government' (Davies, 1968, pp.301-2). It could be argued that, with the

Welsh Office, Wales does possess this regional institution of government capable of taking a comprehensive view of areal variations within the region.

A simple provisions index is formed by the number of GIAs and HAAs approved for each district and by the total number of dwellings covered for each. The basic hypothesis is that districts with larger numbers of approved schemes and dwellings covered are well provided for and *vice versa*. This hypothesis has caveats which can be noted but not fully discussed in this chapter. First, there is the familiar ecological fallacy in the use of aggregate data, operative in this context in the sense that there is no guarantee that all or any of the most substandard houses are those included in improvement area schemes. It is, of course, highly probable that a direct correlation exists. Second, the uneven pattern of approvals raises many questions which cannot be followed up here. Why some districts apply more often or are more successful in applications than others; what are the processes involved in the emergence of a proposal? Third, questions of substitutability cannot be fully explored. Some districts may prefer schemes other than GIAs or HAAs in tackling their problems of housing substandardness or may be committed to longer-term policies which predate the present legislation. It should also be noted that the later of the two schemes, HAAs — which are as yet thinly spread over the region — was more specifically designed to cover areas of worst housing conditions; there was guidance from central government to the effect that GIAs should be declared in areas where prospects for success were greatest (Ministry of Housing and Local Government, 1969).

Map 6.3 shows the impact of recent urban policies on Wales and — from the main content of data on GIAs and HAAs — the mismatch between need (Map 6.1 and 6.2) and provision is a striking feature. A simple correlation test between the scores for districts on need, as indicated by the number of substandard dwellings, and provision, as shown by the number of dwellings covered by improvement schemes, yielded a coefficient of .34 which is not a significant relationship at the 1 per cent level. This measure is not conclusive, however, and more interesting is the areal pattern of mismatch. Some districts with few urban problems have made relatively high demands on the schemes, whilst others — in the core of the highly urbanised industrial valleys — have made very few. Preseli, for example, in South West Wales, has 2,790 substandard dwellings and 1,770 dwellings included in three GIAs. Although a ratio is not strictly valid, the schemes cover 64 per cent of the substandard dwellings. Rhondda, by contrast, has 15,205 dwellings classed

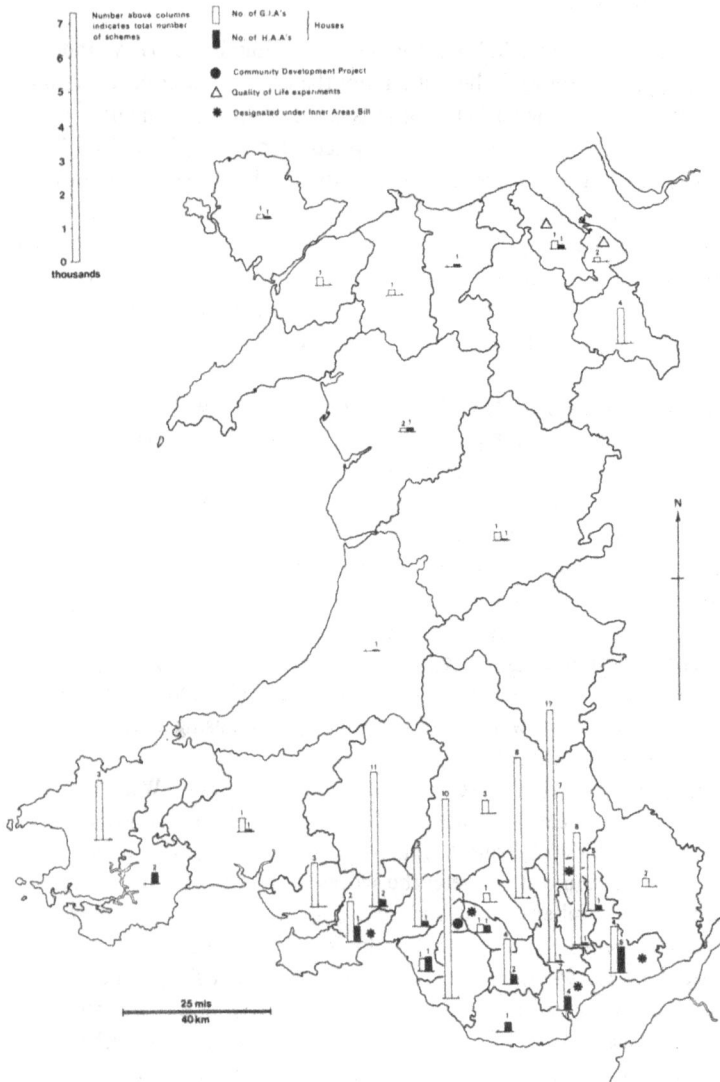

Map 6.3: Urban Policies in Wales

as substandard by the needs index, but has only 413 dwellings covered by one GIA and one HAA — a ratio of less than 3 per cent. This example is striking, but there are others of comparable magnitude. The three largest cities of Cardiff, Swansea and Newport, all with significant numbers of substandard dwellings, have only modest records of improvement scheme approvals. Other districts, some of which do have high need, have been remarkably active in attracting GIAs and HAAs. Rhymney has 18 schemes covering 7,380 dwellings against a need of 9,035; Ogwr has ten GIAs, covering 5,789 dwellings, against a need of 7,820; Lliw has 13 schemes, covering 4,165 dwellings, against a need of 5,435. Outside Industrial South Wales, the scale of scheme approval is small though there are exceptions. Preseli has already been quoted and Wrexham Maelor, the largest urban area in North East Wales, has 1,023 dwellings in four GIAs against a need of 5,250. Most of the housing covered by the improvement schemes is in the private sector, though in some districts, such as Newport, Wrexham Maelor and Delyn, high proportions of local authority housing are included.

The mismatch between needs and provision, as discussed above and shown graphically in Maps 6.1, 6.2 and 6.3, is taken as an indicator of territorial injustice in terms of Welsh housing conditions. There is evidence that the principal contemporary vehicles for residential area improvement are not being properly focused upon those districts of Wales where the need is greatest. Inevitably, however, the two basic stages of analysis followed for the purposes of this chapter raise as many questions as they answer. There is a need to examine much more closely the reasons for differential rates of scheme application and to take a more comprehensive view both of the estimation of need and of the process of provision. Map 6.3 indicates some of the questions of substitutability by identifying projects other than GIAs and HAAs currently operating in Wales. The five districts nominated under the Inner Urban Areas Bill, for example, have comprehensive access to some kinds of aid, whilst large numbers of smaller schemes continue to be approved under the general aegis of the urban programme.

Deprivation at Sub-regional and Urban Scales

For the remaining two scales of analysis, the focus is more exclusively upon urban areas in Wales and is upon the areal variation and nature of urban deprivation rather than upon policies. Industrial South Wales has rural landscapes but is emphatically an urban region. It contains the largest individual cities in Wales and also the distinctive urbanised sub-region of the valleys with its legacy of metal-working and coal-mining industrial bases. This industrial legacy of the valleys has been dramatically reduced in the last few decades but the other legacy of substandard old housing stock and inadequate infrastructure of services remains largely intact (Ty Toronto Socio-Economic Research Group, 1977). At this second stage of analysis, wards and parishes form the units of observation and once again a special extraction of data from the National Classification of Residential Neighbourhoods is used to identify the spatial patterning of deprivation. The same five type-clusters are used and Map 6.4 shows the geographical distribution of these individual residential area types in South Wales. The map is a striking portrayal of the ubiquity within urban South Wales of those five out of 36 residential types from the national classification which were selected as indicative of some level of social and environmental deprivation.

Types 12 and 19 cover much of the valleys area of the coalfield and emphasise the comprehensive reality of their urban problems. The ubiquitous terraced-row districts, almost entirely of pre-1914 construction, still often lacking in basic amenities and housing a population often 'ageing' and of limited skills, dominate this part of South Wales. Type 12, which is the less advantaged of the two types, typifies the central valleys such as Rhondda, Merthyr, Blaenau Gwent and Abertillery, the districts with least stable economic bases, whilst type 19 is more typical of areas such as Neath, Cynon, Gelligaer and Caerphilly, better placed for modernisation and change. Neither of these two types is exclusive to the valleys; type 12, in particular, is found in inner city districts of Cardiff, Swansea and Newport. Residential area type 11 is the other feature of central Cardiff (Adamsdown) and Newport (Alexandra) though it also occurs in three wards of the Rhymney district. Brynmelin, in central Swansea, a large-scale redevelopment scheme of high-rise council flats, is the sole representative of type 21 in urban South Wales. Outside the inner city, residential type 16 identifies wards dominated by large council estates distinguished by low skills, high unemployment, high fertility and poor accessibility. Three wards of Cardiff (Rumney, Ely and Plasmawr) fall into this category together with Swansea's Penderry ward. This residential type does occur elsewhere in South Wales, and the Sandfields Estate at Port Talbot is a clear example of this form of development.

At this scale of analysis, therefore, the diverse nature of urban deprivation in South Wales can be demonstrated. Whilst the classification by five types covers virtually all of urban South Wales, two of

Map 6:4 Urban Deprivation : South Wales

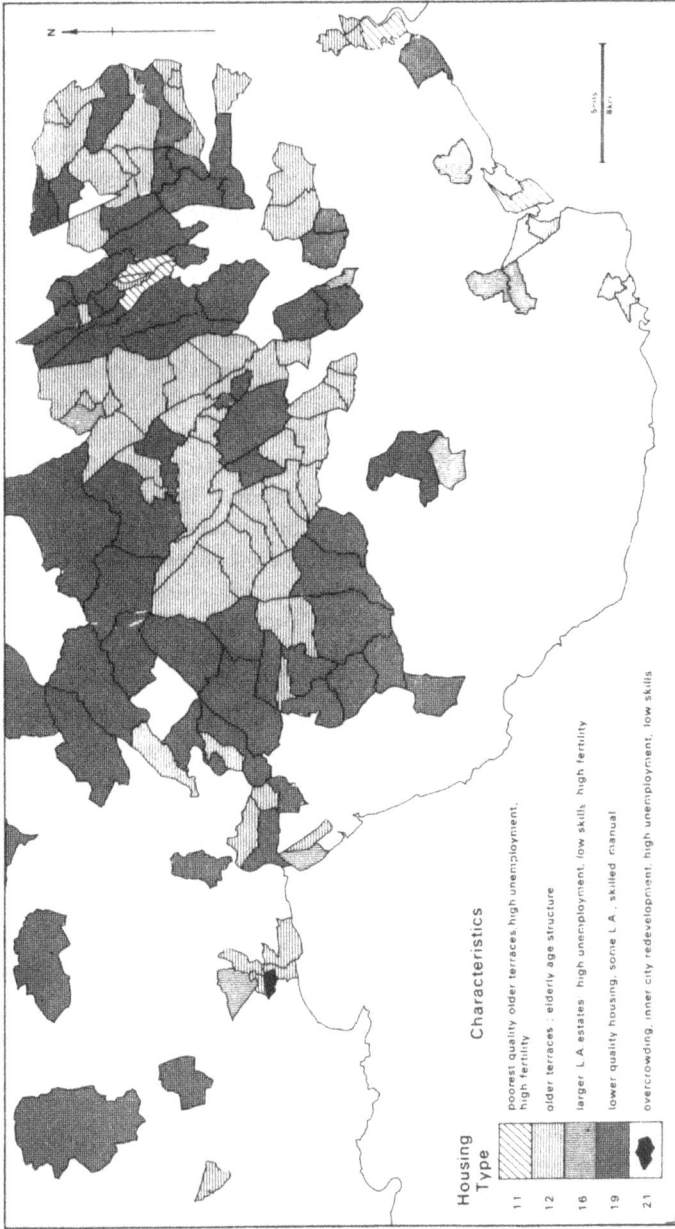

Housing
Type

Characteristics

1.1   poorest quality older terraces high unemployment, high fertility

1.2   older terraces : elderly age structure

1.6   larger L A estates : high unemployment, low skills, high fertility

1.9   lower quality housing, some L A , skilled manual

2.1   overcrowding, inner city redevelopment, high unemployment, low skills those types which correspond largely with nineteenth-century terraced-row housing are dominant. Urban deprivation in South Wales is clearly not restricted to inner city areas as conventionally defined. There is a clear justification for comprehensive government aid to urban South Wales being extended beyond the established industrial development measures to meet the real needs of the urban and social environments.

For the final stage of analysis, intra-urban patterns of deprivation are shown within Cardiff which, with a 1971 population of 279,100, was the largest city in Wales. With enumeration districts as units of observation, a broader model of deprivation based upon research which formed part of the urban programme (Edwards, 1975) was used. For these purposes, the three major competitive markets in urban life were defined as housing, employment and education. Indicators of an inability to compete in these markets were identified and mapped in Cardiff in order to define deprived areas within the city. Three census variables were selected, one from each subject or market. Absence of inside w.c. was taken as an indicator in the housing market, low occupational skill in the employment market and low educational qualifications in the education market. Details of the individual distributions of these indices have been discussed elsewhere (Herbert, 1975) but, for the purposes of this chapter, scores have been combined to produce a measure of multiple deprivation.

Map 6.5 shows a main concentration of deprivation within the inner city but there are also peripheral clusters. A contrast between spatial incidence of types of deprivation — a contrast which is partly demonstrated by the differences between districts classified as deprived on three indices and those classified on two — is that, whereas housing deprivation is almost restricted to the inner city, deprivation in the social environment occurs ubiquitously. Whereas long-term policies have succeeded in reducing the amount of housing deprivation, limiting it to residual and transitional areas in the inner city (Gittus, 1969), they have been less successful in redistributing socio-economic advantages. Local authority housing, at least since 1945, has met norms which place it well above the threshold of substandardness, but its tenants are still generally typified by the low levels of skills and qualifications which were associated with inner city populations. The broad social class polarisation, which has been reduced in housing standards, persists in most other aspects of the quality of life.

These objective measures of urban deprivation within Cardiff provide some insights into the extent and nature of the problem and are valuable in their own right. More recent research, however, has shifted the

Map 6.5: Urban Deprivation: Cardiff, 1971: Census Indicators

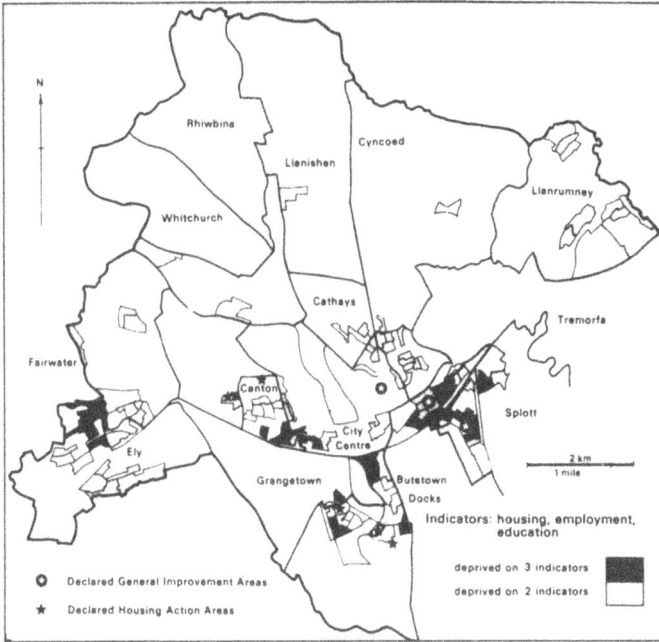

emphasis from objective to subjective measures, i.e. to the nature of the problem as the general public perceives it, to the felt needs of those involved rather than the judgements of outsiders. The reality of these subjective dimensions can briefly be demonstrated in two ways. First, a research project completed in Cardiff (Herbert, 1975, 1976) was able to demonstrate that, even between residential districts which were objectively very similar, there were significant differences in the personal social environments within which people lived. Particular neighbourhoods suffer urban deprivation not merely in terms of the inadequacy of buildings, nor through an inability of their inhabitants to achieve good jobs and better education, but as a result of the prevalent set of values and codes of behaviour which surround children in particular as they grow up. These deprivations are no less real and are possibly more damaging than others.

Another insight into the subjective environment is provided by Map

Map 6.6: Urban Deprivation: Cardiff, 1973: Subjective Indicators

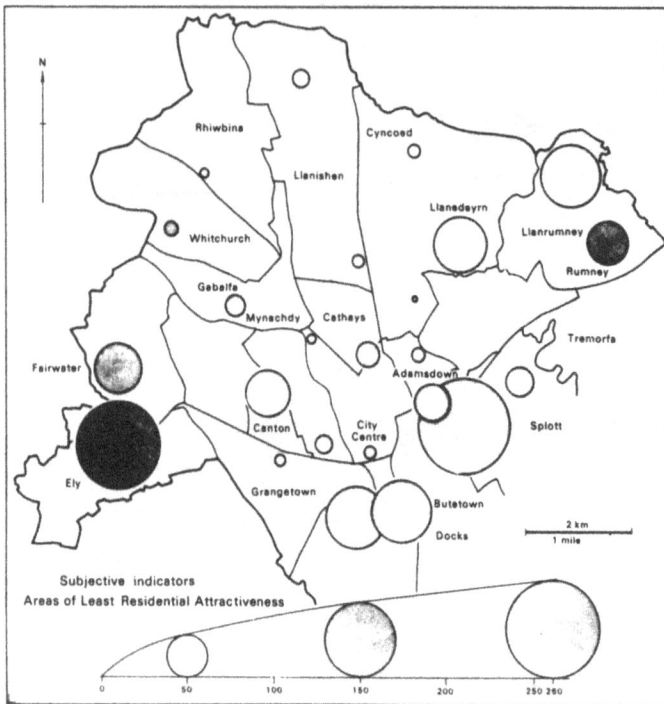

6.6. From a broader-based survey of Cardiff (Herbert, 1976), just under 500 households were asked to identify those districts of the city within which they would least like to live. The map is a spatial image of low residential attractiveness and its close resemblance to the objectively measured pattern of deprivation shown in Map 6.5 is some testimony to the effectiveness of subjective filters of the qualities of the urban environment.

Conclusions

The main thrust of this chapter has been to demonstrate some of the ways in which urban deprivation can be defined and identified on a

variety of spatial scales. Deprivation is a relative concept and is, inevitably, represented to a disproportionate extent among some groups
and in some areas. It is in this sense that deprived areas are identified
both within Wales as a region and within particular parts of its cities.
The fact that deprivation is predominantly an urban phenomenon in
Wales, as elsewhere in the United Kingdom, is in large part a reflection
of the fact that we live in a predominantly urban society. The absence
of any single, really major, city means that the massive concentrations
of inner city deprivation – one expression of problems *of* rather than
simply *in* the city – do not find expression in Wales. Differences between
Welsh towns and those of other parts of the United Kingdom are of
degree rather than kind; all medium to large cities have inner areas but
the enormous social, economic and political problems are those of major
conurbations. It is in Industrial South Wales that the distinctiveness of
Welsh problems finds its clearest expression and we are reminded that
deprivation itself may take various forms and will have different sub-
regional expressions. The sub-region of the valleys is undeniably urban,
unmistakably problematic, and yet has a form and character which is
not easily replicated elsewhere. The universality of deprivation in this
sub-region is a key feature of the Welsh urban problem and provides a
persuasive reason for a specific policy response.

It has been argued earlier in this book that the problem of social
disadvantage is one of ecomomic and industrial organisation, central to
which is the maldistribution of wealth and income. To the extent that
urbanisation is a consequence of such economic processes, this chapter
has inevitably focused upon spatial manifestations of disadvantage
rather than upon its root causes. The form and scale of urbanisation in
Wales *vis-a-vis* the rest of the United Kingdom is in itself an indicator of
the uneven nature of national economic development. A Welsh urban
tradition which is late and limited reflects some of the realities of the
'colonialist' theses; as the Welsh economy has been developed largely by
outsiders to serve outside interests, urban settlements have emerged as
the necessary concomitants to economic change (see Chapter 12, below).
In this context, the absence of large-scale metropolitan development is
a further indicator of regional underdevelopment. Areal variations of
deprivation within Wales indicate intra-regional differences in economic
development. Coastal Wales, for example, which has been affected
advantageously by modernisation and change in the last few decades, is
better placed than 'internal' areas such as the valleys, which have not.
Within the most deprived sub-regions the economic problems are compounded by those of the physical and social environments and change is

slow. From the testimony of earlier chapters in this book, Wales as a
region has greater needs than most United Kingdom regions — twice as
much substandard housing, for example, as the ratio for England and
Wales combined; it follows that the problems of its worst parts are considerable.

Discussion of urban policies has focused upon GIAs and HAAs,
mainly because they are schemes initiated on an area basis for which
good data are available. It is acknowledged that most of the housing
improvement effort is not conducted under these schemes; in 1976, for
example, less than 7 per cent of grant approvals were in GIAs and HAAs.
It is also acknowledged that a range of other area policies are employed
in the attack on urban deprivation. The focus on housing in this chapter
has not allowed discussion of other kinds of urban deprivation, such as
education and the social services, and of the policies such as educational priority and positive discrimination which are designed to tackle
them. A contention here is that, as housing is one indicator of urban
deprivation, so GIAs and HAAs are indicators of the response of local
authorities in urban policy terms. Map 6.3 did include information on
other policies such as the community development project, quality of
life studies and the Inner Areas Bill. This last piece of legislation does
offer an example of a policy, which has been formed in response to the
pressing needs of major urban regions in other parts of the United Kingdom, being applied to Wales in an indiscriminate way. Cardiff, Swansea
and Newport have inner city problems which can be dealt with under
the inner areas policy; though whether they deserve priority over many
other British cities is more contentious. More to the point, however, the
valleys sub-region as a whole is in need of designation as an urban problem area towards which resources should be directed. To designate two
segments of that sub-region, under an Inner Areas Bill, is a totally inadequate response. For many parts of this valleys sub-region the input
in terms of GIAs and HAAs has lagged considerably behind other parts
of the United Kingdom, and the necessity of taking a comprehensive
and objective view of needs from a regional level of policy making seems
paramount.

Area policies have their critics (Townsend, 1976) and are certainly
not alternatives to the more traditional individual policies. This study
has, however, identified some of the areal concentration of deprivation
to which policies must usefully be applied. If any mismatch between
needs and provision results from varying levels of enterprise and competence at a local level, then there is a regional responsibility to recognise
and rectify such anomalies. The range of policies — national, regional,

area and individual – have a continuing contribution to make towards the refurbishing of urban places in Wales; this needs to be paralleled, though, by a continuing scrutiny of the root causes of inequality in British society and its forms of government.

Notes

1. See Ch. 3 (eds).
2. The National Classification of Residential Neighbourhoods was conducted by the Centre for Environmental Studies with sponsorship by the Office of Population Censuses and Surveys. The basic aim of the classification is to summarise as concisely as possible the diversity of residential conditions found in Great Britain in 1971. To this end 16,714 wards and parishes, which in 1971 had a population of 50 and over, formed the input to a classification system based upon cluster analysis – and 40 variables measured from census statistics were recorded for each small area. The procedure reduced this considerable data input to 36 'families' of wards and parishes classified according to their dominant features. Familiar limitations of aggregate analyses and data exist – including the time lapse since 1971 – but the classification provides an invaluable basis for ongoing research and policy guidance.

Part Two

TOWARDS EXPLANATION

7 LOW PAY AND NO PAY IN WALES

Denis Gregory

Without entering the debate as to whether a broad examination of income maintained at either household or national level provides a sufficient exposition of poverty in any particular country, this chapter examines, data permitting, two critical issues: the extent and characteristics of low pay from employment; and the extent and characteristics of 'no pay' from unemployment in Wales.

Data are presented here in an attempt to demonstrate first of all the superficiality of the view that average earnings in Wales remain close to the United Kingdom average (hence Wales cannot be a 'low-pay' region). Such generalisations in fact mask substantial variations within Wales. Secondly, the data try to show that the extent, persistence and continued growth of unemployment in Wales represent a particularly acute form of poverty at both micro (household) and macro (national) economic levels.

Low Pay and Poverty

A number of problems, both conceptual and practical, immediately arise here. Not the least of the former concerns the definition of low pay. The question of a 'yardstick' or datum line beneath which any level of earnings can be held to constitute low pay has proven peculiarly difficult to resolve and continues to elude any form of consensus. Appropriate data can be found ranging from the 'official' subsistence level as defined by the Department of Health and Social Security for supplementary benefit purposes (currently around £35 per week) to the £60 per week minimum wage target demanded by many of the unions in the lower-paid parts of the public sector.

It is also said that regional disparities in living costs (particularly in housing) can materially affect the purchasing power of a wage or salary. Add to this the supposed differences in life style 'quality' between, say, a rural and an urban existence and it can be seen that the linkage between low pay and poverty is not as straightforward as it may at first seem.

Practical problems in the main relate to the availability and quality

139

of data on regional earnings. The two principal series compiled by the Department of Employment — the October survey of manual workers' earnings and the April *New Earnings Survey* (NES) — both record gross earnings (i.e. pre-tax) and neither survey provides much in the way of detailed information on regional earnings, although the NES does permit reasonably useful broad comparisons of regionally based data. The *Family Expenditure Survey* (FES), whilst concentrating on consumption patterns, does provide some information on regional household income which makes a cross-check to the earnings survey material.

Wilding has demonstrated elsewhere (see Chapter 2, above) that, on the evidence of gross weekly earnings, non-manual rather than manual workers in Wales suffer the most when compared with their counterparts in Great Britain as a whole. However, no striking evidence of low pay in Wales is apparent from these comparisons. Whilst this may sound reassuring, it should be remembered that only broad averages, aggregated for all industries and services in Wales, have been considered. There is little doubt, for example, that the dominance of the steel and coal industries distort the earnings figure recorded for all manual workers and that the earnings levels recorded in Industrial South Wales mask the true picture of earnings in Mid and West Wales.

Unfortunately, the NES data on regional industrial earnings are insufficient to make detailed comparisons; however, the evidence that is available from the 1977 survey suggests that only six broad industrial groups can be identified for which the average gross weekly earnings of male manual workers in Wales were above those of their counterparts in Great Britain, and at least ten industrial groups can be identified where average gross weekly earnings in Wales were lower than those recorded for Great Britain. Among the latter groups, male manual workers in food, drink and tobacco, vehicles, distributive trades and public administration appeared to be particularly badly off in Wales as far as gross weekly earnings were concerned.

The variations in earnings levels in the individual counties and major sub-regions (Industrial South Wales, North Wales, Mid Wales and West Wales) are shown in Table 7.1. For male workers it is clear that below-average pay characterises Mid, West and parts of North West Wales. In Powys, for example, average earnings for male manual workers were some 16 per cent below the Great Britain average and some 24 per cent below the highest-paid Welsh counterpart (Clwyd-East). It is also difficult to believe that pockets of very low pay are not present in the rural areas of Wales; unfortunately, official data shed no further light on this beyond the simple average figures listed in Table 7.1.

Table 7.1: Average Gross Weekly Earnings for Full-time Adult Workers in Wales by County, April 1977 (£ per week)

	Manual		Non-manual	
	Male	Female	Male	Female
Clwyd—East	78.7	n.a.	88.4	52.0
Clwyd—West	59.8	n.a.	n.a.	
Dyfed (excluding Llanelli)	62.7	n.a.	79.3	55.3
Gwent	74.5	43.6	85.2	52.9
Gwynedd	68.3	n.a.	82.8	n.a.
Mid Glamorgan	71.2	44.9	85.7	54.4
Powys	60.0	n.a.	n.a.	n.a.
South Glamorgan	72.3	n.a.	89.8	53.3
West Glamorgan	75.4	45.0	79.8	53.4
Wales	72.2	43.3	84.4	53.3

Note: n.a. = figures not available.

Source: Welsh Office, *Welsh Economic Trends* (HMSO, Cardiff, 1978), Tables 50 and 51.

Additional evidence of low pay in Wales can be found in the *Family Expenditure Survey*. Results for the years 1974/75 and 1975/76 show that average weekly household income *per capita* in Wales was some 88 per cent of the Great Britain average, notwithstanding the fact that the make-up of household income in Wales was very similar to that of Great Britain as a whole (in Wales in 1975/76 a slightly higher proportion — around 28 per cent compared with 26 per cent for Great Britain — came from sources other than wages and salaries). Moreover, the indications of low household income revealed by FES are borne out to an extent by the fact that social security spending clearly stands out as the single biggest item of identifiable public expenditure in Wales.

Whilst definitive conclusions on the extent and character of low pay in Wales must await a much improved data base, some general statements and inferences can be attached to the material reviewed in the first part of this chapter.

First of all, the relatively high earnings of manual workers in the metal-manufacturing sector have tended to inflate the over-all earnings figure for manual workers in Wales. It is important to recognise this since the recent employment contraction in this sector may well tend to lessen this upward pressure, thereby bringing the extent of comparative low pay in Wales more sharply into focus. There is little evidence (with the probable exception of the new Ford engine plant at Bridgend) that new additions to the manufacturing base are offering comparable pay to that found in, for example, the steel industry; hence the next decade may well witness aggregate pay for manual workers slipping back against the Great Britain average.

Secondly, there can be little doubt that where one lives and works in Wales is an important determinant of comparative earnings. Although existing data are seriously deficient, enough is known of the generally depressive effect of primarily agricultural employment on over-all levels of wages and salaries in rural areas. The effect this has on the relative standard of living of low-income recipients in rural areas is conjectural given the almost total absence of sub-regional data on living costs.

Thirdly, given the lower average earnings recorded for non-manual workers in Wales, the projected future growth in the proportion of non-manual workers in the labour market will tend, *ceteris paribus*, to exert a downward pressure on aggregate pay levels relative to those for Great Britain as a whole.

Fourthly, the likely increase in the female activity rate in the labour market in Wales, with its potential displacement effect on male employment, may add a further downward pressure on household income. Female earnings in Wales are currently (April 1977) around 62 per cent of equivalent male earnings.[1]

Fifthly, the increases recorded in part-time employment in Wales (for women this grew from 31.2 per cent of total employment in 1971 to 37 per cent in 1976, while for men the increase was from 3.5 per cent in 1971 to 4.6 per cent in 1976) can be taken both as an indicator of low pay and low household income and as a direct contribution to the perpetuation of low pay. Part-time work tends to attract a lower hourly rate of pay; it predominates in the lower-paid sectors of the economy. Hence, for example, in distributive trades 48.9 per cent of female employment and 9.8 per cent of male employment was part-time and in miscellaneous services 57.7 per cent of women and 18.1 per cent of men were in part-time employment in Wales in 1976. Moreover, part-time work is exerting an increasing displacement effect on full-time employment; thus, male full-time employment in Wales between 1971 and 1976 declined slightly, whereas male part-time employment grew. In addition, two-thirds of the growth in female employment over the same period can be accounted for by part-time work. Hence, the lower-paid household, forced to take up additional part-time employment, whilst possibly achieving some monetary improvement in the short term, in the long term merely adds to the continuation of low basic pay and puts a further squeeze on full-time employment opportunities.[2]

Finally, multiple job holding is a further repercussion of low pay which, although under-researched (Alden, 1977) and scarcely touched by official data, undoubtedly exists, particularly in the lower-paid sub-regions of Wales. Anecdotal evidence, for example, suggests that for many lower-paid workers in the milk and dairy products industry (basic wage at the time of writing – a magnificent £37.50 per week) multiple job holding ('moonlighting') is a necessity in order to make ends meet.[3] The effects of moonlighting are, however, double-edged: short-term additions to household income are gained at the expense of a wider spread of employment opportunities. Moreover, the existence of multiple job holding, because it represents essentially-adaptive behaviour, will tend to weaken critically the strength of local trade unions in their efforts to improve low basic rates.

In the same way that the economic totality of Wales is considered problematic because of uneven economic development within Britain, the existence and persistence of low pay in Wales has been determined largely by a parallel unevenness in internal economic development. Thus it can be seen that, where aggregate earnings comparisons reveal no dramatic indications of low pay in Wales, sub-regional analyses (Table 7.1) do provide such indications. Within this generalisation, what might be termed organisational and structural factors also seem to be important. Most apparent in the mix of low-pay determinants are: the size of the employment unit; the type of enterprise; the extent of trade union membership; and the nature of the process of wage and salary regulation.

There is strong evidence to show that the lower-paid sub-regions of Wales exhibit these characteristics. For example, in both West Wales and Powys employment is far more concentrated (67 per cent and 63 per cent respectively) in manufacturing units employing less than 50 persons than is the case for Wales as a whole (55 per cent). Moreover, the rural areas of Wales suffer a higher proportion of employment of which the rates of pay are governed by Wages Council orders – as, for example, in agriculture and milk products – and, as even the government has seen fit to acknowledge (Department of Employment, 1978c), Wages Councils are amongst the most influential villains on the low-pay scene.

According to the Wages Inspectorate in Wales, around one-eighth of the working population (i.e. some 120,000 workers) is covered by Wages Council agreements. Three sectors predominate: retail distribution, licensing and catering, and hairdressing. It is estimated that these account for 90 per cent of Wages Council-controlled workers in Wales. The extent of low pay in these industries and services is readily demonstrable, as Table 7.2 shows.

Table 7.2: Low Earnings in all Industries and Services Compared with Selected Wages Council Industries in England and Wales, April 1978

Full-time men, % with gross weekly earnings less than £50 per week	
Manual men, all industries and services	6.4%
Manual/non-manual, retail food	16.7%
Manual men, hotels and restaurants	43.8%
Manual men, all Wages Councils	18.5%
Full-time women, % with gross weekly earnings less than £35 per week	
Manual women, all industries and services	12.9%
Manual/non-manual, retail food	23.9%
Manual women, hotel and restaurants	39.7%
Manual women, hairdressing	61.0%
Manual women, all Wages Councils	28.5%

Source: Department of Employment, *New Earnings Survey* (HMSO, London, 1978).

Although these data do not relate specifically to Wales, there is no reason to believe that workers in Wages Council industries are any better off in Wales. Indeed, the limited evidence that is available suggests that the reverse is probably the case. The low-pay 'blitz' first carried out by the Wages Inspectorate in the autumn of 1976 revealed that, of the ten towns visited for one week, Newport (the only town in the sample from Wales) yielded the largest sum of wages underpaid by Wages Council establishments. Similarly, of the twelve towns visited for two weeks, Wrexham (again the only Welsh town in the sample) yielded, by an even greater margin, the largest sum of underpaid wages (Department of Employment, 1977). Ironically, the Wages Inspectorate in Wales possesses less staff now than was the case some years ago, and will in the future increasingly rely on postal questionnaires to establishments governed by Wages Councils to ascertain instances of underpayment — an act of faith which borders on the incredible!

No Pay: Unemployment and Poverty

Along with age and family size, unemployment is one of the most significant influences on relative poverty. As is shown elsewhere in this book, post-war unemployment in Wales has persisted at a level well above the average for the United Kingdom, and Wales has always been amongst the four worst hit of its regions. Echoing the position with earnings, unemployment is unevenly spread within Wales. Certain travel-to-work areas, particularly in West Wales, on the North West coast and in South Wales valley 'blackspots' have unemployment rates of truly horrific proportions (see Wilding, Chapter 2, above).

Whilst it is the case that the development of the Welfare State has helped to offset the worst consequences of unemployment and to this extent Wales 'benefits' like any other region in the United Kingdom, it would be wrong to underestimate the scale of hardship and social and economic deprivation which accrue both to the region and to the individual as a result of the persistence of high rates of unemployment. Moreover, it is increasingly recognised that the extent of social and economic impoverishment is crucially determined by both the causes and the characteristics of unemployment.

This is of singular importance since the available data on unemployment in Wales (and the other 'peripheral' regions of the United Kingdom and Europe) suggest that the basic cause of unemployment is no longer primarily related to short-run fluctuations in world trade − the so-called 'cyclical' factors − but rather reflects dramatic and irreversible shifts from labour into capital across a whole range of key sectors in the economy. This structural effect is further complicated by shifts in hiring practices which would seem to reflect basic changes in the nature and organisation of available work − the de-skilling and routinisation of processes enabling women to replace men and part-time increasingly to be substituted for full-time working (see, for example, Massey, 1978).

These changes, together with the effects of recent legislation (for example, the Employment Protection Act and the Sex Discrimination Act), have brought about alterations in the relative price of 'labour power' which have added further to the segmentation of the labour market.[4] Clearly, specific groups of workers have always been more vulnerable to unemployment: for the old and the young, the unskilled and the ethnic minorities, this remains the case irrespective of the underlying cause of unemployment. However, the shift from cyclical to structural unemployment has brought with it a more pervasive and arguably more damaging form of impoverishment in the shape of

Table 7.3: Long-term Unemployment in Wales, by Age Group[a] 1974-78

	Males		Females	
Age group	July 1974	July 1978	July 1974	July 1978
Under 18	1.2	2.3	2.0	3.8
18-19	2.0	6.0	1.6	11.9
20-24	4.6	18.3	4.9	15.1
25-29	8.7	23.9	8.5	14.2
30-34	13.3	29.5	9.9	17.9
35-44	22.8	33.7	17.2	21.8
45-49	33.9	37.2	20.9	28.4
50-54	38.2	41.5	38.1	39.6
55-59	43.4	41.5	51.9	45.6
60-64	53.0	46.3	–	–
Total, all ages	24.1	26.1	12.6	14.7

Note: a. In each case the level of long-term unemployment is expressed as a percentage of the total level of unemployment for the specific age group.

Source: Department of Employment EDS 82A returns, 1974 and 1978.

long-term unemployment.

Table 7.3 shows the build up of long-term unemployment (defined as more than twelve months on the register) in Wales during the current economic cycle – from the 'trough' of mid-1974 to mid-1978.

A number of disturbing features are apparent in the data. First of all, it can be seen that by mid-1978 one in four of all males and one in eight of all females registering as unemployed had been in this position for twelve months or more.[5] Secondly, whilst there is an obvious relationship between age and duration of unemployment (the older the worker, the more likely he/she is to suffer long-term unemployment), it is also clear that in the four years since mid-1974 the incidence of long-term unemployment has grown very sharply amongst the younger age groups. Thirdly, this downward shift through the age range has now brought 'prime-age' workers into the grip of long-term unemployment. For example, between a quarter and a third of unemployed 'prime-age' males had, by mid-1978, been on the register for more than twelve months. It is interesting to note that slight decreases in the proportions of long-term unemployed over the period were recorded in the 55-59 and 60-64 age bands for men and the 55-59 age band for women. This tends to confirm the suggestion that long-term unemployment is becoming relatively less of an older-worker phenomenon and is being felt with increasing force throughout the age distribution of the registered unemployed.

Recent work by the Manpower Services Commission (MSC) (1978) shows a direct relationship between high levels of over-all unemployment and long-term unemployment. To this extent, the dual nature of the labour market in Wales is further emphasised. MSC data show that for males in mid-1978 long-term unemployment was above the Great Britain average in the relatively underdeveloped sub-regions of Clwyd, Gwynedd and Powys, and slightly below the national average in the relatively more developed sub-regions of Industrial South Wales (Gwent, South, Mid and West Glamorgan). In other words, the incidence of long-term unemployment can be seen to be a direct consequence of the characteristic pattern of economic development in Wales.

Long-term Unemployment and 'Micro' Poverty

The relationship between long-term unemployment and poverty at the level of the individual or individual household may, for convenience, be summarised under two broad headings. The first of these, embracing the psychological and social impoverishments associated with the phenomenon, has been fairly extensively researched (Daniel, 1974; Harrison, 1976; Hill, 1977) and it is not the purpose of this chapter to dwell on these aspects. However, since it is equally not the intention to belittle or downgrade these particular hardships, their succinct description to be found in the MSC's recent discussion paper on long-term unemployment is worth reiterating:

> The basic psychological/social problem of long term unemployment is, then, the creation of a vicious circle; boredom leads to loss of drive, laziness and inertia; skills decline and the individual feels less and less capable of taking up work again; at the same time he/she is less likely to secure work because his/her social contacts decline and because insofar as employers regard a long period of unemployment as indicating unfitness they will tend to look to more economically active recruits. Moreover, because the long term unemployed risk being rejected out of hand by prospective employers, they stand less chance of being submitted for vacancies by local office staff of the Employment service. (MSC, 1978)

There can be little doubt that the existence of such a 'vicious circle' represents an insidious form of poverty for those individuals and households trapped within it. There is equally little doubt that such an experience is blighting the lives of an increasing number of workers and their families in Wales. This chapter is, however, limited to a narrower focus on the relationship between poverty and income, and it is to this issue that we now turn.

Numerous studies have established that in the majority of cases long-term unemployment brings with it severe financial hardship (Field, 1977; Hill, Harrison, Sargeant and Talbot, 1973; North Tyneside Community Development Project, 1978; Sinfield, 1968). It is regrettable, therefore, that such widespread ignorance and prejudice should exist on this issue and that the media are allowed to perpetuate and sustain the mythology of 'welfare scroungers'. The MSC discussion document on long-term unemployment does an excellent de-bunking job on the various permutations of the 'scroungers' myth, and provides considerable detail and insight into the privations suffered by individuals and households falling into the long-term unemployed category. In particular, it cites three factors which interact to create conditions of poverty. Firstly, the long-term unemployed are financially vulnerable because 'they have already experienced a prolonged period of reduced income and are that much more likely to be facing the need to make replacements and repairs'. Secondly, 'they have no entitlement to unemployment benefit', and thirdly, in marked contradiction to popular conceptions, 'the social security system is not designed to regard unemployment as a long term experience and treats the long term unemployed less favourably than others'. An extensive study carried out by the DHSS in 1977 revealed that, of the long-term unemployed males in their sample, less than 2 per cent were drawing unemployment benefit, whereas 82 per cent were existing on supplementary benefit and just under 17 per cent were receiving no form of state benefit payments at all. Moreover, it should be noted that supplementary benefit was paid at the ordinary scale rate of £32.60 current at that time, which was £7.60 per week less than the standard rate of invalidity benefit and £4.80 per week less than the long-term supplementary benefit scale rate payable only to the sick after two years on the ordinary scale rate.

Assuming that the unemployed in Wales follow the Great Britain pattern as far as the proportion in receipt of supplementary benefit is concerned (there is little reason to think otherwise, save for the marginal effect that European Coal and Steel Community payments may be having for those workers joining the ranks of the medium- and long-term unemployed following the closures of steel making at the Ebbw

Vale and East Moors steelworks), then by October 1978 some 14,500 of the long-term unemployed men in Wales were drawing only the standard rate of supplementary benefit and for the unemployed men as a whole we calculate some 28,200 — or 46 per cent of total male unemployment — were expected to survive on a 'benefit' of £34.95 per week (the current standard rate). The DHSS survey showed the relationship between duration of unemployment and type of income support received for women to be very similar to that found for men. Hence, using October 1978 data for Wales, we could expect around 40 per cent of all the unemployed women to be drawing standard-rate supplementary benefit.

It has to be said that this very low basic income can be, and is, supplemented by other means-tested benefits available to low-income recipients both in and out of work. However, given the modest levels at which these additional benefits are pitched, their varying take-up rates and the rule that total unemployment benefits must not exceed 85 per cent of previous earnings, it can hardly be said that the totality of state 'handouts' provide anything other than the most meagre of existences to those workers remaining on the register for more than six months (currently around 40 per cent of the total unemployed in Wales).

One further disturbing aspect of long-term unemployment has arisen as a direct consequence of the rising number of ' prime-age' workers affected. This is the increase in the number of dependent children being drawn into relative poverty (DHSS, 1978). The social consequences of this increase may well take a number of forms, including physical and educational underdevelopment, together with an increase in the incidence of children being taken into 'care' (in both the statutory and voluntary sectors of the social services). The point to be made here is that an inadequate basic level of income support for the unemployed will tend to produce subsequent 'downstream' costs for the state as the consequences of poverty make increasing calls on the various services supported by the public purse. This additional 'vicious circle' has further relevance at the macro-economic level, as the next section attempts to show.

Unemployment and Macro-economic Costs

It is only comparatively recently that serious attempts have been made to assess the costs which unemployment generates and which are met from public funds (MSC, 1977). Estimates made so far tend to divide these costs into two categories: firstly, what might be termed the opportunity cost – that is, the value of the margin of production lost as a result of the underutilisation of productive resources (the National Institute of Economic and Social Research estimated on the basis of 1976 levels of unemployment that Gross Domestic Product was some 8 per cent below full employment level); and secondly, the costs to the government made up of transfer payments (unemployment benefits, supplementary benefits, etc.) and lost revenue from direct and indirect taxation. With regard to this latter set of costs, the Wales TUC has calculated that the level of male unemployment prevailing in October 1977 generated a monthly cost to the Exchequer of £21 million and an annual cost of around £250 million (Wales TUC, 1978). In relation to the cost of lost output, it was estimated that a further £140 million should be added for Wales, representing over-all costs (although excluding the cost of unemployed women and young persons) for 1977 of around £390 million. Given the higher levels of unemployment prevailing in 1978 and the increased scale of transfer payments, the over-all cost of unemployment in Wales currently (January 1979) must be approaching £500 million per annum.

Whilst estimates of the over-all costs to the Exchequer arising out of unemployment in Wales are both incomplete (for example, no attempt has been made to 'cost' the extra burdens falling on the personal social services) and imprecise, there is little doubt that they constitute a significant drain on public funds. What is far less clear is the extent to which both the public and policy makers fully appreciate these negative consequences and, hence, the entirely counterproductive effect of public expenditure utilised to support unemployment rather than the positive promotion of employment. The impoverishing effects of this policy are perhaps best illustrated by a recent example from South Wales.

At the end of 1978 a straightforward choice faced the Welsh Office at the Merthyr Tydfil firm of Triang-Pedigree: whether to provide the official receiver with a further £1.5 million of assistance (estimated to be the required cash injection to enable a reasonable chance of viability for the firm by 1980/81) in addition to the figure of £4 million which had been put into the company in the preceding few years (although it should be noted that £2 million of this assistance was siphoned off into paying debts incurred by previous owners of the company); or whether to leave the company to its fate – closure or, at best, the splitting and hiving off of the most saleable parts of the enterprise.

In the face of the strenuous efforts of the workforce, the total support for them by the Wales TUC and the efforts of the local council, the Welsh Office chose to refuse any further assistance. Subsequently, some 300 employees were put out of work in a town which has suffered a succession of recent closures and cutbacks and where the probability of a prolonged period of unemployment is consequently very high. A belated rescue operation was mounted in early 1979 which has resulted in a much reduced enterprise arising 'phoenix-like' from the wreckage of the old Triang-Pedigree company. The new operation, which will trade under the old name, is a joint venture between the Welsh Development Agency and Morris Vulcan, an established toy manufacturer. It is estimated that the new venture will require some 50-60 full-time workers. Hence, whilst this provides some small relief, it remains the case that the totality of the unemployment costs from the closure of the old company, i.e. transfer payments and lost tax revenue from the 250 workers, plus secondary 'multiplier' effects amongst local industry and the reduction in local rate income flowing from this turn of events, are likely to exceed the sum originally requested by the receiver to keep the factory in operation.

Summary and Conclusions

It is perhaps appropriate to summarise the material presented in this chapter in terms of a series of paradoxes. First of all, it is quite remarkable that, given the massive media attention on pay disputes, so little hard data are in fact available at a regional level as far as earnings and relativities are concerned. Classical wage theories, which assume 'perfect' knowledge of any deviations from the 'going rate' in particular labour markets, thus fall at the first hurdle. This lack of information, pre-empting the 'classical' wage earner's 'rational' choice, is, however, one important factor in understanding the spatial inelasticity of labour. The extent to which this represents the most significant determinant of labour immobility, however, remains an issue predominantly for conjecture.

Secondly, although aggregated earnings data suggest that average earnings in Wales are in line with comparable earnings in the United Kingdom, data from other sources, primarily the Inland Revenue and the *Family Expenditure Survey*, present a differing picture. Disaggregated earnings data from the *New Earnings Survey* begin to clarify this, showing the disproportionate upward 'pull' which the high earnings of manual workers in the steel industry exert on the over-all figures. A further twist, however, is added to the paradox as the need for disaggregated data is 'matched' by a supply that rapidly peters out (see, for example, the restricted coverage of Table 7.1).

Thirdly, the shift from manual to non-manual employment within a labour market is normally taken to herald an increase in aggregate income, as non-manual earnings have consistently maintained a higher level than manual earnings. Whilst this remains the case in absolute terms (assuming over-all employment levels do not deteriorate), the shift could worsen Wales's position within the British regional earnings 'league', since average non-manual earnings in Wales compare unfavourably with their British equivalents. Thus, unless non-manual earnings in Wales move closer to the United Kingdom average, any absolute increase in aggregate income accruing from increasing the share of non-manual employment will not be large enough to preserve Wales's comparative earnings position within the United Kingdom.

The fourth paradox concerns multiple job holding by low-paid workers. Low--paid workers, forced to supplement their primary income with earnings from second and third jobs, are in effect caught in what might better be described as a 'survival trap'. In other words, whilst their activity may ameliorate the effects of low pay, it also perpetuates the cause by blunting organisational pressure that might otherwise be brought to bear on the real problem of inadequate basic rates of pay.

The final paradox has implications which extend beyond the issue of low pay. It derives from the increasing work on the net cost of unemployment to the Exchequer. In the light of the Triang-Pedigree experience at Merthyr, it is now a reasonable hypothesis that, for company closures involving more than 200 employees and resulting in a high proportion of long-term unemployment amongst those affected, the costs to the Exchequer are in excess of the costs of a subsidy to keep the company in business. Hence, the argument that Exchequer subsidies to ailing firms are wasteful in fact masks what might be a far more wasteful and socially damaging use of public resources, i.e. the support of unnecessarily high levels of unemployment.

The notion that the labour market in Wales cannot be adequately treated using a homogeneous theoretical model hardly needs lengthy elucidation. The spatial and sectoral distribution of earnings in Wales of itself suggests at the very least the existence of a dual labour market characterised by the industrial sub-regions of North East and South Wales in contrast with the rural sub-regions of Mid and West Wales.

Beyond this we should consider the theoretical implications of 'black' labour markets which could be said to embrace the secondary and multiple job holders. Although a lengthy discourse on the desirability of treating black labour markets as separate entities, rather than as segments of a particular labour market, may have theoretical legitimacy, it could perhaps prove less useful than a simple recognition of the need for a good deal more work to be done in collecting basic data for descriptive rather than proscriptive purposes.[6] Nevertheless, disaggregating and mapping out in more detail the labour market in Wales is only one aspect of necessary future research and, although critical, should not be pursued to the exclusion of the crucial questions regarding the relationship between pay and economic development.

As with unitary labour market theory, classical 'self-balance' theories (which assume entrepreneurs employ cost-minimising strategies in location decisions) are evidently incapable of explaining uneven economic development within Wales. It is increasingly recognised that the existence of low labour costs (implied by low wages and salaries), even when combined with a plentiful supply of labour, provides no automatic guarantee that 'foot-loose' industry will locate new capacity in such areas. Recent events, for example, at Ebbw Vale, where considerable efforts have been made in the form of enhanced financial incentives and tailor-made factory building, have singularly failed to attract even a quarter of the new jobs needed to offset the jobs lost by the closure of steel making at the British Steel Corporation plant which has traditionally dominated the local labour market.

In the light of the evidence that low labour costs and a ready supply of industrially orientated labour do not prove an irresistable attraction to expanding enterprises, it may be more fruitful to examine a reverse proposition to the effect that the persistence of low wages and salaries in fact restrains economic development.

It could be argued that boosting aggregate real income in Wales would lead to an increase in consumer expenditure (notwithstanding the fact that some of this increase in real income would be siphoned off into extra saving), thereby providing some marginal stimulation to both manufacturing and tertiary sectors of the economy. It has to be recognised, however, that marginal increases in demand can easily be met at this time by more efficient utilisation of existing capacity. Moreover, a 'high wage-high productivity' economy may well, *ceteris paribus*, deepen the structural component of the over-all level of unemployment. Offsetting these important *caveats* are the public expenditure advantages which could accrue from the enhanced tax base which an increase in aggregate real income would make available at local (i.e. through the rates) and national levels (through direct and indirect taxation). *Per capita* public expenditure is already higher in Wales than in England (£875 per head in Wales in 1976/77 compared with £754 per head in in England), reflecting in part the nature of Welsh industry, with a considerable nationalised sector, and in part the higher levels of social security spending related to higher levels of dependency in Wales. There is, however, a strong case for increasing public expenditure in Wales, as NALGO has recently pointed out:

> The public service sector plays a particularly important role in any economically deprived and socially disadvantaged region. As the most labour intensive economic sector it represents a valuable provider of employment and therefore could balance the decline of traditional employment sources and the increasing trend towards capital intensity in whatever new industry is introduced into the area. Secondly, it represents the sole means whereby the deficiency of private incomes caused by unemployment, low activity rates, and all the other facets of a deteriorating employment structure, may be offset through communal expenditure — the social wage. Finally, it is arguably as important as direct financial regeneration. A region within which the social services are visibly less successful than elsewhere in the maintenance of the social fabric is unlikely to appear as an attractive option to foot-loose industries. (NALGO, 1979, p. 19)

The difficulty in both theory and practice, and surely the most crucial question as far as the well-being of Wales is concerned, is how to provide an expenditure framework.whereby a sensitive and supportable balance is achieved between the necessary regeneration and productivity improvement in the manufacturing sector and the equally pressing need to advance both employment and standards in the public sector. Currently, the decision-making process surrounding this issue is bogged down by the monetarist orthodoxy ascendant at the Treasury. For Wales, the 'chicken and egg' dilemma of which comes first — increases in productivity or increases in public expenditure — represents a particularly dangerous political and economic impasse which, unless quickly resolved, can only add to the dimensions of poverty and underdevelopment outlined elsewhere in this book.[7]

Notes

1. See Ch. 8 (eds).
2. For a thorough, recent analysis of the impoverishing aspects of part-time work the reader is referred to J. Hurstfield, 'The Part-time Trap', *Low Pay Pamphlet No. 9.* (Low Pay Unit, London, 1978).
3. See Ch. 9 (eds).
4. See Ch. 8 (eds).
5. It is important to stress that the official data recording long-term unemployment understate the true position. Unemployed persons who have been on the register for twelve months or more and who then leave the register through, for example, sickness (and the long-term unemployed because they tend to be older workers are specially vulnerable to sickness 'de-registering') are treated as newly unemployed when they eventually return to the register. It is suggested that, if the recording of long-term unemployed was redefined to include breaks (e.g. sickness, short-duration jobs, etc.), then the recorded level of long-term unemployment amongst males could increase by up to one-third.
6. See Ch. 8 (eds).
7. For an alternative analysis of the functions of state expenditure, see Ch. 11(eds).

8 SEGMENTED LABOUR MARKETS, FEMALE EMPLOYMENT AND POVERTY IN WALES

Robert McNabb

Regional differences in economic well-being are usually examined in terms of unemployment rates and/or income levels. However, one feature of economic disadvantage that does not receive very much consideration is the attachment of people to the labour force, despite the fact that it has a direct bearing on the problem of poverty. Low attachment indicates proportionately fewer wages/salary recipients and more people dependent on them. Changes in the pattern of labour force attachment within a region, moreover, can have important implications for the future economic development of the region. In particular, the nature of the new employment opportunities being created and the increasing role of women in the labour market have been interpreted as part of a process or development which perpetuates or even accentuates regional disparities in economic development.

The purpose of this chapter is to examine the changes in employment patterns in Wales, especially the growth of female employment, and the implications of these changes for the future development of the region. Before presenting the details of these changes we shall outline some of the issues relevant to the relationship between poverty and employment patterns.

Employment Patterns and Poverty

The application of regional policy to areas economically in need has concentrated on creating jobs in these areas and thus reducing unemployment. The success of regional policy is then measured in terms of the number of jobs created over and above those that would have been expected on the basis of past or national employment performance. This is unsatisfactory for a number of reasons (Mackay, 1974). In particular, it attributes to regional policy a success that is independent of the types of jobs that are created and it is becoming increasingly recognised that a growth of jobs in itself is not a sufficient condition for future economic development. Recent studies of poverty and urban deprivation in ghetto areas in the US have, in particular, raised important questions about the role of labour market stratification in determining labour market outcomes. These studies proposed that the role of employment structures in the perpetuation of poverty could best be understood in terms of segmented labour markets. Contrary to the more orthodox approach to poverty which stresses individual inadequacies such as a lack of skills as the root cause of low incomes, it was suggested the types of jobs to which the poor had access were more important, independent of skill.

The basic division in the labour market proposed in the segmentation theory is between 'primary' and 'secondary' segments of the labour market.[1] Jobs in the primary segment are characterised by high wages and employment stability. Firms in the primary segment provide training and good working conditions for their workers and have well-defined promotion ladders with advancement depending mainly on seniority rather than on ability. Jobs within this segment are concentrated in what Bluestone, Murphy and Stevenson (1973) call the 'core' of the economy, which they define as 'those industries that comprise the muscle of American economic and political power . . . the firms in the core economy are noted for high productivity, high profits, capital utilisation, high incidence of monopoly elements and a high degree of unionisation' (p. 29). Primary segment firms are also characterised by highly structured internal labour markets[2] which embody the rules and arrangements governing wage and employment relationships.

Jobs in the secondary segment tend to be low paying and characterised by high turnover and part-time work; workers within this segment have few opportunities for training within the firms and no access to promotion ladders. Secondary segment firms are found in the 'periphery' of the economy − that is, those industries which are 'noted for their small firm size, labour intensity, low profits, low productivity, intensive product market concentration and lack of unionisation' (Bluestone *et al.*, 1973).

The two segments of the labour market are assumed to be characterised by different wage and employment determination mechanisms, as might be expected given the different types of internal labour markets in each segment. More importantly, mobility between the segments, while not ruled out, is severely restricted. The reason for these differences, which Piore (1970) considers to be the most important distinction between primary and secondary workers, lies in the different behavioural requirements of workers within each segment, especially the requirement of employment stability. In the primary segment employers encourage stability by paying high wages and tying promotion to length of service. These incentives are formalised in the structured internal labour markets of firms in this sector. The incentives that give rise to employment stability in the primary segment are largely absent in the secondary segment. Moreover, employment in this segment is by its nature unconducive to the development of stable work habits, since it involves repetitive and boring work which adds an extra inducement to workers to quit their jobs.

The process through which certain groups in society become confined to the secondary segment is explained in terms of a feedback mechanism. Employers in the primary segment require workers who have 'good work habits' — i.e. those who are stable, prompt and reliable workers — and thus provide the incentives necessary to encourage such behaviour. Workers who gain employment in this segment develop such habits, therefore, as a result of these incentives, and these habits are strengthened and reinforced through their working life. Secondary segment employers are assumed to be unconcerned about turnover and so do not reward stable employment patterns. Workers in this segment, therefore, have no incentive to stay in a job and develop 'bad work habits' as a result of which employment in the primary segment is increasingly ruled out.

It is sometimes the case, however, that some groups with the behavioural traits and skills necessary for employment in the primary segment are confined to secondary jobs, either because unanticipated declines in demand trap some individuals in secondary industries or disadvantaged areas (Wachter, 1974) or because their superficial characteristics resemble those of secondary workers. The latter case occurs because employment decisions can be easily and cheaply made on the basis of such readily observed characteristics as sex and race. Such discrimination expands the secondary segment and thus exerts a downward pressure on wages within that segment. Moreover, individuals who are forced into employment in the secondary segment will develop the behavioural traits characteristic of that segment, through the feedback mechanism, ruling out future primary segment employment.

Why then should there develop a dichotomy between jobs that require stable employment patterns and those that do not? In general, two explanations have been provided of the historical forces that generate such a dichotomy: the dual labour market theory (as developed in the work of Piore, 1970; Doeringer and Piore, 1971; and Bluestone *et al*, 1973) and the social control theory (Gordon, 1972; Edwards, Reich and Gordon, 1975). According to the dual labour market approach, segmentation in the labour market is tied to an alleged dichotomy between firms which face stable product demand and those which face unstable demand conditions. Where the demand for a product is stable, firms are prepared to introduce capital-intensive methods of production and develop structured internal labour markets that promote employment stability. Where firms are faced by unstable demand, they are less likely to undertake capital investments because of the increased risks involved. The labour intensive methods of production that develop, it is argued, are generally unskilled and do not necessitate formalisation of wage and employment relationships. The greater chance of lay-off, short-time work and the lack of incentives to remain at work mean that different worker behaviour will result in this segment.

The social control approach to segmentation sees it as a way through which employers can maintain control of the production process both by dividing workers into conflicting groups and by tying those workers who offer greatest threat to the employer (i.e. those who have trades and crafts in common) to the system by rewarding those workers who are loyal, highly motivated and stable employees. According to Edwards (1976), the employer has to be able to translate labour power (the potential to perform labour) into actual labour: 'The problem of translating labour power into labour has led capitalists to create "systems of control" – hierarchical and authoritarian power relations – within their firms' (p. 55). Internal labour markets are thus developed to institutionalise control over workers and enable the employer to translate labour power into labour. The most important aspect of the internal relations that are developed by the capitalist is that those worker behavioural traits that enable the exercise of power by the capitalist are highly rewarded. It is only in situations in which the firm is large and where there is monopoly power that strategies of segmentation can be implemented:

> were it not for the new conditions of monopoly power which emerged during this period, corporations would probably not have had the freedom to devise new strategies for labour management . . . with the rise of monopoly power employers had the freedom to plan longer range strategies for institutionalising internal and external labour markets. (Gordon, Edwards and Reich, 1973, p. 10)

One problem with both explanations of the historical development of segmentation is that they infer a strict dichotomy in the labour market from what they assume to be strict dichotomies either between capital- and labour-intensive industries or in the stability of demand. It is far from clear, however, that these industries can be bunched at either ends of the capital/labour-intensive spectrum or that product demand is simply stable or unstable. Without such dichotomies, however, segmentation in the labour market is difficult to establish.

In a major critical review of the segmentation theories, Cain (1976) has suggested that many of the issues they raise, particularly in their criticism of conventional labour market analysis, are 'not substantial and more or less misguided' (p. 248). It should be remembered, however, that the challenge of the segmentation theories has been primarily an empirical one, with important policy implications. The non-operational nature of the theory, though, has made such testing difficult, with the result that empirical analysis has been piecemeal. Notwithstanding this, several important issues have been raised by segmented labour market economists that have been neglected in orthodox labour market analysis, particularly the importance of feedback mechanisms in determining workers' attitudes and the importance of the historical analysis and the role of institutional factors in determining labour market success.

Segmentation and Poverty

The main implication of the segmented labour market explanation of poverty is that the poor do participate in the economy but it is the manner of their participation that is important; that is the problem. The poor are confined to the secondary labour market and so the problem facing policy makers is not simply one of creating more jobs but one of creating the right kind of jobs.

In particular, if we are to consider the changes that have taken place in the employment structure in Wales and their implications for the problem of poverty, segmentation theories raise the important question of whether the jobs created in the post-war period to replace those lost in coal and steel can be seen as being in the secondary segment. There are several ways this could be examined, though in most instances it requires a detailed analysis of changes at the firm level to consider the types of jobs being created. Data limitations, however, do not permit such an analysis. Consequently, we have considered changes at a more aggregate level. As we shall see, the most prominent feature of changes in the Welsh employment structure has been the increased role of women in the labour force. We have already noted that women

are generally restricted to the types of jobs described as being in the
secondary segment. As Andrisani (1973) remarks, women are often
confined to the secondary segment at the onset of their labour market
careers independent of their abilities or skills. Moreover, the

> social definitions of family and sex roles continue to under cut
> employment stability among women. And, as the percentage of
> women in the labour force continues to increase, some employers
> seem more and more likely to move many jobs into the secondary
> market in response to the (expected) behavioural characteristics
> of secondary women employees. (Gordon, 1972)

For the United Kingdom, Bosanquet and Doeringer (1973) have
argued that 'many of the symptoms of duality exist in Britain as well
as in the United States' (p. 432) and cite as evidence the fact that
women are over-represented in low-paying jobs and face employment
and wage discrimination, noting a survey of 44 major firms which showed
that 91 per cent of them had 'women only' jobs (mainly in clerical
occupations) and 73 per cent had jobs that were closed to women.
Similarly, women experience much less occupational upgrading and
female earnings are low, even after such things as education and skill
are taken into account. While the evidence Bosanquet and Doeringer
present does not definitely establish the existence of labour market
duality, it does indicate the inferior employment conditions faced by
women.

Labour Force Attachment, 1961-71[3]

As we saw above, low labour force attachment has a direct bearing on
the problem of poverty and urban deprivation since it provides some
indication of the relative number of wage and salary recipients compared
to those dependent on them. In Table 8.1 we present activity rates
for males and females for the years 1961, 1966 and 1971.

For both men and women activity rates are lower in Wales than for
Great Britain as a whole, though the difference is especially large for
women. If we transform these percentages into absolute numbers
their significance can be more readily seen. If we standardise the Welsh
figures by assuming that Wales has the national average activity rates
and the same population, in 1971 there would have been 105,000 extra
income recipients in the region. Of this, 76,000 would be women and

Table 8.1: Activity Rates for Great Britain and Wales, 1961, 1966 and
         1971

	Males		Females	
	Great Britain	Wales	Great Britain	Wales
1961	86.3	85.1	37.5	28.1
1966	84.0	81.0	42.1	28.7
1971	81.4	78.5	42.7	35.7

Sources: OPCS, 1961 Census, 1966 Sample Census and 1971 Census.

29,000 men. Together with the further income that would be generated
by so many extra wage and salary earners, the importance of low labour
force attachment for Wales is apparent.

Of equal significance, however, are the changes in the activity
rate figures in Wales, especially since 1966. For men the national
trend has been one of decline, though this has been greater in Wales
than for the rest of the country. Between 1961 and 1971 the over-all
activity rate for men fell by 4.9 percentage points compared with a
decline of 6.6 percentage points in Wales. On the other hand, the
performance of female activity rates has been more favourable in
Wales, though this involves some element of 'catching up' with the
national pattern. Still, over the five years between 1966 and 1971, the
female activity rate in Wales increased by nearly 6.0 percentage points
more than the increase for Great Britain as a whole.

One important feature of the growth in the number of economically
active females in Wales is that it has been accounted for solely by an
increase in the number of married women in the labour force. Between
1966 and 1971 the number of economically active married women
increased by about 26 per cent or over 50,000, while the number of single
women fell by more than 10 per cent. This mirrors, to some extent, the
changes in the pattern of female activity rates nationally, though the
growth in the number of married women economically active is much
smaller (14 per cent) despite a larger decline in the attachment of
single women to the labour force.

It is possible, of course, that the increased importance of married
women in the labour force reflects a relative increase in the number of
married women in the population generally or, alternatively, it is
because of a change in their age distribution such that there are now
relatively more married women in high-activity age groups. There has,
in fact, been very little change in the proportion of women who are

married − 62.9 per cent in 1966 and 63.1 per cent in 1971 − while the age distribution of married women in 1971 is much the same as it was in 1966. The fact is that more married women are now entering the labour force than was the case in previous years. This can be seen by looking at the age-specific activity rates presented in Table 8.2.

Table 8.2: Age-specific Activity Rates (Females), 1966, 1971 (per cent)

Age group	Married Women		Single Women	
	1966	1971	1966	1971
16-24	35.6	37.5	66.7	60.8
25-44	33.5	40.8	76.2	74.3
45-59	32.4	41.8	58.1	60.8
60+	7.4	9.2	9.3	7.6

Sources: OPCS, 1966 Sample Census and 1971 Census.

For married women there has been an increase in the activity rates of all groups, the largest being for those aged between 45 and 59. For single women the reverse is true, with the exception of those aged between 45 and 59 whose activity rate was increased by nearly three percentage points.

Male-Female Employment Patterns

The changes in activity rates described above, with male attachment to the labour force declining and the increased role of married women in the labour force, suggest some important changes in the over-all employment structure in Wales. These changes can be seen in Table 8.3, in which we present the changes in male and female employment in Wales for selected years. Again the striking feature is the contrasting patterns of change between men and women.

Table 8.3: Employment in Wales by Sex (000's)

	Males	Females	Females as % of total
1953	676	250	27.0
1963	686	297	30.2
1971	629	333	34.6
1973	636	364	36.4
1976	612	383	38.4

Source: Department of Employment, *British Labour Statistics: Historical Abstracts*, (HMSO, London, 1971) and Welsh Office, *Welsh Economic Trends* No. 5, (HMSO, Cardiff, 1978).

The number of men declined by nearly 10 per cent between 1953 and 1976 while female employment has increased by more than 50 per cent; or, in relative terms, the proportion of total employment accounted for by females has increased by over eleven percentage points. Despite this, however, it is still the case that the region has an above average ratio of males to females resulting from the still significant, though declining, dominance of male-intensive industries.

The extent of decline in such male-intensive industries as coal mining can be seen in Table 8.4, in which we present employment change by broad industrial group. As might be expected, the extractive industries have accounted for the largest loss of male jobs, this being mainly due to a decline in mining, though the fall in employment in metal manufacture has also been significant (about 20,000 jobs were lost between 1967 and 1976 in metal manufacture). The growth of new jobs, on the other hand, has been primarily in the service sector, and this presumably accounts for the changing pattern of male-female employment in the region. By 1976, 65,000 more females were employed in service sector industries than had been the case in 1967. In fact, by 1976 industries in this sector accounted for 76 per cent of all female employment in Wales. Most notable sources of new employment opportunities were in professional and scientific services (34,000) and miscellaneous service industries (20,000).

Table 8.4: Employment in Wales by Broad Industrial Sector, 1967 and 1976 (000's)

	1967			1976		
	Males	Females	Total	Males	Females	Total
Extractive	104.9	10.6	115.5	59	8.5	67.5
Manufacture	232.4	75.6	308	225.2	77.6	302
Construction						
Gas and	89.3	5.8	95.1	81.5	6.8	88.3
Electrical						
Services	250.0	225.4	475.4	246.3	290.5	536.8

Source: Welsh Office, *Welsh Economic Trends* (HMSO, Cardiff, 1978), Table 22

The types of jobs that have been created within these industries reflect the general pattern of female employment found in them. In particular, there has been a growth in the number of clerical workers. especially machine operators, professional workers (nurses and teachers) and service workers, including cleaners and kitchen hands. Together these occupations accounted for over 80 per cent of the total growth in female labour between 1966 and 1971.[4]

Some Implications of the Growth of Female Employment

As we have already seen, the types of jobs that are typically available to women are those described as 'secondary' in the dual labour market literature, jobs in which the employment characteristics are inferior in many respects to those available to men. Female wage rates are substantially below those of male workers and the jobs that women do are often unskilled or semi-skilled and available on a part-time basis. Moreover, there are significantly fewer opportunities for women to boost their earnings by working in incentive payments schemes, since the amount of overtime and shift work they can do is limited by law. In Wales, women earn £26 per week less than men and nearly 40 per cent are employed on a part-time basis, compared with only 4 per cent of men. Similarly, 80 per cent of female workers are employed in intermediate / junior clerical work or in unskilled or semi-skilled manual jobs, while only 34 per cent of male employees are in such occupations.

These figures apply to female employment generally in Wales, so need not be indicative of the new jobs coming to the region. However, in the jobs that have grown, it is the case that a significantly larger proportion of females work part-time and that their earnings are below the national average for females in other jobs.[5]

What then are the implications for poverty of the changes that have taken place in the employment structure in Wales? An unambiguous answer to this question is difficult to give since the changes that have occurred can be interpreted in more than one way and since these changes are part of an ongoing process of change; a lot will depend on whether the pattern of change that has taken place over the past ten years continues. What we have experienced is a fairly dramatic change in the sex composition of the Welsh labour force, with more married women entering the labour force as more employment opportunities for them have become available, while the old problem of declining male-intensive industries remains with us. To date the growth of jobs for married women has just about kept pace with the loss of jobs in such industries as coal and steel, and it is possible that, for many families, incomes have been supplemented by more wives going out to work.

However, it is not clear that this process will ultimately benefit the region. The types of jobs that are being created are really ones that can be described as 'peripheral', in the sense that they do not really involve employment stability since they include a high proportion of part-time work and are characterised by high turnover rates, nor do they have the permanence or security of the more stable, full-time work that characterises male employment. Because of this, such 'peripheral' employment will not adversely affect the Welsh economy if it supplements a strong – and much larger – 'core' of stable jobs.[6] However, if it is in fact replacing these 'core' jobs, at least for certain groups of previously 'core' employees, then the implications are far more serious, since it involves the substitution of low-paying jobs, that are characterised by employment instability, for better-paid and more stable employment.

The picture that emerges, then, from the limited data available is that in Wales there has been a considerable growth in the service sector and that these new jobs have been directed towards the employment of females, especially those who are married. These jobs tend to be poorly paid, semi- or unskilled and characterised by job instability. On the other hand, the traditional 'regional problem' continues to rear its ugly head. Male employment is declining, more so than would be expected on the basis of national trends (Welsh Office, 1978c), and male unemployment remains well above average. Regional policy has done something to reduce the impact of industrial decline (Moore and Rhodes, 1975, who estimate that over 50,000 jobs have been created as a result of regional policy). Nevertheless, rather than creating new employment opportunities which would meet the excess supply of male labour, what in fact has happened is that the jobs which have been created have resulted in an increase in the supply of married women in the labour force. Moreover, it is not the areas within Wales which suffer most from industrial decline that receive these jobs, but rather the other more prosperous areas, increasing the hardship and poverty in the former and generating more over-all inequality.

Conclusions

In this chapter we have outlined an explanation of poverty based on the view that the labour market is segmented into two or more self-contained parts. The problem of poverty arises not simply because of a lack of jobs but because the poor are confined to the secondary segment, though secondary segment workers often move between employment and unemployment. Within such a framework it is possible to view the changes that are taking place in the Welsh employment structure as a growth of the secondary segment. However, since the women who have entered the labour market are typically married, the growth of these jobs – notwithstanding the fact that they are often part-time, low paying, etc. – must in many cases involve an increase in family income.[7]

In terms of the future economic development of Wales, however, these changes are more serious if these trends continue, since the new employment opportunities being created are significantly inferior to the jobs that are being lost. In order to judge the usefulness of the segmentation theory, however, much more analysis needs to be undertaken. First, we need to know a lot more about the employment circumstances of the poor. Is it the case that they can find employment but only in secondary jobs? If so, what factors limit the jobs available to them? Second, a more detailed longitudinal analysis is needed to consider the importance of feedback mechanisms. Finally, a more detailed analysis of the nature of the new jobs being created is required, in order to provide a more useful basis for manpower policy recommendations than a simple concern with the number of jobs created.

Notes

1. This distinction is the most commonly used though other types of segmentation have also been suggested (see Gordon, 1972; and Gordon, Edwards and Reich, 1973).
2. According to Doeringer and Piore (1971), an internal labour market can be defined as 'an administrative unit within which the pricing and allocation of labour is governed by a set of administrative rules and procedures'. It is distinguished from the external labour market where wages and employment are determined by the working of market forces.
3. Figures for estimating the extent of a region's population which is economically active are available only in census years. Activity rates are the usual measure of labour force attachment and are measured as follows:

$$EA_i = (Employed_i + Unemployed_i)/Population^i$$

where EA_i is the proportion of group i who are economically active (i.e. the activity rate for group i) and $Employed_i$, $Unemployed_i$ and $Population_i$ are the numbers employed, unemployed and total population in group i.
4. Detailed occupation data are available only for the census years. In 1971 a high proportion of female occupations were included in the 'not classified' category and were excluded from these estimates.
5. Over 50 per cent of women working in the professional and scientific services and miscellaneous services industries in Wales are employed part-time, compared with an over-all average of 37 per cent for all industries and 14.7 per cent in manufacturing. For clerical and related workers average incomes in the UK are £46.5 per week compared with an over-all average for all occupations of £46.9 per week and £49.2 in non-manual occupations.
6. This is not to say that employment discrimination against females does not have an adverse effect upon the position of women in the Welsh economy, but simply that these extra jobs involve a supplement to family incomes, thus reducing the over-all problem of poverty.
7. See Ch. 7 (eds).

9 INDUSTRIALISATION, INEQUALITY AND DEPRIVATION IN RURAL WALES[1]

Glyn Williams

Disadvantage cannot be adequately understood simply by reference to a range of social indicators which demonstrate the existence of 'deprivation', but must be viewed in the context of inequalities set by the class structure of the general population. Certainly, any discussion which does not consider this context can do little to explain poverty as a social phenomenon. In fact, however, it is rare to encounter discussions of social disadvantage which do incorporate an awareness of the problems of production, reproduction and legitimisation of poverty embodied in class formation and change. As a result, most discussions fail to make the essential link between poverty, inequality and the nature of economic change. In this chapter, I shall attempt to remedy this situation by reference to an analysis of rural Wales. In doing so, I shall draw particularly on some of the theoretical perspectives current in the sociology of development.

Development Theory and the Sociology of Rural Wales

Two perspectives which dominate in recent discussions of poverty and economic development can be labelled 'diffusionist' and 'dependency' models. Advocates of the former argue in terms of government aid programmes, private investment, etc., generating economic development through the 'trickling down' of capital, technology and organisational methods from the 'core' capitalist areas to the 'backward' areas of the 'periphery'. In contrast, advocates of the dependency model argue that the contemporary underdevelopment of peripheral areas is the product of the uneven development of capitalism. This second perspective views peripheral underdevelopment as a consequence of core penetration and claims that poverty at the periphery can be eradicated only if both its internal structures and its relationship with the core undergo a fundamental change. In these terms, of course, rural Wales may be seen broadly as a peripheral area.

The orthodox social science paradigm has focused on the diffusion model. This perspective is evident not only in the way that economic development itself has been approached, but also in the discussion of the sociology of rural society and, more specifically, Welsh rural society. An almost exclusive focus of sociological studies of Wales has been on the rural areas in which cultural distinctiveness is most apparent. The best known of these studies are the various 'community studies' undertaken immediately after the Second World War (for example, Rees, 1950; Davies and Rees, 1960). Operating within a structural-functional framework, they tended to view the various communities as closed, static entities, where face-to-face interaction involved status group differentiation rather than class-based polarisation; the communities were portrayed as the converse of a differentiated, almost anomic, urban-industrial society. The dichotomy which developed in the limited discussion of external influences comprised urban-industrial influences acting as anglicising forces which threatened an ill-defined 'Welsh way of life' (Day, 1979).

In contrast to the studies undertaken by these 'native' social scientists, two studies from the Manchester School of social anthropology (Frankenberg, 1957; Emmett, 1964) adopt an evolutionary perspective. English culture is seen as the source of change in an again loosely defined Welsh way of life; English culture is the point towards which Welsh culture necessarily moves. The impression is given that Welsh rural society is a somewhat endangered, primitive form of social organisation which must yield to the larger, more complex forms of British society. The Welsh are placed in Nature, where basic instincts are given rein; whereas the English are the source of a civilisation which diffuses slowly to encompass Welsh society and culture.

It is no great step from this kind of perspective to an explanation of poverty in terms of cultural 'backwardness', with the actors themselves responsible for their situation. Such explanations refer to attributes such as language, values, attitudes, etc. as factors which prevent 'progress'. Significantly, this view seems to be prevalent among many of the agents of state planning and welfare institutions, to the extent that it would appear to have been legitimised, with the 'community studies' mentioned above providing the supporting evidence!

The alternative orientation to rural Welsh society which I shall adopt in this chapter derives, at least broadly, from the dependency model. Its focus will be the control of resources by externally based (i.e. to rural Wales) powers, which denies the indigenous population the ability to sustain a locally based pattern of balanced economic development. The process whereby core areas organise the production of the periphery has the effect of concentrating resources at the core and creates a progressive economic and political dependence of the periphery on the core. This characteristic form of economic development has the consequence within the periphery of creating particular types of class structure and conflict (Cardoso and Faletto, 1969). New class interests are generated which are committed to the new forms of production introduced to the periphery to serve the essential interests of the core and which threaten those classes already established in the periphery (Hirschman, 1977). In short, these changes have the effect of creating new structures of inequality and poverty in the peripheral areas. In the context of rural Wales, those who lose out most in these processes appear to respond by mobilising on the basis of the socio-cultural resources of the area. In the following sections of the chapter, I shall attempt to exemplify and expand upon the themes that I have presented in an abstract form by reference to developments in rural Wales since the beginning of the twentieth century.[2]

The Restructuring of Rural Wales: the Demise of the Old Economic Order

The twentieth century has witnessed the wholesale restructuring of the economy and society of rural Wales. Agricultural production has been transformed by the changing patterns of land holding and ownership and by the massive substitution of capital for labour in the process of production itself. In the primary sector (predominantly, of course, slate quarrying, with some metal extraction), there has been a decline, progressive almost to the point of extinction. The other side of the coin, obviously, has been the introduction of manufacturing industry into rural Wales, often with state encouragement and sponsorship. Clearly, these enormous changes have had a profound effect on the occupational and class structures of the area.

The extension of the franchise during the nineteenth century led to the collapse of the old political regime. The landowning class's control over the state was considerably weakened and the new order introduced fiscal penalties on unearned income and inherited wealth. These were major factors which contributed to the break-up of the vast rural estates, although the changing fortunes of agricultural *vis-á-vis* other forms of investment also played their part. The result was a transformation of the patterns of landownership in Wales (Davies, 1974b) which mainly involved former tenants purchasing their (relatively) small-holdings. Hence, between 1909 and 1941 the proportion of Welsh agricultural holdings occupied by the owner increased from 10.6 per cent to 37 per cent, this figure rising to 58.4 per cent by 1960 and 63.7 per cent by 1970. However, most of the units involved were of less than fifty acres in area, which made them highly susceptible to subsequent economic changes.

The intervention of the state — frequently justified in terms of controlling food prices — has been of major significance in generating these latter economic changes. Hence, in upland Wales, the policy of extending sheep farming by the introduction of hill farm subsidies had enormous repercussions. As associated policy aimed to extend the proportion of 'commercial agricultural units', which were defined as those capable of employing one full-time labourer in addition to the occupier. For example, the Small Farms Act of 1959 went as far as to limit aid to farms in this category (which, in some senses, were those least in need of government aid). Moreover, this Act made aid conditional upon the acceptance of a production plan devised by the National Agricultural Advisory Service. These programmes have, at least in part, been responsible for the reduction in the number of agricultural units in Wales from 55, 402 in 1951 to 32,495 in 1971. During the same period, the number of units larger than one hundred acres in area increased by 17 per cent, while those less than twenty acres diminished by 71 per cent. Hence, Welsh agriculture has been transformed from a predominantly tenant farmer and small-holding basis to owner-occupation of larger, more 'rational' units.

Contemporaneous with these developments was a process of substitution of capital for labour in agriculture. Hence, between 1921 and 1971, the numbers employed in agriculture fell from 106,835 to 52,750. The effects of this capitalisation were especially marked on the smaller upland farms with relatively unproductive land. Such units had been unable to extend their capitalisation very far, nor were they able to afford to hire labour.[3] Thus, many of the farmers who purchased their independence from the large landowners subsequently went out of business and were proletarianised in the process. State intervention to purchase small farms to convert them to timber production has had similar consequences.[4]

These changes in agriculture have been paralleled by an equally profound transformation in the primary sector of the rural economy, both of which, in turn, have contributed to the vast depopulation of rural Wales since the 1920s. Quarrying was a major employer in many parts of the area, with 17,000 men being employed at one time in the slate quarries alone. By the 1970s, only a few hundred remained in the slate industry.

The consequences of this decline have been felt in all sections of the localities affected, amongst both owners and workers. For example, at the end of the nineteenth century, two-thirds of the income of the huge Penrhyn estate derived from the slate quarries. It was this dual interest which allowed the estate to exploit the labour resources of its tenants, who were also quarrymen, as well as to shift capital from one interest to another as necessity and/or advantage dictated. Clearly, the decline of quarrying undermined this lucrative system. Similarly, a large part of the local proletariat was adversely affected. Both quarry-men and farm labourers were impelled to migrate in large numbers (often across the Atlantic), leaving behind a population which was in many respects impoverished. Furthermore, as T. Davies (1976) has shown, much, although by no means all, of the quarrying interests were financed by local capital. Whilst we know little about what use was made of the profits which derived from these enterprises, it is significant in terms of the dependency model of development (see above) that their demise signalled the end of what was virtually the only source of local capital which could have been used for subsequent industrial development.

By the end of the 1950s, then, it was clear that rural Wales had experienced a profound restructuring of its economy. Changes in the occupational base had generated a population loss which was so severe that the ability to reproduce a labour force was in doubt. Although he focuses on agriculture exclusively, Hannan (1978) has summarised the situation well:

> The model of transition in a modernising Western peasant society — where the oversupply of labour in agriculture is absorbed in a relatively smooth transition into urban industrial employment — to a considerable extent overstates the ease of transition, even in those countries with rapidly expanding employment opportunities. The process of 'modernisation' leaves stranded a large number of older, low income, dependent people who have not been able to adjust fast enough to the rapid economic changes occurring.

Yet the policies which were implemented ostensibly with the intention of generating new employment opportunities in rural Wales have been less than wholly successful in alleviating these problems.

State Intervention and Industrial Development

Since 1945, the state has played an increasingly major role in the organisation of the rural economy. I have already referred to its operations within the sphere of agriculture. However, a number of policies have been aimed at the introduction of new economic activities into rural Wales, quite distinct from the pre-existing economic structure. Among these developments have been the location of large, capital-intensive projects in rural areas; the encouragement of new manufacturing industry by means of 'regional development programmes'; and the expansion of the leisure industry.

There is a general tendency for that sector of industry which has reached the highest level of replacement of labour by capital to locate in peripheral areas, usually in the form of extractive, energy-related and port-related enterprises. In rural Wales, such enterprises take the form of power stations (for example, Wylfa on Anglesey), aluminium plants (for example, at Dolgarrog and Amlwch), oil terminals and refineries (for example, at Milford Haven and Amlwch) and various hydro-electric and water storage schemes (for example, Dinorwic). The extent to which developments such as these are beneficial to their localities is highly dubious (see Carter, 1974, for a theoretical treatment of the parallel situation in the Scottish Highlands). They require a large labour force during the initial construction stages, but subsequently employ only a small number of highly skilled and supervisory personnel. In consequence, during the initial stages, labour is attracted from local employers by the relatively high financial rewards. In addition, supervisory and skilled workers are drawn in from outside the locality. Hence, for example, a recent study of the construction of the Dinorwic pumped storage scheme (Williams and Howell, no date) indicated that most of the professional staff were English, the supervisory staff Irish, and the majority of the local workers in the lower-paid, unskilled categories. This pattern is, of course, partly attributable to the contracting of construction work to firms outside rural Wales, which naturally bring with them certain workers from the core areas. Moreover, the dependence of the peripheral area is further emphasised during the working life of these enterprises. The situation arises in which the natural resources of the area are exploited and in which the environmental costs (for example, pollution) are borne by the peripheral area, but the latter derives little or no benefit in terms of new, stable employment opportunities (Buttel and Flinn, 1977). In fact, projects such as these may have a positively *de*stabilising effect on the local

labour market. Despite being among the lowest paid of the workers
employed during the construction stages, local people can still earn
more then than previously. Accordingly, there is a reluctance to
exchange new-found 'affluence' for the lower rewards available locally
after construction is completed. Hence, among the local workforce at
Dinorwic, 67 per cent of those under 30 years of age expressed the
intention of leaving the area when they were made redundant. Thus, a
project which was presented as one which, in part, was intended to
ameliorate levels of unemployment and associated out-migration may
well serve to stimulate the latter (this is not to say, however, that such
out-migration is not beneficial to the individuals involved).

Perhaps the most far-reaching aspect of state intervention in rural
Wales has involved the 'regional development programmes'. Their
purported objective is to entice private enterprise (especially manufacturing industry) from the core areas by offering incentives which
will induce firms to locate in the Development Areas. Conventionally,
this sort of policy approach is justified by the claim that without
monetary inducements industry would not locate in peripheral areas;
that is, it does so against its 'natural preferences'. By offering such
inducements, the state thereby ensures the creation of job opportunities
in areas of high unemployment; a rationale clearly couched in social
welfare terms.

However, it should be recognised that this sort of argument implies
a particular view of the role of the state generally and of its activities
in peripheral areas in particular. The state is seen as an essentially
benign institution, which is concerned solely with the development of
peripheral areas along the lines suggested by the diffusionist model.
In contrast, it needs to be recognised that the state exists primarily
to further the development of capitalism and employs the ideological
apparatus to make this development acceptable. Whilst the definition
of areas such as rural Wales as ones which are in need of state aid may
acknowledge the deficiencies of past state policies, it also serves to
legitimise what may be viewed as the transfer of capital via the state to
capitalist enterprises. Hence, the presentation (as above) of state aid
as a form of welfare plan plays down the local impact of the extension
of capitalism, and the local agents of the state can play the creation of
local employment opportunities against any negative effects (T.M.
Davies, 1978). As Poulantzas (1973a) has recognised, the channelling
of state resources through local government has the diversionary effect
of making these resources appear to be used in local interests, in solving
local problems. In reality, the state spends on the social infrastructure

the minimum that is necessary in order to retain the necessary labour force, to reproduce it and to avert any political protest (Poulantzas, 1976). In order to avoid expanding its costs and also to convey the impression of reducing local unemployment in real terms, it will resort to various relocation schemes when these serve the interests of capitalism. Such a policy serves to retain a local workforce, which has limited but specific skills, while the residual population is encouraged to leave. Thus, there is no real contradiction between a policy which is claimed to reduce out-migration by means of the introduction of job opportunities and the simultaneous offering of incentives to leave the area.

Clearly, the incentives offered by the state are of some value to those capitalist enterprises which come to rural Wales; however, there are other attractions which may well be more significant. Hence, Thomas (1966) lists, for example, the existence of a non-unionised, non-militant labour force and the presence of a large, untapped female population, willing to work part-time for relatively low wages, as major reasons for locating factories in rural Wales (see also, Massey, 1978). Moreover, the result of state policy tends not to be the wholesale relocation of plants, but the extension of enterprises through the establishment of branch factories. This means that the managerial and decision-making functions remain firmly located in the core and that there is little integration of the industrial development of rural Wales into the mainstream of the economic structure. Again, the tendency is for these firms to import their own middle management and key workers, leaving only the relatively poorly paid, unskilled work for the local workers: a situation compounded by the absence of local industrial training schemes. Once more, the dependent relationship between the periphery of rural Wales and the core is underlined.

The final aspect of state intervention in the economy of rural Wales involves the promotion and extension of tourism. Between 1961 and 1971, the income from tourism in Wales doubled from some £50 to £100 million. By and large, wages in this sector are extremely low, although, it is argued, they are in some instances supplemented by free accommodation, meals, etc. For example, a recent survey of Mid Wales (Wenger, 1979) indicates that average wages in the tourist industry were not only well below the average for Wales as a whole, but also well down on the figure for the study area itself (which is generally a low-wage area). Moreover, employment in tourism is seasonal and also involves considerable part-time work. In consequence, many of the customary benefits — holiday pay, sickness benefit, etc. — are forfeited. Given the nature of this work, it inevitably draws in a large proportion of female workers, but offers little prospect either of stable attachment to the labour market or of skill acquisition and occupational mobility.

However, perhaps the most conspicuous effect of the increase in tourist activity involves the use of local resources. The vast number of tourists who visit rural Wales during the holiday season places intense pressure on the social infrastructure, which is designed principally to cope with the 'normal' population level. This often is clearly disadvantageous to the local population. In short, the costs of maintaining this infrastructure fall upon a population which is denied the fullest access to it; and it is by no means clear that these costs are balanced by the benefits accruing to the majority of the local population from tourism itself.

The picture that emerges, then, is one in which the periphery of rural Wales is dependent upon the core areas. The intervention of the state has operated to a considerable degree to accentuate that dependency. However, it is important to consider what is happening not only at the highly aggregate level of core and periphery, but also at the level of the changes in class structure and inequality that are taking place within the periphery as a result of its dependent relationship with the core. It is to the latter that I shall turn in the following section of the chapter.

Polarisation in Rural Wales: Spatial, Class, Cultural

The patterns of development which I have sketched in the preceding sections have had profound consequences for the internal structure of rural Wales. The latter's dependent position has generated what may be termed a polarisation which assumes spatial, class and cultural dimensions. It is by an examination of this polarisation that the nature of inequality in rural Wales may best be understood and its relationship with dependent patterns of economic development recognised.

The spatial dimension of polarisation is, in part, a simple result of the uneven nature of capitalist development. However, in rural Wales, this natural pattern has been accentuated by the policy of 'growth pole' industrialisation, which has been implemented by the state since the 1960s.[5] The objective of this policy has been to focus economic development at certain pre-selected centres (such as Milford Haven, Aberystwyth, Brecon, Newtown, centres along the North Wales coast) which are assumed to have the greatest 'potential' for sustained growth. New employment opportunities are to be created at these centres and workers from the surrounding hinterlands are expected to travel daily to these opportunities. Thereby, the larger part of rural Wales would reap benefits from a concentrated pattern of development.

In fact, there has been a clear tendency for the benefits to cluster close to the poles, with a subsequent lack of benefits away from them. Indeed, it becomes possible to draw a clear distinction between an 'enclave' of relative prosperity in the poles and the increasingly 'marginalised' hinterlands — a typical configuration of dependent economic development (Quijano, 1973). Workers living in these marginalised areas and working in the poles are obliged to find their own transport; given the pattern of withdrawal of public services (Rees and Wragg, 1975), private access becomes an essential job qualification. These workers tend to spend their earnings in the relatively large enterprises at the pole and the resultant fall-off in trade in their home areas leads to a decline in the small businesses run by the local petty bourgeoisie. Nor is this tendency for growth in the enclave to be complemented by decline in the marginalised areas confined to private enterprise. It becomes increasingly 'rational' for the state to locate its collective facilities, such as educational and health services, in the poles, largely as a result of the population decline in the marginalised areas, which is itself a response to the marginalisation process.[6] Of course, these relocations serve further to isolate the population of the marginal areas from essential societal services.

A more specific illustration of these rather general points may be given from a recent study of Gwynedd, based upon the 1971 census (Grant, 1979); whilst the picture that emerges is admittedly crude, it serves to highlight the process of spatial polarisation. Along the Merionydd, Aberconwy and Anglesey coasts, enclave areas, indices of 'deprivation' are low. In particular, housing tends to have all the amenities and there is a considerable amount of recent housing construction. These areas are also characterised by high rates of in-migration, some of which is attributable to new employment opportunities, the remainder to retirement migration (which, of course, imposes considerable pressure on some of the centralised service facilities). Unemployment is seasonal. In contrast, the inland areas, well away from the growth poles, exhibit high 'deprivation' scores, with housing conditions being amongst the worst in Britain. These marginalised locations are occupied by a population with a disproportionate number of old people, often living alone, mixed with younger families, frequently living in overcrowded conditions and with the head of the house-

hold unemployed. Not surprisingly, levels of in-migration to these
areas are relatively low.

There are clearly dangers in conceiving of the generation of inequalities within a peripheral area such as rural Wales purely in the
spatial terms of enclave and marginalised areas (Rotman, 1974). However, further insight into the nature of conditions in the marginalised
areas may be derived from a second empirical study, a survey-based
analysis of the general economic and occupational structure of Mid
Wales (Wenger, 1979). Taking first of all the occupational structure of
the male labour force, Wenger's study draws attention to the fact that
a relatively high proportion of male workers is self-employed.[7] Whilst
a significant part of this figure can be explained in terms of farming,
Wenger argues that the absence of employment opportunities, particularly in what I have termed marginalised areas, is also a significant
factor. Quite simply, for many (especially skilled) workers, the choice
is between self-employment and unemployment. A second, and clearly
associated, trend is towards multiple job holding, with 12 per cent of
household heads 'moonlighting'. Hence, self-employment is not
necessarily seen as a means of social mobility, offering lucrative returns
and prospects, but rather as an adaptation to the shortage of employment opportunities. This is further borne out by the average levels of
income of the self-employed. Despite working anything between 37
and 112 hours per week, and receiving assistance from family members,
average incomes were only slightly higher than skilled workers in
Wenger's sample, ranging between £50 and £60 per week. It is this low
return which presumably accounts for the high rates of mobility between
the self-employed and skilled worker categories, with 18 per cent of the
male employed population being upwardly mobile from skilled to self-
employed status, whilst a further 16 per cent was downwardly mobile
between the two categories.

In many ways, then, the occupational structure for males in the
marginalised areas is highly reminiscent of what Bonacich (1978) has
termed the 'cheap labour' sector of a 'split labour market'.[8] She says:

> The concept of 'cheap labour' refers not only to the wages paid a
> group of workers, but also to hours worked, standard of living, and
> degree of organisation and militance, or in other words, to the total
> cost of employment holding productivity constant.

Within the marginalised sector, limited job opportunities oblige the
worker to accept lower-paying employment or to seek some form of

work (even if it be self-employed) outside the regular, integrated market. It is in the self-employed category that the notion of 'cheap labour' is most clearly manifested. The self-employed person frequently works very long hours. His income is generally rather low, profits often being reinvested into the business. Extensive use is made of labour from family members, further reducing the household return for labour. Almost by definition, workers of this type are non-unionised. Certainly, income (per hour) and working conditions amongst the self-employed are far poorer than would be acceptable to workers in enclave areas. Nevertheless, this 'cheap labour' confers major advantages on the bourgeoisie of the enclave areas; it constitutes a 'threat' to the workers of these areas, as well as providing a source of cheap services.

However, as should be clear, to leave the analysis at the level of the spatial distinction between enclave and marginalised areas would be to paint too simplistic a picture; it is important as well to examine internal differentiations. Hence, Wenger's analysis of the occupational structure for women is instructive at the general level of her survey. She emphasises the importance of part-time employment for women, with 50 per cent of employed women in her sample falling into this category. Such work often consists of employment in the service sector, where earnings levels are very low; hence, Wenger reports averages of between £25 and £30 per week for the female labour force as a whole. However, Grant's study (1979) suggests that a pattern of low-paid female employment (whether part or full-time) is by no means confined to the marginalised areas. In fact, he suggests that female employment is rare in some of these areas and tends to be concentrated in the urban areas of the enclave. In this situation, it tends to be married women, drawn from a local population with poor housing conditions and low car ownership, who are in employment. Moreover, there is a relationship between female activity rates and male activity which suggests that the income derived from the woman's work is essential to the maintenance of household earnings. In short, a highly complex set of interrelationships emerges between patterns of inequality and poverty both within and between enclave and marginal areas.

A similarly complex situation emerges from an examination of the more general consequences (in terms of income) of the process of marginalisation. Wenger's study of mid Wales indicates that the average weekly income in the survey was 33 per cent lower than the figure for Wales (itself a relatively low average). Similarly, the figure for manual workers (males) was substantially below those for Wales and for Britain as a whole: 44 per cent earned less than £50 per week, compared with some 18 per cent in Britain. In contrast, however, there was a higher percentage of household heads earning more than £68 per week than in Britain as a whole. Hence, there is some reason to believe that differentiation exists within the marginalised areas, as well as within the enclave (see above).

This theme of class differentiation within the enclave and marginalised areas of the periphery can be usefully extended by examining in more detail the changes that have taken place within the enclave. As I have shown, recent state intervention to restructure the economy of rural Wales has had the effect of introducing new capitalist enterprise, to a large extent from the English core. This, in turn, has had the effect of generating quite significant in-migration of English personnel, mainly in middle management and key worker categories. Again, as I have argued, this introduction of a new group of relatively affluent individuals is paralleled by a decline in the economic structure which supported the (limited) local and traditional petty bourgeoisie, deriving from the historical circumstances of the nineteenth century (see note 2). Only in the expanded activities of the state (for example, in reorganised local government) has this indigenous middle-class group been able to retain a secure employment base. Clearly, these changes have had consequences for the material well-being of the individuals involved — for example, the small businessman proletarianised by failure to compete with new, larger-scale enterprises. However, it is also possible to trace out consequences at a more structural level.

It is important not to regard the new middle class in rural Wales as a homogeneous group. Whilst most incomers are 'spiralists', combining occupational with geographical mobility, it is possible to distinguish three categories. Some are 'non-integrating spiralists' (Payne, 1973) whose period of residence in rural Wales is likely to be relatively short. The nature of their employment does not demand integration, nor does it result in any advantage to them or their families. Their attitude towards the local social and institutional structure often consists of a mixture of withdrawal and antagonism. In contrast, 'integrating spiralists', either by the nature of their jobs or of their own volition, seek to accommodate and become part of local social networks and institutions. Finally, there are 'blocked spiralists', whose mobility has been arrested. Many of them see their rightful place to be higher up the occupational ladder and, in consequence, outside rural Wales. They frequently seek an explanation of their circumstances in the nature of their local environment.

The importance of these distinctions and of that between new and indigenous middle-class groups lies in their relationship with political mobilisation and conflict. Most clearly, conflict arises between the indigenous groups and the integrating and frustrated spiralists over the control of local institutions – for example, should they be of a 'Welsh' or 'British' nature. The indigenous middle class is able to carry a large part of the local proletariat because of the antagonism among the in-migrant groups towards the Welsh language, which serves as a point of identity for the local population, and because of the manifestly privileged position of the newcomers in the local social structure – a clear 'cultural division of labour' (Hechter, 1975). The new English midddle class, on the other hand, is able to mobilise those of the local petty bourgeoisie who stand to gain from industrial development and who may be used as 'front men' in confrontation. In many respects, then, these conflicts are more pervasive than anything based upon conventional party politics alone, as the official parties have to accommodate the conflicts. The entire process is reminiscent of Gonzales Casanova's (1974) discussion of colonial exploitation and native capitalism. Moreover, these conflicts are critical to a discussion of poverty because, in part at least, it is in the outcomes of the conflicts that future changes in the material conditions of rural Wales lie. In this context, the role of cultural issues occupies a central importance; they interact with questions of economic development to produce a characteristic structure of political conflict in rural Wales.

It is here that the final dimension of polarisation – the cultural one – is of significance. Given that the control of the means of production associated with the industrial development of the enclave lies outside Wales, it is not surprising that the relations of production do not involve the Welsh language. As a result, the Welsh language has the minimum of relevance for social mobility and enclave integration. In fact, it is of relevance only in a limited number of jobs in the public sector and then at the cost of vociferous opposition from the lobby of non-integrating spiralists. Not surprisingly, the incidence of Welsh speaking in these enclave areas is low.

In the marginalised sector, the Welsh language assumes a different status. Especially in areas where the compensatory welfare functions of the state have difficulty in penetrating, the welfare functions are assumed by voluntary community organisations and institutions which operate through the medium of Welsh. Hence, the language serves an important function of 'risk minimisation' in such areas. Nevertheless, it is not surprising that the population of these areas holds ambivalent views towards the language (Lewis, 1975); it is viewed as useful in terms of 'risk minimisation', whilst at the same time detracting from one's social status.

In the light of this cultural/linguistic polarisation in adaptation to the process of marginalisation, it is again not surprising that it is the marginalised areas which have adopted political nationalism as a means of improving their situation. However, it would be mistaken to interpret this as a narrowly 'cultural' response. Rather, the processes at work *seem* to correspond remarkably closely to those outlined by Touraine (1977):

> there is a reaction against dependence. Here it is not a class but a territorial collectivity, whether regional or national, that is defending itself against an external domination. This dimension may separate itself off from others in order to give birth to a vague, very easily manipulated nationalism or populism, but it is necessarily present in a dependent social movement. It is fairly directly linked to the existence of *'marginality'* which is to say, the powerlessness of a dependent society to bring a large section of the population into participation in economic growth.

In short, nationalism is seized upon as a response to the disadvantages of the marginal sector.

However, Touraine's analysis, whilst it does have certain strengths, does not fully comprehend the situation which I have described. The heterogeneity of the low-income groups in the marginalised sector, together with the false sense of economic opportunity associated with self-employment, militates against the development of any proletarian consciousness amongst marginalised workers. The economic arrangements characteristic of marginalised areas tend to individualise the problems of making a living. These circumstances make class-based action difficult. It is also evident to many that the policies of the state, in collusion with external capitals, are, in part at least, responsible for the very process of marginalisation. Hence, the 'adversary' can only be defined as a capitalism imported to the area and controlled by 'foreigners'. However, the class group which makes this definition is itself restricted to a marginalised position. Therefore, class struggle cannot be characterised as embodying 'progress', as class struggle appears to be directed against the means of achieving that progress — 'foreign' capital. It is in this situation that the tendency to align along ethnic lines, in opposition to a 'foreign master', arises.

Conclusion

In this brief chapter I have attempted to sketch an outline of inequality in rural Wales that is in conscious contrast to the conventional explanations deriving from a diffusionist perspective. I have emphasised the dependent nature of economic development in this peripheral area; development is controlled by a 'foreign' bourgeoisie, aided and abetted by the state; in consequence, this development is produced in the primary interests of core capitalism, rather than in the interests of the local population. Such development has had clearly identifiable consequences in terms of the generation of inequalities and poverty within the peripheral area; more specifically, it has had the consequence of generating enclave and marginalised populations. Whilst internally differentiated, these populations have manifestly unequal material circumstances. Finally, I have argued that it is in these conditions of economic change, allied to the cultural distinctiveness of rural Wales, that the explanation of political conflict must be sought and that it is in the latter that a major avenue of change in material conditions lies.

I take the arguments that I have presented to be a specific illustration of the point made recently by Holman (1978); he says:

> If poverty and the poor are to blame, then a divided and stratified society is accepted as normal and just. It follows that if poverty justifies the existence of lower strata in society, then the position of higher strata is also legitimated.

Conversely, if poverty is seen to be a function of the general structure of societal inequality, then the whole of that structure must be questioned. Such questioning is clearly not in the interests of those in power. Hence, those who focus their attention upon social indicators, perceptions of poverty or even the poor themselves, in isolation from more general structures, are inadvertently serving the interests of those in power. The analysis must bring into focus the fact that explanations of poverty in terms of the deprived themselves serve ideological purposes in the maintenance of inequality itself.

Notes

1. I am grateful to Gareth Rees for substantial comments on earlier drafts of this chapter.

2. Clearly, a full analysis requires a treatment of the historical processes by which capitalism became the dominant mode of production for rural Wales and of the class and ethnic groups generated in these processes. An outline of such a treatment was included in an earlier vision of this chapter, but has been excluded for reasons of space. However, see Williams (forthcoming).

3. Some 83 per cent of farms in Wales draw exclusively on family labour.

4. Between 1947 and 1969, the land in Wales devoted to forestry increased from 86,000 acres to 300,000 acres.

5. The basic policy is set out in the document produced by the Welsh Council, *A Strategy for Rural Wales* (1971).

6. See Ch. 5 (eds).

7. In rural Wales, 21 per cent of the male labour force is self-employed.

8. See Ch. 8 (eds).

10 UNEVEN DEVELOPMENT, STATE INTERVENTION AND THE GENERATION OF INEQUALITY: THE CASE OF INDUSTRIAL SOUTH WALES[1]

Gareth Rees

Any attempt to understand the nature of poverty in Wales must come to grips with the processes of industrialisation and urbanisation. Quite simply, it is these that have set the structures of material inequality within which any meaningful discussion must locate poverty. A pervasive feature of these processes is that they have taken place unevenly over geographical space: and Wales provides a dramatic example of this. At one level, this is illustrated by comparing Wales as a whole with other parts of Britain; hence, for much of the present century, Wales has been acknowledged as a 'problem region'. However, this sort of comparison ignores the heterogeneity that is internal to Wales. Since the nineteenth century, the industrial south has dominated the remainder of Wales. The development of heavy industry (iron and, above all, coal) in the counties of Glamorgan, Monmouthshire and, to a much lesser extent, Camarthensire produced an overwhelming concentration of population, economic activity and urban settlement. Thus, by the First World War, these counties contained well over three-quarters of the total Welsh population.

It is also well known that this period of competitive capitalism in South Wales (as elsewhere) generated a class structure of the harshest inequality. This was as clear to contemporary observers as it is to us today; as the Report of the Royal Commissioners of Inquiry into the State of Education in Wales of 1847 put it:

> I regard their (i.e. the workers') degraded condition as entirely the fault of their employers, who give them far less tendance and care than they bestow upon their cattle, and who, with a few exceptions, use and regard them as so much brute force instrumental to wealth, but as nowise involving claims on human sympathy. (p. 293)

Now, this is not to say that average wages in either coal mining or metal manufacture were lower than in possible alternative occupations (and, in particular, agriculture). On the contrary, despite considerable variations within both industries, the opposite was the case and this goes

a long way towards explaining the continued flow of workers into
Industrial South Wales. However, it has to be recognised that the life
of the industrial worker and his family was an essentially precarious
one. Upward occupational mobility tended to take place within the range
of manual jobs (the coal industry provided some notable exceptions –
Morris and Williams, 1958). Moreover, the relatively high levels of
earnings obtained only during periods of economic prosperity: given
the direct relationship of the staple industries to an export market,
there were violent fluctuations in trade that had severe repercussions
for the working people. Where family incomes fell or were actually
halted – whether as a result of trade conditions or simply as a result
of injury or illness – there were virtually no mechanisms of support,.
apart from the despised poor law. Nor were these conditions confined
to the coalfield areas. In the coastal settlements (Cardiff, Newport
and Swansea), although there was a far greater occupational diversity,
the working class also experienced more seasonal and long-term
unemployment, a greater amount of casual work and a higher incidence
of pauperisation. In addition, it appears that the conditions of the
urban settlements of the industrial valleys compared favourably with
those of the working-class areas of, for example, Cardiff (Daunton,
1977); although, given the chaotic nature of both, poor water supplies,
overcrowding and almost non-existent sanitation were characteristic of
all working-class areas in South Wales.

The economic crisis of the inter-war period marked the demise of
this characteristically nineteenth-century structure. As is well known,
the staple industries collapsed and massive unemployment, outward
migration and enormous economic hardship were the inevitable consequences. The trauma of this period and the demands imposed upon the
state by the organisation of the war effort between 1939 and 1945 led
to a fundamental alteration of the situation: a change that has become
increasingly apparent since 1945. Quite simply, the state has become
massively involved not only in the provision of key welfare services, but
also in the management of the economy. It is undeniable that the
growth of this involvement has dramatically changed the material
conditions in which the majority of the British population live
(including, of course, the section living in South Wales). The commitment by successive governments to the maintenance of 'full employment' and the pursuit of economic growth, allied to the supports and
guarantees provided by the Welfare State, have (in my terms) removed
the 'precariousness' from the lives of the vast majority of working-class
families. These families no longer face the actuality, or even the threat,

of destitution in a way comparable to the period of early industrial and urban growth.

However, as numerous commentators have pointed out (for example, Westergaard and Resler, 1975), this is a long way from demonstrating that the structures of inequality, both social and spatial, in British society have been eradicated. It is in the context of these inequalities that poverty is to be understood. In spite of the growth of state intervention, it is still the case that certain groups in the population and certain geographical areas are manifestly disadvantaged in terms of their economic and social prosperity.

It is for this reason, then, that I believe it is important to examine critically the relationship between state intervention and patterns of inequality and poverty in contemporary Britain. Necessarily, I shall have to go beyond what the state itself *says* these relationships are: I shall have to question the view that governments act disinterestedly to benefit the 'nation as a whole'. In contrast with conventional accounts, I shall sketch an analysis which locates the changing configurations of material inequality in the shifting requirements of the system of economic production, which is itself determined by the necessity of generating sufficient levels of private profit. I shall argue, moreover, that the state has a primary function of facilitating the conditions conducive to generating this private profit (irrespective of whether it actually succeeds in doing so). The state is thereby itself involved in the processes by which inequalities are produced between different groups in the population and between the geographical areas in which they live.

Of necessity in a relatively short chapter, I can present only the outline of this analysis; I shall have to ignore many of the complexities of the argument. Hence, I shall confine myself to what I take to be the key determinant of inequality and poverty, as well as the major area of state intervention: economic development. Empirically, I shall be concerned with what has happened in South Wales since the end of the Second World War.[2] Most significantly, however, I shall be obliged to simplify the processes which operate within the state. Clearly, the state in my terms comprises many distinct parts: for example, central government, local government and, increasingly, supra-national government (most notably, the European Economic Community). Internal to these various parts are numerous separate groups: politicians, administrators, representatives of 'pressure groups' and so forth. Any thoroughgoing analysis of the functions of the state would take account of this diversity and, more particularly, the conflicts that occur. That I do not do so here is simply the result of the constraints of space imposed upon me. (However, for a discussion of some of these issues in the context of Industrial South Wales, see Rees and Lambert, 1979).

The Post-war Restructuring of the Economy in South Wales

South Wales emerged from the Second World War with an economic structure still overwhelmingly dependent upon coal mining and metal manufacture (predominantly steel making by this time). Its history since then, and particularly since the late 1950s, has been one of the progressive 'diversification' of this industrial base. More specifically, the numbers employed in coal and steel have been substantially run down, whilst manufacturing and, more dramatically, the service sector have expanded to a major extent. The activities of the state have been central to this process of restructuring. At a general level, economic development in South Wales has reflected the fluctuations of the British economy as a whole and the attempts at economic management by successive governments. However, in a more particular sense, South Wales's status as a 'problem region', dominated, moreover, by nationalised and state-controlled industries, has elicited much more direct interventions by the state: through, for example, regional planning, key infrastructural investments, the 'rationalisation' of the coal and steel industries and, more recently, the activities of specialist agencies such as the Welsh Development Agency. It is on this level that I shall concentrate here.

A simple picture of what has happened to the economy in South Wales is given in Table 10.1. After the immediate post-war boom, major retrenchment took place in coal mining during the late 1950s and 1960s and in steel making during the 1970s. In contrast, the 1960s and 1970s have witnessed the marked growth of manufacturing industry (other than steel making) and of service sector employment.

However, this treatment masks a much more complex pattern — a pattern of characteristically uneven development. Obviously, the decline of coal mining has primarily affected the coal-mining areas: deep mining has now ceased along the north-east and south-western edges of the coalfield, whilst even in its centre mining has been abandoned over quite extensive areas. Hence, for example, the Rhondda valleys, once the heart of the coal-mining industry, now have only three pits remaining and two of these (Maerdy and Fernhill) are under threat of closure. It is not surprising that over 5,000 jobs in mining and quarrying were

Table 10.1: Changes in Employment in Wales, 1951-71

Employment sector	1951-61		1961-71	
	Male	Female	Male	Female
Fishing	− 604	+3	+ 260	+ 20
Agriculture	−18,227	−3,797	−16,100	+ 1,150
Metal manufacture and engineering	+ 29,940	+6,565	+17,750	+5,640
Mining and quarrying	−30,530	−12	−42,970	+ 40
Professional, technical and artistic	+ 19,394	+9,196	+9,420	+9,320
Services, sport and recreation	+ 2,720	+531	+ 4,830	+27,640
Clerical	+ 8,605	+ 18,207	−4,020	+21,820
Total	−4,483	+ 36,189	−48,650	+ 91,680

Source: L.J. Williams and T. Boyn, 'Occupation in Wales, 1851-1971', *Bulletin of Economic Research,* 29, (1977), pp. 71-83.

lost from the area between 1965 and 1975 (Mid Glamorgan County Council, 1977a). Similarly, the consequences of 'rationalisation' in steel making have been felt most acutely in quite localised areas; for example, the closure of the steel-making plant at Ebbw Vale in 1977 has created problems primarily for the town itself and the immediately surrounding areas.

Moreover, it is precisely these communities which have been especially adversely affected by the changes in coal and steel, which have done relatively badly out of the growth in the manufacturing and service sectors. For example, the Cynon Valley, in the north of Mid Glamorgan, lost over 3,000 jobs in mining and quarrying during the ten years before 1975: however, it also lost about 1,500 jobs in manufacturing industry and made only very marginal gains in the service sector (Mid Glamorgan County Council, 1977a). In contrast, not only have the towns of the 'valley mouths' and the coastal plain benefited from the growth of manufacturing, but also these gains have not been offset by the decline of any major employers. Perhaps the most striking example of this sort of employment growth is the area around Llantrisant which recorded a remarkable increase of 2,000 jobs in the three years between 1971 and 1974: an amazing irony in view of the decision not to proceed with the designation of a new town at Llantrisant following a contentious public inquiry in 1972. Similarly, the expansion of service employment has been concentrated in these localities: they have benefited both from the relocation of major services from other parts of Britain (as, for example, in the resiting of numerous government departments) and from the centralisation of services within the region. The major exception to this pattern of 'dualistic' development is the city of Cardiff itself; here, the uneven patterns of growth and decline are manifest within the city. Hence, the loss of some 3,000 to 4,000 jobs following the closure of the East Moors steel plant has come on top of a decline in other sorts of manufacturing industry in the city. However, there has been an over-all expansion of employment in the service sector and, more particularly, in certain types of service activity such as public administration, professional and scientific services, distribution and finance (these grew by some 9,000 jobs between 1961 and 1971 — South Glamorgan County Council, 1976). What is perhaps most significant here is that it is these sorts of employment that provide jobs which tend to be filled by women. This, in turn, raises the general question of the nature of the new jobs being created in South Wales.

The critical point to be made in this context is that a significant proportion of the new jobs in South Wales have been filled by women; what were historically very low rates of female activity have risen to levels much closer to the British average. For example, in Mid Glamorgan, the largest in terms of population of the counties of South Wales, there was a net increase in employment of some 6,300 jobs during the ten years up until 1975. However, by far the greater part of this is attributable to changes in female employment, which rose by 7,700 jobs between 1965 and 1971 and a further 8,600 jobs in the subsequent four years. These striking increases were recorded in both manufacturing (and especially electrical engineering) and the service sector. The general trend that emerges, then, is one of employment losses in the traditional, male-dominated industries being counter-balanced by gains in new, female-dominated industries.

Allied to the growth of female employment is the question of the 'skill profile' of the jobs being created in South Wales. Certainly, McNabb (Chapter 8, above) argues that a great many of the new jobs in the tertiary sector are part-time and/or semi- and unskilled, and therefore badly paid. Equally, Davies and Thomas (1976) have shown that for their sample of overseas firms (significant providers of new jobs) there is a concentration of workers in the unskilled category (58.2 per cent) with only 5.2 per cent in the senior administrative category, 5.4 per cent senior scientific, 20.9 per cent skilled workers and 10.3 per cent clerical workers. And Lovering (1978a) suggests that a similar pattern may be characteristic of those other non-Welsh-owned firms which comprise some 60 per cent of all manufacturing employment. Clearly, much more detailed information would be required to make any definitive assessment of the situation. However, there are at least some indications that employment growth in South Wales is concentrated toward the 'low skill' end of the spectrum. As we shall see later, it is this sort of consideration that has led some commentators to question the very basis upon which we conventionally analyse the nature of the 'regional problem' and its consequences for changing structures of inequality and poverty (Lovering, 1978a; Massey, 1978).

In this section, I have done little more than to sketch some of the major changes that have taken place in the employment structure of South Wales in the fairly recent past. However, I believe that, by drawing attention to the spatial unevenness of these changes and to the nature of the new jobs which are being created, I have done enough to cast considerable doubt on the more simplistic analyses which have been made of what has happened in the region. The dramatic changes that have taken place are frequently characterised as evidencing a successful 'modernisation' of the economy. However, the question that is begged by this sort of analysis is *for whom* have these changes been a success. It is the answer to this question, of course, which provides one of the central concerns of this chapter and I try to give a direct answer in the next section.

New Patterns of Inequality

One of the most forceful recent studies of industrial change (Community Development Project, 1977) argues that:

> The costs of industrial change are borne by local working class communities. These communities grew up in response to the demand for labour from new industries, yet over time changes in these industries have destroyed their original role. The decline of each area's traditional industrial structure sets off a chain reaction of economic and social consequences, undermining every aspect of life in the local community. (p.32)

Although this study was based on a group of 'inner city' areas and industrial towns in England, this conclusion is equally applicable at a general level to South Wales. Although it has been shown elsewhere in this book (see Chapters 2, 7 and 8, above) that South Wales as a whole is quite 'prosperous' when compared with other parts of Wales, this ignores the spatial unevenness of this 'prosperity' within the region.

The process of economic development that we have outlined has indeed imposed the severest costs on many working-class communities, both in the coalfield areas and the 'inner city' of Cardiff. So much is clear in the statistics of unemployment, low economic activity, poor housing, population decline and so forth which characterise such areas. Hence, for example, the Rhondda valleys have, during the 1970s, experienced male unemployment rates double the level for Mid Glamorgan, which itself has had unemployment well above the average for Industrial South Wales and, indeed, for Wales as a whole (Mid Glamorgan County Council, 1977a). The housing stock is old and basic amenities are poorly provided (see Chapter 3, above). Not surprisingly, population fell by some 11,000 during the decade 1961-71, largely as a result of outward migration. Similarly, the decision to close the steel plant at East Moors in Cardiff has had a massive impact on the immediate locality (in spite of the well-publicised payments made to some of the redundant workers!). The enormous loss of jobs entailed has exacerbated the already chronic problems of unemployment in the 'inner areas' of the city: unemployment in these areas was as high as 6 per cent in 1971, before the major effects of the closure (South Glamorgan County Council, 1976). Given the past inability to attract new manufacturing to Cardiff, it seems likely that these working-class communities are destined to share the fate of their valley counterparts (although the effects of substantial investment by the Welsh Development Agency remain to be seen).

There is, of course, an ambivalence about the decline of these communities and the industries on which they were dependent. This ambivalence emerges frequently in discussion with those who have actually experienced the changes that have taken place. Something of this is captured in the following extract from an interview with a former miner, who had left his home area (Glyncorrẅg in West Glamorgan) in order to seek work in Herefordshire.

> They have closed our collieries and that is good. It's good to get men from underground, although there is millions of tons still there. (But) when a way of life depends on one means even to the extent of buying a loaf of bread and that means is taken away, you have destroyed that entire way of life. That is what has happened in the valleys. (unpublished interview, Upper Afan Migration Study: see
> Rees, 1976a, 1976b)

Coal mining and steel making are extremely arduous, unhealthy and dangerous industries (see Chapter 5, above); clearly, to remove the necessity of working in such conditions is highly desirable. However, equally clearly, it is not on these ground that changes have been made in these industries in South Wales. Moreover, given only limited replacement jobs, the net outcome of industrial restructuring has been for many communities the increase of their relative impoverishment and the loss of much of the less tangible aspects of a 'way of life'.

However, as we have stressed, it would be quite wrong to suggest that these sorts of costs have been borne by every community in South Wales. The corollary of the collapse of some localities is the growth of others. This point is made quite explicit in P. Davies's (1976) study of economic 'well-being' in the valley areas. She was concerned with the extent to which factors such as population change, economic activity, income and unemployment (as measured, for the most part, in the 1971 Census of Population) were distributed unevenly across those local authorities which were designated 'Special Development Areas' in the language of regional economic policy. Clearly, I cannot reproduce the detail of her analysis here. However, perhaps it is sufficient to note that her data reveal a clear distinction between many of the 'valley mouths' (and, in particular, the area around Llantrisant) and the areas further north on the coalfield proper (P. Davies, 1976, *passim*). In other words, the distinction that I drew in the previous section between those areas which are gaining jobs and those which are losing them is, not surprisingly, reflected in indicators which measure 'well-being' more directly (although the caveats which I made about the types of job being created may also be relevant here). It is also significant that this study provides evidence of a pattern of uneven development and its consequences. Nevertheless, the spatial unevenness of ecomomic change itself and, accordingly, of its consequences is only part of the story. It is also the case that these consequences have been felt differentially within afflicted communities. The developments within the region have created a new set of requirements which must be fulfilled if individuals are to gain entry to the labour market. Quite simply, working people vary in their ability to respond to these new requirements.

I can perhaps illustrate this point by reference to a study carried out in the Amman valley, in the extreme west of the coalfield (Town, 1978). The pattern of industrial change in this area appears to conform well to the general processes that I have described: pit closures, especially as a result of rationalisation during the late 1950s and 1960s, with only limited replacement by manufacturing and services, leading to a general shortage of employment opportunities. However, what is especially instructive is that Town demonstrates clearly the way in which these changes created widely varying pressures on different types of local working people. He says:

> local manufacturing industry is able to 'manage' the labour market to suit its own needs; this was equally true of most of the factories in the clothing, textile and footwear field, who were in general reluctant to take on and train older women (usually defined as any married woman who has started a family) from scratch. The net result was that older people were debarred from a large and prosperous sector of employment. In effect such recruitment policies split the labour force into two distinct categories when it came to finding a job. On the one hand there were those who by virtue of their age and possibly the possession of certain skills constituted high quality labour; on the other there were those who did not. (p.73)

In other words, those employers who did move into the area were in a particularly powerful position: they were able to specify precise criteria which had to be met by those seeking work. The tragedy is, of course, that this sort of specification excludes precisely those workers who were worst affected by the decline of the previously dominant industry — redundant miners.

This very local pattern is repeated throughout South Wales. It is no coincidence that in Mid Glamorgan, for example, of the men who have been out of work for more than six months, some 44 per cent are over 50 years of age. Similarly, it is no coincidence that such a significant proportion of the new jobs created in the region have been given to women. In part, of course, this proportion is determined by the sex composition of applications, particularly given the types of job involved. However, it is also the case that women are often highly desirable as workers in the eyes of employers: their levels of pay are generally lower; they are frequently prepared to take part-time work; levels of unionisation are low; and so forth. It is thus a necessary feature of economic change that not only will new patterns of growth and decline be generated over geographical space, but also that workers will vary in their ability to 'make out' in these changing conditions.

I can draw together these two strands of the argument by a brief consideration of population movement. Two forms of population movement are of critical significance in the region: daily journeys to work; and permanent migration to a new place of residence. The former has been central to the strategy of regional development adopted by the state (of which more later). It has been argued that daily commuting offers the means of maintaining the established coalfield communities, as well as reaping the benefits of new employment opportunities at the 'valley mouths'. Clearly, many people do travel daily to the jobs available at places such as Llantrisant, Bridgend, Pontypridd and, above all, at the service centre of Cardiff (Davies and Musson, 1978). However, equally clearly, costs are imposed by this necessity to commute: not simply the obvious financial costs, but also those of time and social disruption. These costs are, in turn, exacerbated by the generally poor provision of public transport in areas of low car ownership (for an especially acute example, see Rees, 1974). Moreover, daily journeying to work is a selective process. In much the same way that working people vary in their ability to meet the requirements set down for jobs, they vary in their ability to travel to the locations where they are available. Most obviously, car owners are in a highly favourable position (although this solution to the travel-to-work problem in itself creates problems for other members of the household in terms of their access to work, school, shops and so forth). Equally, other factors such as age and family commitments play a significant role.

A second sort of response to the changing spatial distribution of economic activity is for workers to migrate to the new 'growth areas' — to the areas where employment opportunities are available and, to simplify, standards of living are higher. As we have seen, this form of population movement has been a pervasive feature of industrial development in South Wales. In the most recent period, for example, the Central and Eastern valleys (broadly equivalent to the valley areas of Mid Glamorgan and Gwent) lost some 21,000 people during the decade 1961 to 1971, in spite of a natural increase of almost 23,000; it is, of course, no coincidence that this was the period during which the closure programme in the coal industry was at its most severe. At a more detailed level as well, the patterns of growth and decline within the region have called forth distinctive population changes. Hence, as we should expect, many of the 'valley mouths' have experienced considerable population growth as a result of net inward migration, whilst many of the coalfield areas have experienced major population losses (Rees, 1976b).

It is much more difficult, however, to say anything about the effects of these population changes. Conventionally, population loss is treated as an index of the poverty of the areas experiencing it. However, it may well be the case that the individual migrants themselves benefit from their move. Certainly, it seems that those families leaving the coalfield

communities for the towns of the 'valley mouths' and the coastal plain
do so in order to take advantage of better employment opportunities,
shorter journeys to work, improved housing conditions and so forth,
although many of them are reluctant to detach themselves from the
dense social networks of their places of origin (Rees, 1976b). Perhaps
the crucial point here, however, is that only certain kinds of people are
able to take this option. Analysis of the 1971 Census of Population, for
example, shows that migrants in South Wales differ sharply from those
who do not move. Migrants tend to be drawn from the younger, economically active sections of the population; they are also more likely
to be owner-occupiers and to be from high or middle socio-economic
groups. A study of migrants from one valley area showed that they
tended to be better educated and qualified (Rees, 1976a). In other
words, these are the sorts of people who are able to respond in a very
direct way to the changes in the organisation of the economic and urban
structure that are going on around them. The other side of this coin is,
of course, that in making this response they are distancing themselves
from the less fortunate members of working-class communities, not only
in a literal, spatial sense, but also in terms of the material conditions of
their lives. In a very real sense, the costs of industrial change have been
borne by the local, working-class communities of South Wales. However,
it is also important to take account of the differential severity of these
consequences within the working class. I suggest that for some groups
of working people the costs have been disproportionately heavy.

Alternative Frameworks of Analysis

The critical question that is begged by the account that I have given of
economic changes and their consequences in South Wales is how we are
to make sense of what has happend. As I have suggested earlier, the
state has played a central role in shaping the course of economic
change in the region. It has been directly involved in restructuring the
coal and steel industries; it has pursued regional economic policies
aimed at the encouragement of new manufacturing development; it has
made major investments in the transportation infrastructure; it has
contributed to the growth of the tertiary sector by its policy of resiting
government offices. And all this is over and above the state's more
general involvement as a direct employer in the health service, education and public administration generally: it is with some justice that
Humphrys (1972) has described South Wales as 'the closest to a

nationalised region that existed in Britain' (p.64).

However, it is characteristic of the sort of 'liberal democracy' in which we live that the state has also provided a rationale for the interventions which it has undertaken. Necessarily, it has presented analyses of the problems confronting Industrial South Wales which, in turn, have provided the justifications for the policies it has adopted. These official analyses have not only reflected a 'conventional wisdom' about the economy in South Wales, but have also played a major part in establishing and shaping this 'conventional wisdom' (for a fuller account, see Rees and Lambert, 1979). Therefore, I begin my discussion in this section by looking at what the state has had to say about the developments I have described in earlier parts of the chapter.

Now, it is clearly an extremely complex task to do this. I propose, however, to focus my attention on the major statement by central government on the Welsh economy during the post-war period: the 1967 White Paper, *Wales: the Way Ahead* (Welsh Office, 1967). Whilst obviously a limited approach, I maintain that the White Paper gives an adequate indication of the essential elements of the state's analysis, at least up until the mid-1970s.[3]

As has been argued in detail elsewhere (Rees and Lambert, 1979), the first element of the analysis is that, by the early 1960s, there had already been a successful modernisation of the economy in South Wales. State intervention had effected a shift from an overdependence upon 'archaic' coal and metal industries to a situation in which the region enjoyed the benefits of a variety of modern, manufacturing industries and a complementary infrastructure. The major remaining problems seen in the White Paper related to the industrial valleys, where there had been inadequate replacement of jobs lost through the cutbacks in the coal industry. The solution to these problems was seen to lie, at the general level, in the continued application of regional policy incentives to attract more manufacturing industry to the area. More specifically, however, this new development was to be directed to the 'valley mouths' (and, to a lesser extent, the 'heads of the valleys'). This strategy would thereby capitalise upon the supposed locational advantages of these areas to entrepreneurs and, at the same time, provide residents of the coalfield communities with job opportunities within daily commuting distance. In this way, the government's avowed commitment to the preservation of 'the substantial valley communities' (p.102) could be fulfilled.

This analysis is in most respects typical of a number of other strategies for 'problem regions' (and, indeed, sectors of industry) prepared during the 1960s (for example, Scottish Development Department, 1963; National Economic Development Council, 1963). Concern with the general lack of competitiveness of British industry generated numerous proposals for state intervention to 'modernise' obsolescent industrial structures, thereby achieving 'balanced regional growth' and restoring national economic prosperity.

At a more general level, it is also remarkable that the analyses contained in these various reports present the 'problems' with which they are concerned in a remarkably consistent fashion. Hence, *Wales: the Way Ahead,* for example, views the circumstances confronting the communities of the coalfield (and the same could now be said of the depressed steel-making areas) as comprising residual problems: pockets of economic and social disadvantage left behind in the inevitable process of 'modernisation' and, hence, progress. As the Community Development Project study (1977) again puts it: 'Such an approach . . . puts across the problems of these areas . . . so that they seem *marginal* — not in the sense of unimportant, but certainly peculiar to these areas; while things in general, of course, are fundamentally alright and "normal"' (p.55). Moreover, it is typical of such analyses that these localised economic problems are presented as deriving in an unproblematic way from the inadequacies of the areas which they afflict. Hence, *Wales: the Way Ahead* argues that it is impossible to generate significant industrial development in the valleys themselves because of the absence of sufficient land for building (Welsh Office, 1967, p. 102). Or again, the decline of the coal industry is attributed variously to the exhaustion of reserves, the failure of many pits to maintain 'economic operations' and the inability of the industry to adjust to changing 'market conditions' (Welsh Office, 1967, p. 42). Now, the point here is not simply that these arguments can be disputed on purely technical grounds, but more importantly that the context in which they are rooted is not made explicit. Arguments of this type divert attention from the economic and political imperatives which underpin them and which derive from the particularities of the way in which British society is currently organised.

It is at least partly in this context that we should interpret the stability of the state's analysis and the relative absence of opposition to its strategies, in spite of their manifest failure to achieve the objectives set for them.[4] As I have sketched in earlier sections, men 'released' from coal mining and, more latterly, steel making have only to a limited extent been absorbed into new, high-productivity manufacturing. Moreover, major growth — unpredicted in *Wales: the Way Ahead* — has taken place in service activities and this growth has, to a considerable degree, generated low-paid, low-skill jobs, many of which have been filled by women (see also Carney and Lewis, 1978). Even at a more specific level, the consequences of concentrating development at the 'valley mouths' have not been the ones suggested in the 1967 White Paper. Again as we have seen, far from stabilising population and promoting economic and social prosperity in the valley communities, many of the latter have continued to decline (it is, of course, difficult to say what would have happened if the state's strategy had been different). In other words, although dramatic changes have taken place in the economic structure of South Wales, they have not been the ones predicted in *Wales: the Way Ahead*.

This leads us to question the validity of the analysis presented in the White Paper. Crucially, it fails to relate the economic and social problems with which it deals to the changing nature of economic production in which the former are based. Similarly, it assumes that the state has certain powers and capabilities which it uses to shape economic development in the general interests of the British people. In short, it is a highly conventional analysis of the problems of social and spatial inequalities. That the state's analysis should take this form is not, of course, surprising. It is clearly functional to the state: areas for debate are restricted and alternative analyses and strategies are ruled out of court.[5]

In contrast to this approach, a number of recent analyses have taken as their starting-point the nature of capitalist production itself and its uneven workings over geographical space (for example, Carney and Lewis, 1978; Lovering, 1978a; Massey, 1978). Hence, 'regional problems' are interpreted in relation to the dominant trends in production. These, in turn, are explicable in terms of the central imperatives of ensuring continued capital accumulation and maintaining adequate rates of profit — that is, in terms of the necessity of making production profitable and competitive (for a fuller account, see Carney and Lewis, 1978). Quite simply, at any given period, the conditions necessary for such production are distributed unevenly over geographical space: different areas have varying degrees of attractiveness as locations for economic activity. It is this fact — to put it somewhat simplistically — which accounts for the unevenness of economic and social prosperity both within and between geographical areas. It is in this quite specific sense, of course, that I intend the term 'uneven development'.

Hence, Lovering (1978a) has recently argued that the decline in the traditional, extractive industries in Wales (as a whole) has been paralleled by the emergence of an 'enclave' of advanced manufacturing activities. This 'enclave', comprising the vast bulk of large and medium-sized

plants, is dominated by the branch establishments of overseas and UK-
but not Welsh-owned firms (Davies and Thomas, 1976; Tomkins and
Lovering, 1973). It is suggested, moreover, that these branch plants are
major contributors to the significance of semi- and unskilled and part-
time work for the economy in Wales; in addition, part of the growth of
female employment is associated with these establishments. Lovering
goes on to argue that employment in this 'enclave' yields relatively
high wages (in comparison with the available alternatives in Wales) and
'may even offer fairly stable employment, since they are governed by a
corporate strategy which responds only marginally to changes in
activity in Wales' (1978a, p. 17). It is on this basis that Lovering appears
to draw a distinction between the relative prosperity of, in particular,
South East Wales – where the 'enclave' is most strongly represented –
and the relative poverty of 'the rural areas of Inner Wales' (although, he
emphasises, the various activities of the state are sufficient to ensure
that these areas are by no means completely impoverished).

  This analysis of the specific conditions of Wales is closely related to
the much more general analysis presented by Massey (1978). She
argues that the changing nature of production – and, in particular, the
growing size of firms, the progressive separation of different stages of
production (both functionally and geographically), the increasing
importance of 'deskilled' methods of direct production and the rising
significance of research and development – has yielded a new 'spatial
division of labour', which is characteristic of the advanced sectors of
production. Lovering (1978a) describes the form of this new spatial
configuration in Wales as follows:

> The transformation of industry in Wales can be seen as part of the
> more general process of capitalist restructuring which involves
> transferring production away from the traditional core areas – lead-
> ing to unemployment in the inner city zones – and setting up a new
> spatial hierarchy. In Wales we might visualise the consequences in
> the image of a 'headless capitalism'. (p. 17)

In other words, Wales (and, in particular, the industrial south) is one of
those areas that is attracting new employment – of particular kinds –
because of the changing requirements of production for private profit.
As Massey (1978) puts it, under competitive pressures, standardised and
automated production, requiring semi- and unskilled labour,

  is increasingly located in areas where semi-skilled workers are not only available (since they are everywhere), but where wages are low, and where there is no tradition — at least among these workers — of militancy. Typically this will involve the incorporation of workers with no previous experience of capitalist relations of production — drawn either from the remnants of pre-capitalist modes, (or) from the collapse of a previously-dominant industrial branch (in which case it will be the women, not the workers employed in the former specialisation, who will be employed). (p. 117)[6]

However, it is worth noting that the distributional consequences of these changes are by no means as straightforward as Lovering (1978a) appears to suggest. Hence, for example, whilst the growth of female employment (especially among married women) in the 'enclave' may be taken as an indicator of increasing household incomes, this is obviously true only where there is no dramatic decrease in the income of the male member(s) of the household. Yet it is precisely such a decrease that has befallen so many male workers in Industrial South Wales.

It also has to be borne in mind that a major part of employment change has taken place in the tertiary sector, about which both Lovering (1978a) and Massey (1978) say very little. Moreover, it is in this sector that a large number of the low-paid jobs have been created. In part, this growth is symptomatic of the wholly general trend of expansion in services which is characteristic of the particular division of labour associated with the contemporary period of capitalism (Mandel, 1975); hence, for instance, the rapid expansion of the distribution sector has generated large numbers of (often) low-paid jobs. However, equally dramatic has been the growth of state activities. This growth has given rise not only to a burgeoning 'professional' workforce (teachers, social workers, administrators and so on) but also to an increase in jobs that are both menial and badly paid (for example, cleaners, home helps, canteen workers, clerical workers, etc.). In the context of Wales as a whole, Lovering (1978a) has argued that the effect of public sector employment is to counteract some of the consequences of uneven private development. The former is more evenly distributed geographically than the latter and therefore provides sources of income in areas which otherwise may well be impoverished. What is less clear is whether this is true within South Wales, given what I have already said about the centralisation of services within the region and the attraction from outside of major government agencies (and, indeed, private enterprises) to the principal settlements of the coastal plain.

We should also be clear as to the extent of the state's role as

employer. Lovering (1978a) reports that some 40 per cent of employment in Wales is accounted for by the public sector: 15 per cent in the
nationalised industries, 16 per cent in the National Health Service,
education and the Post Office, and the remaining 9 per cent in local
and central government. As I have suggested, these figures reflect the
general expansion of state activities. However, these activities have a
particular significance in Wales in that employees in the public sector
comprise a relatively high proportion of the total workforce. It seems
likely that for Industrial South Wales this special significance of the
state is attributable to some extent to the growth of central and local
government, but more particularly to the still massive presence of the
nationalised industries.

The question that now has to be answered is why the growth in the
significance of the state has taken place. As I have shown, many of the
changes that have occurred in the economic structure of South Wales
are directly attributable to the actions of the state. This involvement is
only one manifestation of the general trend of expansion in government
intervention in the British economy as a whole. The specific character
of that intervention in South Wales derives from the region's role within
successive 'spatial divisions of labour' (hence, for example, the importance of the nationalised industries). I suggest that this long-term
development is explicable — at least at a general level — in terms of the
progressive inability of private capital to sustain the levels of investment (and to bear the consequent risks) necessary to maintain its
profitability and competitiveness.[7] Hence, the state steps in to undertake these investments and to ensure what Mandel (1975) terms 'the
general conditions of production'. Thus, for example, the state has
come to provide in Britain not only the minimum of a currency and
legal structure, but also a transport system, power supplies and, increasingly, direct subsidies to capital. Moreover, although Welfare State
provision may be regarded (with some justice) as the product of working-
class pressure to improve living conditions, this provision is also useful
to capital in producing an educated, healthy and adequately housed
workforce, which is maintained when not in employment, ready for
re-absorption into the labour process when necessary (Cockburn, 1977).[8]

Viewed from this general perspective, the specific role of the state
in the restructuring of the economy in South Wales appears in a very
different light. Hence, for example, the contraction of the coal industry
during the 1950s and 1960s must be interpreted in relation to the
state's commitment to ensure cheap fuel supplies to private industry.
This commitment led to the adoption of a state policy to convert

Britain from a broadly single-fuel economy based on coal to a multi-fuel economy using oil, gas and nuclear energy as well as coal (Carney and Lewis, 1978). It is these circumstances that are explained away in *Wales: the Way Ahead* by reference to unspecified 'market conditions'. Similarly, the considerable investment that has been made by the state in the development of the transport system in South Wales is explicable at one level by the need to subsidise private industrial production in the region in order to ensure the appropriate conditions of successful accumulation. Moreover, this latter point must be considered alongside my earlier arguments to the effect that South Wales (in view of its labour force, in particular) was in any event an attractive location for new industry, given the changing nature of production itself. Certainly, the logic of Lovering's (1978a) and Massey's (1978) analyses is that the pattern of economic development in South Wales cannot be attributed in any straightforward way to regional economic policy. Indeed, regional policy incentives would appear in some cases to be little more than cash subsidies, with only limited effects on the locational decisions of certain categories of firms (Pickvance, 1979). This point is further borne out in the report *Regional Development Incentives* (Department of Industry, 1975): it is suggested that, at least amongst the 'biggest 500' category of firms, only 15 per cent gave regional incentives as a major reason for their investment decision, although 51 per cent did say that regional incentives had influenced their location decision.

What I am outlining here, then, is an alternative form of analysis of social and spatial inequalities to the conventional one embodied in the pronouncements of the state. This alternative begins from the nature of economic production and is able to derive an account of the economic changes we have described earlier, in which the state's role is shown to be crucial and, indeed, highly problematic. Hence, the restructuring of the economy in South Wales is a consequence of the region's position within a national and world-wide economy, the *raison d'etre* of which is production for private profit. This is to say, of course, that the inequalities and deprivations which I have described in South Wales are entirely normal consequences of this economic order. Moreover, the state has functioned to facilitate this restructuring process; indeed, it has been, in many respects, indispensable to it. In this sense, the failure of the strategy set out in the 1967 White Paper to fulfil its stated objectives must be set against what it has achieved in terms of 'modernising' the economy and thereby providing conditions of continued capital accumulation. In this sense as well, the state can be seen to be closely implicated in the consequences of the economic changes which it has facilitated.

204 Industrial South Wales

As we have seen, these effects have been mixed. The collapse of some working-class communities and the impoverishment of significant proportions of their inhabitants must be contrasted with the growing economic and social prosperity of other parts of the region – a prosperity upon which some working-class families are able to capitalise. Moreover, I should emphasise, it is in the nature of capitalist development that new patterns of material inequality of this kind are constantly being created. Thus, on the one hand, it is incontrovertible that the circumstances of working-class people have improved with the growth of state intervention; on the other, the state is itself involved in the generation of new inequalities as a result of its relationship with a system of production for private profit. The fact that certain members of the working class benefit from these processes of change in no way denies the point that their motor force is the creation of private profit. Indeed, the creation of divisions within the working class may well be a critical condition of the continuation of this private profit system.

Notes

1. A number of people made extremely helpful comments on earlier drafts of this chapter. I should like to thank Geoff Mungham, Richard Spooner and, in particular, Philip Cooke, John Lambert and Teresa L. Rees. Any errors, of course, remain my own.
2. I define 'South Wales' as comprising the three counties of West Glamorgan, Mid Glamorgan and South Glamorgan, as well as the industrial south-east of Dyfed and west of Gwent. Within this region, the major division is between the 'valleys' and the 'coastal plain'. The former correspond broadly to the areas of the coalfield; they are a series of deeply incised valleys running north to south and stretching from west to east right across our study area. Before reaching the coast, these valleys run out on to a flat, mostly agricultural plain, on which the major urban settlements (Cardiff, Swansea and Newport) are also located. I shall also refer in the chapter to the 'valley mouths' and 'heads of the valleys': not surprisingly, these are intended to refer to those areas where the valleys join the coastal plain and those where the valleys reach the northernmost edge of the coalfield and merge into the mountainous country beyond.
3. For example, the *Note for Guidance on Employment/Industry and Population* (Welsh Office, 1975b) issued to the four county authorities in South Wales repeats the central elements of the 1967 White Paper. Indeed, it says: 'On the whole the original strategy for Industrial South Wales has needed little change and although constrained somewhat by the overall problems and uncertainties of the national economy, the rate of progress in implementation has been satisfactory' (p. 4). This stability is remarkable in view of the numerous exogenous changes that have taken place: for example, the crisis of the steel industry and the consequent closure of the plants at Ebbw Vale and East Moors; the changes in regional economic policy consequent upon the 1972 Industry Act; the public expenditure cuts introduced as a result of the crisis of the British economy; and the limited stabilisation of the coal industry, following the re-orientation of fuel

policy post-1974 (although, in fact, a major programme of pit closures is planned for South Wales).

4. This is not to say, of course, that there was no opposition to the strategy set out in the White Paper. Indeed, at several planning inquiries since its publication (and, most notably, at the public inquiry over the proposed designation of a new town at Llantrisant in 1972) the strategy has been vociferously attacked. However, the basic parameters set by *Wales: the Way Ahead* have not been challenged on these occasions. It is arguable that only Plaid Cymru offered a radical alternative; however, even this alternative was confined to the limited context of political and administrative change. (See Rees and Lambert, 1979 for a fuller account of some of these issues.)

5. I am not, of course, suggesting that this limitation of debate is simply a function of the form of the state's analysis. What I am suggesting is that it is one aspect of the massively more pervasive process of 'legitimation': the process by which the willing acceptance of the existing order is obtained, even from those who manifestly are disadvantaged by it. (For a straightforward account of this process, see Miliband, 1969.)

6. There is no incompatibility here between Lovering's claim that wages in the 'enclave' are high and Massey's emphasis upon the significance of low-wage areas. Lovering's comparison is with wage levels in other sectors of the economy in Wales (and, in particular, the 'marginalised' sector). From the point of view of the firms, however, these wages may well be lower than they would have to pay in other regions (and countries), especially where the workforce taken on includes significant proportions of women; and it is in these terms that Massey's argument is couched.

7. Clearly, I have presented only the barest outline of the analysis here. Perhaps the most complete account is presented in Mandel (1975).

8. In the fulfilment of this role, the state is, however, beset by contradictions. For example, O'Connor (1973) has argued that the financial demands of this role are such as to precipitate what he terms 'the fiscal crisis of the state', which imposes the necessity of complex fiscal, monetary and, in particular, public expenditure manipulations by the state.

11 CAPITAL RELATION AND STATE DEPENDENCY: AN ANALYSIS OF URBAN DEVELOPMENT POLICY IN CARDIFF

Philip Cooke

This chapter seeks, by means of an analysis of the forces of urbanisation in metropolitan Wales, to demonstrate the extent to which a variety of superficially unconnected phenomena are manifestations of the unfolding of a particular form of the relationship between the British state and the capitalist mode of production. The use of the term 'metropolitan Wales' may strike the reader as unusual in the light of received knowledge of the historical configuration of Welsh industrial, institutional and cultural development. In terms of industrial development it has been remarked that Wales never really experienced a true industrial revolution since it never moved beyond the primary extractive and manufacturing phase (Hobsbawm, 1968). This is reflected in the pattern of urban concentration which for the most part still reveals the effects of the early phase of competitive capitalism. The development of institutions in Wales has frequently been recorded in the form of footnotes to those of England, with the notable exception of those reflecting linguistic, religious and, to a lesser extent, educational divergence. Finally, the cultural distinctiveness of Wales receives its inspiration from modes and forms of existence which are almost exclusively pre-capitalist in origin; even the Anglo-Welsh industrial novel emphasises the family relations of a peasant economy rather than class relations of the industrial reality (R. Williams, 1978). There is, thus, no metropolitan tradition in Wales.

However, the thesis to be advanced here is that change in the nature of Welsh dependency, contingent upon significant change in the role and function of the state in late capitalism, is condensed in the emergence of a metropolitan Wales centred upon Cardiff. The new form of dependency derives, it will be shown, from a massive increase in the intervention of the state in the total ensemble of Welsh life, not from choice but from necessity. The process of transformation entails, it will be argued, new forms of the contradictions inherent in the capitalist mode of production, contradictions which have the effect of intensifying the appropriation of profit from the working class and thus further impoverishing its economic condition. These contradictions are revealed with crystal clarity in the processes involved in the restructuring of the built environment of the capital city of Wales to meet the exigencies of its emergent metropolitan status.

The argument will be structured as follows: the first part will be devoted to a critical analysis of the existing treatment of the state as a theoretical object. This key topic must perforce be dealt with in attenuated form but its importance to the general argument warrants its inclusion. Both mainstream social science theorisation (here referred to as 'disciplinary') and varieties of Marxist theorisation of the state are discussed. The second part is devoted to the formulation of a theory of state dependency based upon the most rigorous of the recent Marxist theories of the state. The final part is devoted to an historical analysis of the complex of urban development policies which appeared in Cardiff during the 1960s and 1970s, with particular emphasis being placed upon the relationships between state and capital and the more general politics of urban space entailed by this nexus.

Theories of the State

Disciplinary Theories of the State

While the tradition of explicit theorisation of the state has been discontinued within the social sciences, the symptoms of two main strands can be inferred from writings the focus of which is usually on specialised and abstracted aspects of the capitalist state.

On the one hand, there is that complex of 'integrationist' theory within sociology, the lineage of which may be traced from Parsons (1966) back at least to Durkheim, in which the state is an essentially anomie-inducing institution the power of which is nevertheless indispensable if the collective goal of societal order is to be fulfilled (Durkheim, 1951, 1957). This work is permeated with ambiguities for, first, it is unclear whether all political action is meant to be explained in terms of compliance with cultural norms, or only that part which is thus orientated; and second, state power is presented as simultaneously concentrated and diffused, as it must be if the voluntaristic assumption of normative consensus on which the integrationist perspective rests is to be sustained.

Associated with this perspective is the political theory which identifies the political system as open, responsive and with a relatively weak, arena-like state which acts as a focus for bargaining amongst private interest groups. This theory is shared by those who believe power to be shared pluralistically, such as Dahl (1961), as well as, for example,

Easton (1965), who appears to believe that political life is not concerned with power but with cybernetic steering. Common to this
approach is the radical separation of the political from the economic,
with classes based on the division of labour being one among many
disparate interest groups. Since control of the state is dispersed, it is
located firmly at the political rather than the economic level. Ambiguity
is also the main problem with this theory since the state seems to be
located externally to society, as the arbitrating arena, yet to depend
utterly upon societal power configurations for its content. As with
integrationist sociological theory, the whole hangs together through a
consensus on what constitutes the 'democratic creed' (Presthus, 1971,
p.336).

Lastly, the neo-classical economic view of the functions of the state
corresponds in all essentials to those discussed above. The state's only
obligations are to furnish conditions whereby markets can function, by
securing life and property and a basic framework for production, and to
intervene in the market when its own efficiency is impaired or when a
pricing system cannot be devised (O'Connor, 1969, pp.388-91). The
main criticism of this view of the state is that its radical separation of
the political from the economic simply produces erroneous prescriptions. The worst of these was that a labour market in a state of equilibrium was inimical to involuntary unemployment. The wage-cuts of the
1930s, prescribed to restore that temporary disequilibrium, produced
increased involuntary unemployment consequent upon reduced demand;
this ushered in the era of state management of the capitalist economy.

On the other hand, a strand linking 'institutional' sociological
theory, elite political theory and Keynesian economic theory may be
identified. The first of these can be found in contemporary 'managerial-
corporatist' theses, which derive from the work of Weber (1964) for
whom capitalism is formed through the agency of the state with its
bureaucracy which acts as the rationalising instance imposing the spirit
of the age upon society (Bell, 1973; Dahrendorf, 1959; Winkler, 1977).
Power resides with the bureaucratic elite as the state comes increasingly
to serve its own interests through its extension of rational uniformity
throughout the social system. This theory combines theology with taut-
ology; first, no scientific explanation for the immanent rationalising
tendency is offered and, second, the existence of an elite whose incum-
bents have the necessary rationalistic qualities is the equivalent to pro-
posing that 'power begets power'.

Elite and neo-elite political theory is an extension of Weberian
sociology and suffers from identical problems. Briefly, the recent

findings of a widely cited study by Bachrach and Baratz (1970) serve to demonstrate the poverty of this approach. The state is seen to be un-responsive to the poor and to stifle their grievances, if they have any, by creating a political culture which favours the maintenance of elite power. Bachrach and Baratz's central failure is their inability to estab-lish the nature of the socio-economic interests served thereby.[1]

Finally, in the economic sphere, the failure of neo-classical theory was mitigated to some extent by the development of demand manage-ment after Keynes (1936), in which the state complements the neo-classical 'securing' functions with those of regulation and stabilisation for the economy as a whole. To this extent the theory postulates the need for the sort of bureaucratic elite capable of comprehending and adjusting economic arrangements which Weber and the managerialists claim to have identified. The state is thus required to achieve economic growth without inflation and involuntary unemployment by regulating consumption through fiscal, budgetary and monetary measures. It is required to stabilise the economy by direct and indirect involvement in stimulating levels of investment. Equilibrium is reached when the volume of production equals consumption, state expenditure and intended private investment. The fact that equilibrium can be achieved even with substantial unemployment or inflation is what makes the state the crucial source of demand management to absorb unused capa-city and increase employment. The overriding point of criticism of this approach to the state is that, by bringing the state to the heart of the economy by adoption of deficit financing, guaranteed by state central banking, it crystallises the permanent institutionalisation of inflation. This is exacerbated by increasing the disequilibrium between level of production and effective demand (Friedman, 1962; Mandel, 1975).

It is plain that for many reasons, only some of which are touched upon in this brief outline, the theories discussed above are generally unsatisfactory as a basis for the analysis of change in the form and function of the contemporary state. This is for two main reasons. First, they do not treat the historical dimension seriously, but rather present existing arrangements as eternal, or subject to only marginal modifica-tions, as is particularly clear in the first complex of theories. Where change is at least alluded to, as in the Weberian institutional theory, its source is located, in Hegelian fashion, externally to the material world. Second, though it has been possible to identify parallels within the disciplines which might enable a structured approach to be adopted, the perspectives are ultimately of such uneven quality and disparate emphases that such an exercise could only prove futile.

Marxist Theories of the State

By contrast with the material discussed above, in the Marxist tradition the state is both taken as a fundamental theoretical object and treated coherently, rather than as a fragmented series of problem areas. Concretely, it is usually taken to include government, armed forces, police, judiciary and civil administration.[2] While Marx never developed his proposed theory of the state, the sporadic references to it in his work were structured by Engels (1968) and Lenin (1965), who summarised the basic idea as follows:

> The state is a product and a manifestation of the *irreconcilability* of class antagonisms. The state arises where, when and insofar as class antagonisms objectively *cannot* be reconciled. And, conversely, the existence of the state proves that the class antagonisms are irreconcilable. (Lenin, 1965, pp.10-11, emphasis in original)

From this it can be seen that the state is an essential attribute not of societies in general but only of those where politics — the institutionalised form of struggle between classes with irreconcilable interests — is necessary. In addition, politics is only necessary in societies where surplus product is not distributed collectively, but appropriated by a ruling class as property. Finally, the state is not separate but is an intrinsic effect of this type of society; its apparatus is the vehicle for the maintenance of such property relations. The single point of coincidence between disciplinary and Marxist theories of the state lies in the recognition of a separation between the political and the economic under capitalism. However, Marx's explanation of this is in terms of the contradiction between freedom and compulsion which is entailed in the transition from feudalism to capitalism. In capitalism, the separation of the worker from his means of production compels him to sell his labour power as a commodity. This provides an infinitely more plausible derivation of the state — as the means of enforcing this relation — than the Hegelianism of Weber's immanent rationalising tendency. For Marx, therefore, the state is an effect of the social relations necessitated by the division of labour in the process of production under capitalism.

Contemporary interpretations of the Marxist theory of the state can be divided into two categories the respective theses of which will be referred to as 'fusionist' and 'relationist'. There are four basic propositions associated with the fusionist theories. First, it is correctly posited that in the monopoly phase of capitalism the dominance of the economic level in the reproduction of capitalism is displaced by that of the political (state) level, albeit acting in an economic role. Second, this displacement takes the form of a merger or fusion between the state and the monopoly fraction of capital, other fractions such as the petty bourgeoisie being relegated to the subordinate class. Third, monopoly hegemony ensures that the state functions to reproduce monopoly conditions through its intervention in the development of productive forces. This technical-rational function means that the state can be dissociated from sustaining private property relations by a change in state power. Lastly, the state is thus conceived as representing in instrumental form the fusion of the political and economic levels characteristic of the present phase of state monopoly capitalism.

The problems associated with this thesis focus, first, upon the assumption that the monopoly fraction is capable of self-organisation and fusion. This view negates the basic function of the capitalist state which is to organise the interests of the dominant class against those of the subordinate class. Second, the emphasis upon the intervention of the state in the sphere of productive forces (technical organisation of production) rather than production relations (mode of appropriation of surplus value) presents the state as the sort of neutral technical arbiter beloved of disciplinary theorists. Lastly, the conception of the state as an instrument – 'it is not only its hierarchical organisation which determines the role of the capitalist State as an instrument of bourgeois rule' (Mandel, 1975, p.493) – removes from consideration its relative autonomy, as represented in state concessions to the non-monopoly fractions.

The relationist thesis will be outlined only briefly here since it forms an important part of the next section of the chapter. The principal points are as follows:

1. The appropriation of surplus value from producer (i.e. worker) by capitalist forms the fundamental social relation in capitalism and the basis of the class struggle. The state, as a particular form of the enforcement of the abstraction of labour from the means of production, represents the separation of the political from the economic under capitalism.
2. The continued existence of the state depends upon its success in ensuring the cohesion of the social, political and ideological superstructure (social formation) and the reproduction of the capitalist mode of production.
3. The functions of the state demand its relative autonomy to organise the interests of the dominant class and disorganise those of the

subordinate class, thereby sustaining the process of capital accumulation against its contradictions.

4. The contradiction determining the state's centrality to capital accumulation in the monopoly phase is the falling tendency of the rate of profit.[3] This entails the constant restructuring of the capital relation through increased state expenditure. This in turn causes the contradictions of capitalism to be assimilated to the state apparatus, which increasingly reflects the basic capital relation and, depending upon the stage of class struggle, appears increasingly disarticulated (Hirsch, 1978; Poulantzas, 1975).

A Theory of State Dependency

The Capital Relation Thesis

It would be misleading not to point out that the relationist thesis as presented above constitutes an amalgam of the work of two authors, one of whose work (Poulantzas) has been criticised quite severely by adherents of the work of the other, though interestingly both authors seem to find each other's work complementary. Most notably, both depict the state as 'shot through' with the contradictions of capitalism condensed in the class struggle. However, where Poulantzas's point of entry is the political level, allowing him to locate the state's foundation in the class struggle, Hirsch's is at the level of production, which means the two analyses produce different effects. For Poulantzas, the state ensures the cohesion of the social formation; whereas, for Hirsch, it is capital which performs this function. Nevertheless, their points of convergence become more rather than less apparent as one moves towards the more detailed levels of their theorisations.

First, and at the most general level, the fundamental functions of the state are conceived by Poulantzas as being twofold. On the one hand, the state safeguards the cohesion of the social formation by means of policies the effects of which appear beneficial for both main classes, but the ultimate effect of which is the reproduction of the labour force. On the other hand, the state must function to present dominant class interests as being in the general, public interest. For Hirsch, the equivalent functions logically entail those identified above: they are, first, that the state's key function is to ensure the reproduction of the process of capital accumulation; and second, that where necessary it must reorganise the social relations of production in the interests of capital and at the expense of labour.

Second, both Hirsch and Poulantzas conceive of the form taken by
the state under monopoly capitalism as reflecting the separation of the
political and the economic, though this is elaborated by the former as a
surface form of the contradiction between the forces and relations of
production. State expenditure constitutes a necessary investment for
reproducing the conditions of accumulation in Hirsch's analysis, while
for Poulantzas it has the cognate function of countering the falling rate
of profit. This means, respectively, that the state's capital relation involves the subsidisation of expanding capitals, backward monopolies
and state consumptions, or increasing the socialisation of production
and concentration of capital in the interests of the monopoly fraction.

Finally, for both Hirsch and Poulantzas, the state's relations with the
dominated class involve the intensification of the extraction of surplus
value by, for example, investing in research and development in the
sphere of technological innovation with a view to increasing productivity or reducing those deductions from surplus value represented by
state consumption expenditures. The limits to state action are defined
in both cases by the exigencies of capital accumulation in the context
of the prevailing balance of class forces. Here, Poulantzas emphasises
the contradiction posed for the state by its increasing absorption of the
crises of capital which become reflected within the state apparatus itself; Hirsch simply notes that the limits of state action are predetermined
by the tendency for the rate of profit to decline, to which it must react
positively. Lastly, both authors see the state as necessarily responding
to the processes of combined and uneven development contingent upon
capital concentration. This takes the form of subsidies to declining
sectors of the economy; Poulantzas, though, sees uneven development
as also entailing a crisis of fragmentation in advanced historic nation-
states, as the internationalisation of capital intensifies.

State Dependency

To a considerable degree, therefore, it is clear that markedly similar
forms and functions for the state under monopoly capitalism are
postulated. On this basis, the following theory can be elicited with a
view, specifically, to offering an understanding of recent change in the
Welsh social formation, as a reflection of long-term change in the underlying mode of production, beginning with the implantation of competitive capitalism in the eighteenth and nineteenth centuries.

1. Competitive capitalism produces uneven economic, political and
ideological development, specific combinations of these instances being

locally determined by the particular, dominant mode of production. This phase of capitalist development is accompanied by political action to secure the integrity of the nation-state. Where cultural and ideological discontinuities occur between the core (metropolis) and the periphery (dependent social formation) these may replicate the discontinuities in the imperial nexus, necessitating the implantation or underlining of core ideological and political traits in the periphery. This varies with the importance to the core's structure of industrial capital of the periphery's production. Where this is high, pre-capitalist instances will be dissolved; otherwise they will tend to be conserved. Exchange is of primary products for commodities, with some core export of investment capital. Class struggle occurs at the level of individual capitals.

2. The development of extensive and intensive imperialism is concomitant with the predominance of monopoly over competitive capital in the metropolis, as large enterprises concentrate at the expense of small firms. Archaeo-capitalist enterprises in dependent social formations are compromised by monopoly technical innovation and imperial competition. The state co-ordinates the interests of capital under monopoly hegemony and, in dependent social formations, it intervenes to re-structure archaeo-capitalist enterprises, whilst also conserving pre-capitalist modes of production. Exchange is of primary (and some commodity) products for core commodities, with export of productive and unproductive state capital to the periphery. Class struggle is focused on state expenditure and relict archaeo-capitals.

3. The scope of state involvement in the dependent social formation becomes more extensive as the monopoly capitalist mode of production establishes predominance within the periphery. The relation of dependency begins to be transformed from a wholly core-periphery one to an internalised relation, as the peripheral state apparatus grows in the process of organising the interests of monopoly capital. Growing state involvement reproduces forms of the contradictions of monopoly capitalism within the peripheral state apparatus and between the peripheral and core state apparatuses. Contradictory policies which result in waste occur as decisions of the state's productive apparatus conflict with those of its reproductive apparatus. Intra-state conflicts are magnified as the state is perceived as contributing to the uneven development syndrome. This is concretised in the growth of demands by the peripheral bourgeoisie for political self-assertion against, on the one hand, state inadequacy and, on the other, the manifestations of monopoly

capital's concentration and centralisation tendencies. Alliances between hitherto indirectly affected, marginal, culturally pre-capitalist fractions and the remnants of the dominated class of archaeo-capitalism emerge with this development. Economically, complexes of monopoly capital — themselves instances of the internationalisation of capital under an Americanised hegemonic fraction — accentuate the change in the dependency relationship between historic core and periphery. Class struggle in the incipiently state-dependent social formation reflects the fission of the historic nation-state and entails intensification of demands for social investment and social consumption expenditure by the state.

4. The failure of increased state expenditure seriously to mitigate the effects of the secular replacement of a labour-intensive competitive capitalist economic base with capital-intensive monopoly capitalist enterprises brings a further and intensified round of state activity, which increasingly reflects the chaotic relations of capitalist competition. This takes the form of a proliferating miscellany of branches of the state apparatus at the level of the peripheral quasi-nation-state, each charged with stimulating private capital accumulation. Increasingly,the state is involved not only in provision of infrastructure and collective consumption goods (housing, urban renewal, health services) but also in productive expenditure (equity-sharing schemes and investment in private firms) and monopoly concentration through core-based nationalisation. Growth in devolved authority in private and public institutions reflects the extent of internalised state dependency at the economic level. This is crystallised with the introduction of the formal parliamentary mechanism of control over the burgeoning state apparatus at the political level, confirming quasi-nation-state status. The extended state apparatus intensifies the introduction of monopoly forms of economic growth in the culturally pre-capitalist margin, producing effects of intensified cultural dissolution and the necessity for new forms of state intervention to mitigate these effects. The state-dependent social formation is thus permeated at all levels by the monopoly-capitalist state form. Class struggle is almost exclusively focused around the state which is charged with maintaining the cohesion of the social formation, while restructuring the capital relation at the expense of the working class. This function necessitates the maintenance of complex relations by the state with the various dominant class fractions and the working class, resulting in increasingly arbitrary and conflicting policies. Either the state, to maintain the preconditions of its own existence, ceases all pretence of neutrality and becomes overtly authoritarian; or the crises

of capital intensify to the extent that the capital relation and the state are transformed in the total socialisation of production.

Urban Planning: an Emerging Nexus of Contradictions in the Capital Relation

Urban planning theory has been dominated by the integrationist-pluralist-neo-classical triad in both its analyses of urban development and in its conception of the planning process. The latter has depended upon the theory of 'incrementalism' (Dahl and Lindblom, 1976) which formalises pluralism into a *modus operandi*. More recently, these approaches have been complemented by an institutional, managerialist orientation (Pahl, 1975) at the urban development level and a more technical, corporate, model of the planning process (Chadwick, 1971), neither of which can be said to have made a lasting contribution to the improvement of analyses and prescriptions regarding the urban crisis. Better explanations have been sought in both the fusionist and relationist branches of Marxist theory. The former is reflected in the work of Lojkine (1977) and to some extent Harvey (1973), who has been characterised as adhering to the 'manipulated city hypothesis' (Roweis and Scott, 1978).[4] The tendency to view city governmental machinery as potentially benign if freed from manipulations is more marked in Lojkine's state monopoly capital theory of urban development which sees the road to socialism lying in splitting the state-monopoly fraction alliance by encouraging the coalescence of non-monopoly fractions and the working class, evidence of which is adduced for the Lyon region (Pickvance, 1977, p.245). In both cases the authors seem oblivious to the incorrigibly capitalist nature of the state.

The relationist thesis is represented in the work of Castells (1975, 1977a, 1977b) who is principally concerned to show how the state's function in the reproduction of the labour force has the effect of politicising and focusing class struggle. Urban policy is crucial here, since its rhetoric of rationality appears to meet the interests of the property and finance fractions, as well as those of the working class, until its demystification to the latter provokes the rise of 'urban social movements' struggling for 'collective consumption' goods. But Castells's analysis is fatally flawed by his inscription of relations of distribution on to technical production relations, a characteristic identified and criticised by Marx as the classic bourgeois formulation of the concept of production. Castells's problem stems from the Althusserian structuralism which informs his work and from which Poulantzas's work has also suffered. This chapter represents an attempt to apply aspects of

Poulantzas's more recent materialist analysis of the capitalist state which converges much more closely with the capital relation theory developed by Hirsch.

Urban Development Policy in Cardiff

The urban development policy analysed in this section was a three-part policy: to redevelop the city centre shopping area, to restructure the road system, and to develop a higher education precinct. In varying forms it has endured throughout the post-war years. In other British cities the process could simply be presented as an instance of state intervention in the extended reproduction of monopoly capitalism. However, the situation of the Welsh social formation, Cardiff's function as its capital city, and the context of the extended dissolution of archaeo-capitalist modes of production command extra attention. It is hoped that this is provided by an analysis based on this combination of capital relation and state dependency theory. Ideally this would be carried out in such a way that the competitive capitalist epoch would receive the same attention as the more contemporary periods, but space limitations prevent this. This section will consequently be divided between analyses based on moments three and four of the state dependency theory.

Urban Development and Incipient State Dependency

Fundamental Role and Functions of the State. The extensive destruction of cities during the Second World War had stimulated, amongst other things, planning legislation which gave local authorities the right compulsorily to purchase land for redevelopment and, through the Public Works Loan Board, a source of loan-capital at privileged interest rates. Most local authorities were, in fact, unable to carry out redevelopment and were encouraged to form partnerships with the only company equipped to do so, Ravenseft Properties Ltd. After the bombed city centres had been rebuilt, the central state, committed to further urban containment and restructuring policies, invited successful urban planners to form consultancies to bear the creative brunt of this work. These included the Buchanan and Wilson-Womersley consultancies.[5] The role and functions of the state at the early post-war stage had thus been the establishment of the legal superstructure for local state intervention in the appropriation of rent as a form of surplus value, while fixing the conditions for the further privatisation of what Lefebvre (1970) refers to as a secondary circuit of capital. This compensates for reduction in the rate of appropriation of surplus value in the sphere of industrial capital with an increase in the sphere of property development. Thus, while at the ideological and political levels the state performed its function of maintaining social cohesion by generating policy which gave the appearance of being in the general interest, at the economic level it was actively assisting in the process of reconstructing the social relations of production to counteract the declining tendency of the rate of profit.

State Form, State Expenditure and Capital Relation. Cardiff, not unlike other British cities of the early post-war period, lacked the competence to comply with the new legislation and its plan for the city centre was rejected by the Ministry of Housing and Local Government in 1959. At the same time, Colin Buchanan[6] had been appointed chairman of an investigation into urban traffic congestion. The Buchanan Report's key principles were: first, unrestricted use of the motor car in urban areas was a demand to be satisfied; second, conflicts between this demand and present urban structure should lead to a change in the latter; and third, central area redevelopment in large cities would be massive and thus necessitate the formation of consortia of financial institutions (Buchanan, 1963). A year after the publication of the Report, Colin Buchanan and Partners were appointed as planning consultants to Cardiff City Council, on ministry advice. To induce Cardiff to be a laboratory for the application of the Report's principles, the Ministry of Transport proposed to pay half the £300,000 consultancy fee. At the political level the appointment was presented as a *coup* for three reasons. Cardiff was to be the prestigious first recipient of the Buchanan treatment; as the leader of the City Council had noted: 'When his report appears it will become a text-book for the redevelopment of central areas throughout Britain' *(South Wales Echo,* 13 November 1965). Moreover, the newly established Welsh Office (October 1964) was keen to incorporate the findings of Buchanan's 'probe study' into Welsh regional policy: 'The City Council have accepted in principle the recommendations of the Probe Study report and in their implementation they will have the full support of the Secretary of State' (Welsh Office, 1967). Finally, the appointment was officially seen as a significant step towards making Cardiff a worthy capital city of Wales, which it had not been since its inception in 1956,

> Whatever restraints are practicable on the growing use of private cars in the city and whatever steps are taken to make increasing use of

public transport, Cardiff can develop as an administrative and commercial centre and as the capital of Wales only if vehicles of all kinds can move around and within the city in reasonable comfort. (letter from Secretary of State for Wales to E. Rowlands, MP, 6 March 1969, quoted in Welsh Office, 1972)

and 'The City Council believes that development as a university city is an important part of the city's role as capital' (Welsh Office, 1971). There was no party political conflict over the Buchanan appointment or, even initially, on the main proposals; the parties 'were working as one team for the benefit of the city' *(Western Mail,* 27 May 1966). The plans were presented as meeting the general public interest: 'The basic concept of the redevelopment is to make a better city centre for Cardiffians and South Walians' (Welsh Office, 1972). State form at this stage constituted a unified political and ideological surface separate from but establishing the conditions for capital accumulation.

State expenditure on 'the biggest scheme of urban renewal proposed in Britain' (Welsh Office, 1972) is outlined in Table 11.1. The scheme arose from the condensation of Buchanan's extensive proposals for expanded commercial and administrative activities into, effectively, one city centre site. This, in turn, arose as a result of the City Council's appointment of Ravenseft Properties Ltd as development partners. Ravenseft's consultant planners, Wilson and Womersley, produced first a (September 1968) plan which remained unpublished because a Council financial and estates appraisal had shown that the deficit to the city would require a nineteen pence in the pound rate burden and, second, a scaled-down (April 1969) version in which, as Table 11.1 shows, the over-all rate burden was reduced to roughly twelve pence in the pound, of which ratepayers would have to pay five pence initially.

For this, the city's return was based on an equity-sharing agreement, some details of which are illustrated in Table 11.2 Essentially, once Ravenseft had received an average 9.25 per cent on capital investment, remaining profits were to be shared fifty-fifty. However, the somewhat dubious 'residuals' method of valuation tended to overestimate actual returns to the city, since it took no account of inflation in building costs or rack rents. The former were already increasing rapidly, while the latter were likely to stabilise given the increase of shopping and office floorspace, from 3.4 million to 3.9 million square feet and 3.75 million to 4.97 million square feet respectively between 1969 and 2001 (Welsh Office, 1972).

The principal function of state expenditure on land assembly,

Table 11.1: Cardiff City Council Expenditure on Centreplan, 1970, 1973

		1970		1973	
Capital expenditure:					
Public buildings:	Land	1,802,230		2,172,517	
	Construction	1,966,500		2,500,000	
			3,768,730		4,672,517
Roads:	Land	1,623,750		1,887,445	
	Construction	3,476,650		6,126,000	
			5,100,400		8,013,445
Car parks:	Land		3,533,012		5,284,985
Commercial sites:	Land		10,634,092		13,562,468
			23,036,234		31,533,415
Revenue account					
Expenditure:					
Loan Charges		2,027,057		2,799,593	
Lease rents payable		143,253		225,644	
			2,170,310		3,025,237
Income:					
Rack rents		2,977,453		4,865,317	
Less return to Ravenseft		2,295,177		4,117,253	
			682,276		748,064
Annual deficit			1,488,034		2,277,173
Rate equivalent		£. s. d		p.	
Public buildings		— — 9		4.68	

Table 11.1 (continued)

Commercial sites	—	—			0.64
Roads	—	—	10		5.84
Car parks	—	—	10		5.63
	—	2	5	(11.87p)	16.79
Less: Additional rateable value	—	—	10		6.75
Land already purchased	—	—	7		3.64
				(6.84p)	10.39
				5.03p	6.40p

Sources: Joint Report of the Cardiff City Council Chief Officers to the Finance Committee and the Defined Areas Sub-Committee, 7 March 1973.

Table 11.2: Residuals Valuation of Shop and Office Elements

Development	Building costs	On-costs	Total development costs	Developers' return		Rack rent income	Residual ground rent surplus
Shops/dept. store	3,122,756	624,551	3,747,307	8.75%	327,889	907,492	579,603
Offices	6,737,150	1,347,430	8,084,586	9%	727,612	801,500	73,888

Source: City of Cardiff Estates Department, Central Area Redevelopment Estates Appraisal, 1969.

infrastructural investment and so on was clearly to secure the basis whereby the private sector partner could get a commercial return on its investment. However, under conditions of sharply rising interest rates on variable interest, short-term loans at 1.5 per cent above the norm (which property companies have to pay), stable rack rents and, finally, only 50 per cent of any residual ground rent surplus accruing to Ravenseft, the deal was vulnerable. Table 11.3 shows the increasing costs of the Centreplan scheme, as it was called, from 1968 to 1975.

Table 11.3: Centreplan: Capital Expenditure Increases

	1968	1973	% increase	1975	% inc. cf. 1968	cf.1973
Cardiff	£23.0m	£31.5m	38	Estimated		
Ravenseft	£24.9m	£44.3m	78	Over-all cost		
Total	£47.9m	£75.8m	58	£126m	163	66

Sources: Joint Report of the Cardiff City Council Chief Officers to the Finance Committee and the Defined Areas Sub-Committee 1973; *Western Mail*, 24 January 1977.

By 1975, Ravenseft had terminated the partnership, presumably because the 16-18 per cent interest rates to them over the period 1973 to 1975 meant that most of their rental income from past developments was absorbed in loan charges, possibly producing a shortfall between rental income and liabilities, a situation exacerbated by the equity-sharing arrangements. Equally, taxation changes were progressively reducing the profitability of property development companies (and hastening their absorption into larger financial institutions); a government rent freeze was followed by Labour land tax proposals (Massey and Catalano, 1978); and, after local government reform, commitment to the project was lost with the removal of Cardiff's unitary status. All these contributed to the deal's demise. To develop Cardiff's capital city function, 10 per cent of the city's annual capital programme (1968 figures: Welsh Office, 1972, para.286) would have had to be committed between 1970 and 1981, with deficits met by rate increases. Effectively, a regressive tax was being proposed to subsidise the development of a secondary circuit of capital. However, central and local state policy conflicts, on the one hand penalising property development, while on the other hand joining forces with that fraction to achieve political and economic objectives, resulted in only the interests of the concentrating monopoly finance fraction being served.

Dominated Class, State Limitations and Uneven Development. Centreplan represented a non-political form of the class struggle, with gains
being made by the dominant class at the expense of the dominated
class. The other two components of the development complex, the
higher education precinct and what came to be referred to as the Hook
Road, were instances of politicised class struggle. Both involved housing
loss and induced popular opposition which, in the first case, was
successful following a public inquiry (Welsh Office, 1971). The Hook
Road was the main Buchanan proposal for restructuring the city's
highway network which the city saw as integrated to Centreplan: 'the
schedule also shows the proposed phasing of the C.D.A. (Centreplan)
roads. Since these are essentially dependent on the construction of the
Hook Road, the phasing has been carried out as one overall integrated
exercise' (Welsh Office, 1972, para.718). Seventy-five per cent of the
£20 million cost of the road would be borne by the Welsh Office, but
the scheme was eventually defeated politically, despite attempts to
'mobilise bias' (Bachrach and Baratz, 1970) by the use of 'selective
mechanisms' (Offe, 1976) on the part of the City Council;[7] the abstain-
ing Chairman of the Planning Committee noted that, 'on present
indications, the Hook Road proposal does not receive the sort of back-
ing from the citizens of Cardiff which is required if it was to be successful' *(South Wales Echo,* 30 January 1973).

Centreplan and the Hook Road reveal the opposing limits of the
relative autonomy of the state. On the one hand, when dealing with
private capital its autonomy is totally governed by the exigencies of
capital accumulation. On the other hand, state intervention is also
limited even in its attempts to counter the declining rate of profit,
through increased state expenditure, by the conjunctural stage of the
class struggle. Finally, this complex of state policies cannot be understood except in the context of the legacy of uneven development inherited by Industrial South Wales, as the city's evidence at the Centreplan public inquiry makes clear:

> changes in the region from coal and steel production . . . require
> more commercial, professional and technical services . . . If Cardiff
> does not grow to fulfil this function . . . Bristol would . . . (and) the
> whole of South Wales west of Cardiff would have its peripheral
> character emphasised and its economic development handicapped.
> (Welsh Office, 1972, para.21)

Despite its rhetorical absurdities, the dependence of the impoverished
social formation upon state intervention, the alternative of a form of
neo-colonial relationship, and the role of the state in fragmenting
historic nation-state ties are clearly demonstrated.

Urban Development and Formalised State Dependency

The sole survivor of the policy complex described above was Welsh
Office approval for central area redevelopment. However, in the post-
property slump period, the secondary circuit of capital had been re-
structured and concentrated.

Fundamental Role and Functions of the State. When the City Council
re-advertised the prospect of partnership with a development company,
its key conditions were: (1) no financial involvement by the city in the
scheme; (2) the developer accepted for prime office site development
should also develop the shopping centre. The Labour Council was
attempting to turn back the capitalist clock to pre-monopoly times.
The new partner selected was a conglomerate with oil as well as
property interests, the Heron Development Corporation. Its negotiations with the city demonstrate the bizarre manner in which central
state land legislation (the Community Land Act, 1975, and Development Land Tax, 1976) aimed at diverting property development
profits to the community, limited the state's autonomy further and
benefited the monopoly finance fraction at the expense of the community.

State Form, State Expenditure and Capital Relation. The attempt by
the local state to underline its independence from the immediate processes of the secondary circuit of capital was short-lived. The first condition to be broken was the second one (above) and it directly involved
the financiers of the Heron scheme, Coal Industries Nominees, the
investment branch of the National Union of Mineworkers (NUM)
pension fund. The success of Heron in setting this condition aside was
a form of initiative test, upon the passing of which would depend
further joint enterprises. Citing the need to start development before
Development Land Tax took effect, the Labour Council agreed to
Heron's office development proposal. The City Council, as freeholders,
would grant a 150-year lease to the NUM pension fund without assur-
ances regarding the shopping centre.[8] More significantly, the Community Land Act condition preventing the sale of freeholds was easily
circumvented when the shopping centre negotiations did eventually

begin. Heron's estate agents, Powell and Powell, had assembled a con-
sortium of developers including Debenhams, Boots, Woolworth and
Marks and Spencer, but to attract Debenhams Heron first negotiated a
999-year lease from the City Council, approved by the Welsh Office,[9]
which Debenhams then bought for £525,000. Subsequently, the other
stores did the same with their 150-year leases. The need for these sales
became apparent when in November 1976 the Conservative Council
announced the abrogation of the first condition (above). Heron had
claimed they were £4 million short of the estimated £20 million cost of
the proposed shopping centre. High interest rates were cited as cancel-
ling out the rents which the developers could afford to pay the city, so
the Council agreed to invest £2.8 million in city centre land purchase
which, added to the £1.05 million from sale of leases, virtually made up
the deficit. Lastly, the equity-sharing scheme was agreed on the following terms: Heron/Coal Industries Nominees 80 per cent, Cardiff City
Council 20 per cent of residual ground rent surplus (Dumbleton, 1977,
p.53).

Central state land legislation may thus enable traditional sale and
lease-back arrangements to be replaced with more congenial lease and
lease-back arrangements, notwithstanding the view that it might severely
affect property companies and eliminate urban land as a long-term
investment (Massey and Catalano, 1978, p.183). The relative autonomy
of the state even to negotiate a reasonable return on investment is
compromised by the necessity for increased non-productive expenditure as the monopoly financial institutions further involve the state in
the appropriation of surplus value.

Dominated Class, State Limitations and Uneven Development. What
this example reveals is the extent to which not only the dominated
class but also the hegemonic fraction are state dependent under monopoly capitalism; but the principal effect in Cardiff is to remove from
the social consumption fund to the social investment fund a 1978
figure of £10 million[10] during a period when UK public expenditure
for 1977/79 was cut by £3,500 million and Cardiff's housing expenditure was cut by half. Clearly, the state's main vector of relative autonomy points towards the dominated class as a prime source of necessary
non-productive expenditure, from whom this function must be con-
cealed. Occasional glimpses of this exploitation must make the state
more vulnerable.

Finally, the function of both state and NUM pension fund in direct-
ing contributions from wages earned in areas suffering the worst

features of uneven development towards investments which exacerbate the associated problems, as is happening not only in Wales but in other coalfield areas *(Sunday Times,* 10 September 1978), presages the daunting prospect of workers in declining industrial sectors subsidising private sector development in the favoured tertiary sector and marks a sublime twist to the intrinsic contradictions of uneven development.

Conclusions

Three main conclusions emerge from this analysis of the form and functions of the British state in a traditionally dominated and dependent social formation under monopoly capitalism. First, under the capitalist mode of production the basic relation of production, the capital relation, entails the progressive assimilation of the state and concentrating and internationalising monopolies. In Wales this is realised in the growth of the state apparatus, the branches of which are charged with extending monopoly enterprises as replacements for archaic remnants of competitive capitalism. In the field of urban development, massive assimilation of state and financial-institutional fractions is one form of countering the decline in the rate of profit through increased valorisation of private capital.

Second, the assimilation of state and capital in Wales, as a peripheral social formation, internalises the traditional core-periphery dependency relation to one of state dependency in mediating the extension of monopoly capitalism. Dependency is through the state to whatever international industrial and financial capital can be attracted. This reflects back on the form of the state in a growing fission of the unity of the historic nation-state, represented in administrative and political devolution and ideological, political and economic exploitation of the role of Cardiff as Welsh capital city at the expense of the dominated class.

Third, these processes have severe implications for the intensified reproduction of conditions of uneven development focusing upon the nature of the economic base which the quasi-nation-state is promoting and the demands necessarily made upon state expenditure to counter the declining rate of profit in both the primary industrial circuit of capital and, increasingly, the secondary property circuit of capital. The working class is subsidising, by deductions from social consumption expenditure and rate increases, which affect them disproportionately, the development of metropolitan Wales.

228 Capital Relation and State Dependency

Notes

1. Lukes (1974) argues that this work goes little further than the pluralist material it criticises since it retains a focus on observable disputes over conflicting preferences. His own advocacy of a radical investigation of objective interests and their hegemonic denial has itself been condemned as utopian and relativistic (Hindess, 1976).

2. Poulantzas (1972, p.251) has argued that this set should be referred to as the state repressive apparatus and complemented by a state ideological apparatus including the church, political parties, unions, schools, mass media and the family. This rests on Gramsci's argument that ideology is more than ideas; it comprises institutions which articulate them.

3. The falling tendency of the rate of profit is one of the fundamental laws of capitalism discovered by Marx (1959, pp.211-60). It results from the fact that surplus value can only be extracted from living labour (variable capital), whereas machinery (constant capital), though helping increase productivity, represents dead labour and depreciating capital. Capital's continuing need to accumulate tends to drive out living labour from the production process through increased investment in constant capital – hence the falling tendency of the rate of profit. State expenditure, being unproductive, tends to equalise the rate of profit in the short run.

4. Whereby the alliance of finance and real-estate capital manipulates urban spatial form to extract enormous super-profits (class-monopoly rents) from powerless citizens.

5. The Town and Country Planning Act 1944 was of key importance, as was the more extensive Act of 1947, which introduced a 100 per cent betterment levy on 'windfall' gains in land value (soon removed). Government-controlled building licences were only granted in the early post-war period 'for replacing bombed shops or for shops on new housing estates. This spurred the local authorities to busy on with developments and quickened the flow of work into Ravenseft's eager hands between 1950 and 1955. In these crucial years Freedman and Maynard had virtually no opposition' (Marriott, 1969). The latter were the two estate agents who founded the Ravenseft partnership. The consultancies were closely connected with property development; Buchanan had, in 1959, been the government inspector at the public inquiry into Jack Cotton's Monico scheme for Piccadilly; Wilson had been the officer responsible for the redevelopment of blitzed Canterbury.

6. See note 5.

7. A co-ordinating committee of seven action groups opposed the scheme and by 1968 this had led to a split between the ruling Conservative and Labour groups. The latter had been out of power since 1965. The 'selective mechanisms' included guillotining public meetings and expedient transformation of (open) committees into (closed) sub-committees (Welsh Office, 1972, para. 747). Despite 17 dissenting votes (mostly Labour), by 1971 the Council had initiated compulsory purchase procedures which elicited 5,000 objections heard at the public inquiry, December 1971 to March 1972. Before the minister's determination a by-election in a solid Conservative ward produced an anti-Hook Road Labour victory and, at a final Council meeting to consider a Labour motion to abandon the scheme in January 1973, the Hook Road plan was defeated.

8. Recently, in line with Council policy, the finance committee approved the sale of this lease and an adjoining one to the NUM pension fund for £285,000 (*Western Mail*, 12 October 1978).

9. Welsh Office approval was necessary because the intention of the Community Land Act was for leases of much shorter periods to be granted.

10. Land purchases (1977 estimate) £4,332,000 (*Western Mail*, 24 January 1978)
    Concert Hall (1978 estimate)   £6,665,316 (*Western Mail*, 11 October 1978)
    Less: Welsh Office grant   £1,000,000

    Total   £9,997,316

12 WALES, THE REGIONAL PROBLEM AND DEVELOPMENT

Graham Day

In their different ways the various contributions to this book add weight to one central observation: that over a very long period it has been possible to conceive of Wales as 'backward' when compared to other parts of Britain. The emphasis has varied with regard to the stress placed upon the cultural or economic symptoms of backwardness, and more or less significant exceptions have had to be made for particular parts of Wales, but in general it has appeared to 'lag behind'. At the present time we find pockets of Wales that will stand comparison with almost anywhere else in Britain for their prosperity, yet they are surrounded by, and often in very close proximity to, real deprivation. Viewed in terms of the full gamut of scarce and desirable conditions of life, the people of Wales are on average less well endowed than people in most other parts of Britain. As the essays in Part One demonstrate, this 'on average' conceals, as usual, considerable differentiation and diversity; but the examination of this, while important, takes second place to the fundamental point that, although the dimensions change and the comparisons alter, the striking feature is the persistence of relative deprivation. It places Wales among a number of areas which present, within their respective national territories, an acknowledged 'regional' problem.

The preceding essays also illustrate something of the range of ways in which these issues can be tackled, depending on which of the great variety of available perspectives has been adopted. In this chapter, an effort will be made to pull some of the threads together and identify leading issues which will require systematic attention in the future. Building a comprehensive framework for the understanding of modern Welsh society and its potentialities involves cutting a swathe across many of the standard academic frontiers and bringing together some rather disparate themes: current efforts are unavoidably preliminary.

Issues in Regional Development

We can set out from Paul Wilding's assertion that 'poverty and inequality are rooted and grounded in the particular nature of the Welsh economy' (1977, p.13). However, in order to elucidate this claim adequately, we will find ourselves compelled to go beyond straightforward 'economics' to consider the broader context within which that economy has come to have its specific character; since its formation, and hence the likely direction of future development as well, has been responsive to the general social and political condition of Britain. While there is much that is peculiar to Wales, its basic social nature is shared with the rest of Britain, and there is nothing intrinsically 'Welsh' about its problems. Wilding himself notes this when he comments 'No claim is made either explicitly or implicitly that Wales is an area of unique deprivation. It isn't. There are English regions — notably the North and North West — which present a similar co-existence of social problems' (1977, p.1). Again, this locates the discussion in a framework of 'regionalism'.

Regional diversity has become a topic of growing importance for social science. Its very existence offers a challenge to expectations derived from some of the influential models of development. Rather than being reduced to merely 'local' colour in a pattern of basic homogeneity prevailing throughout the advanced societies, differences of economic and social conditions between regions have remained marked, showing no sign of spontaneously withering away; and in a number of instances they have interacted with other factors to produce overt political forces of a kind not allowed for by the main tendencies of social science analysis. Thus, consideration of the bases of regional differentiation leads one towards an examination of the nature of 'ethnoregionalism' and nationalism, and their expression in separatist movements. The past few years have seen some major attempts to incorporate a more adequate recognition of these phenomena into both academic research and political debate, and the theories and hypotheses deployed in those analyses have an obvious relevance for interpreting the situation in Wales.

The inability of dominant approaches to account for the prevalence and persistence of regional inequalities has stimulated a series of conceptual innovations, with the result indicated by Brookfield: 'the sort of analysis now being undertaken into the regional and metropolitan problems of the richer countries is creating a thickening web of methodological and theoretical links with the study of development' (1975, p.188). In other words, there has been a new emphasis on the essential unity of the questions which must be answered concerning interregional disparities within countries and those which concern relations between countries within the world economy. This is not to say that the answers will be identical, but that the problems are of the same order: 'development' is a continuing process, and not a gateway through which societies pass at a particular point in their history.

The presence of regional differences within the advanced or metropolitan societies during the course of their development is as self-evident as the existence of differences between countries. What is in dispute is the genesis of these differences and their continuation in the long term. At both international and intranational levels there have been arguments to the effect that differences diminish over time and can therefore be chiefly attributed either to states of initial endowment, the most obvious of which would be the 'natural' factors of resources, climate, geography, population and so on, or to the relative point in time at which a particular part became attached to a larger system. Given integration, a variety of processes of gradual assimilation come into play. There are strong parallels between the theories of 'modernisation', proposed by certain sociologists and political scientists operating at the societal level, and the regional theorising of economists and geographers, although the mechanisms they refer to may be quite different. In each case, the effect of transactions occurring across unit boundaries is said to be one of equalisation.

In the case of neo-classical regional economics the central mechanism which achieves this result is the market, which induces a series of flows and counter-flows acting to even out disparities; these continue until an equilibrium position is reached whereby the crucial indices, such as wage-rates and profit levels, are approximately the same in all regions. Equilibrium may not be reached in practice because of obstacles like the 'frictional' reluctance of labour to move due to sociological, or other, reasons, but 'according to much regional theory there should be no regional problem. Its premises assume a harmonious self-adjustment in an idealised capitalist system' (Holland, 1976a, p.1). However, for the realisation of these outcomes we are asked to assume, among other things, perfect competition, constant returns to scale, no technical progress and a fixed supply of labour (Richardson, 1978, p.137). When we start from the standpoint that there *is* a regional problem, and that it is of sufficient size to disconfirm the predictions of the model, then we can reject the approach on the grounds of both empirical weakness and theoretical unreality: none of the assumptions is remotely like conditions actually encountered in contemporary society, and many of the processes relegated to the category of friction or imperfection are of fundamental importance in the relationships of regional development.

The comparatively smooth progression of the various regions

towards balance and towards equality of condition with respect to income and profit levels, productivity and employment rates, suggested by the neo-classical theorists, runs counter to experience, and its theoretical validity was challenged during the 1950s by the work of Myrdal (1957) and Hirschman (1958), who instead proposed models of vicious circles. Myrdal's theory of 'cumulative causation' postulates that 'the play of forces in the market normally tends to increase, rather than to decrease, the inequalities between regions', at least in the earlier stages of national economic development. The neoclassical model allows that a developing region will exercise some attraction over others which are not moving as fast, drawing in labour, investment and so on; but whereas it anticipates a reasonably quick emergence of counterbalancing movements, Myrdal points instead to the drain of skill, enterprise and capital from stagnating regions, the ability of the developing region to extend its market into the less developed, and the tendency for further innovation to occur within it. Hirschman (1958) similarly contrasted the growth of some regions with the retardation of others, and included in his account subjective factors which could contribute to the perpetuation of this situation — 'growth mindedness' in certain areas and relative fatalism in others. These 'backwash effects', as Myrdal termed them, have been expanded upon by subsequent writers. Superior economic performance in growth regions provides the basis for better public services, such as health, education and infrastructural investment, which add further dynamic impulse. Holland argues (1976b) that a high-wage sector, while attracting labour, also provides a bigger market and hence attracts more capital investment embodying technical progress and increasing productivity. The availability of labour in areas of slower growth cushions the expanding region against rising labour costs and labour shortages, and so allows continuing capital accumulation.

There are counteracting forces: the benefit of growth in one region may 'trickle down' to others. These 'spread effects' (Myrdal, 1957) would include increased demand for the products of less developed regions among the more affluent population experiencing growth, relocation in the face of mounting congestion in certain areas, investment of surplus capital where labour was cheap, and so on. Myrdal suggested that there was no reason to expect these effects to restore a general equilibrium, and argued that their impact was greatest in economies which were already relatively developed and therefore equipped with 'improved transportation and communications, higher levels of education and more dynamic communion of ideas and values'. We catch echoes here of the thesis that increases in transactions enhance the prospect for equalisation, but Myrdal's arguments were addressed to the stability displayed by inequalities between rich and poor countries: by extension, they have equal bearing on the persistence of intranational inequalities.

The debate initiated by Myrdal in the context of economic analysis has its counterpart among theorists of 'modernisation'. Once again one finds a tendency to assume original differences that are progressively weakened by the creation of social and economic arrangements which cut across them. The inclusion of distinct regions, countries or societies within a common framework of socio-political institutions, with con-comitant values, sets in train a process of homogenisation: 'traditional' structures give way to those which are characteristic of the advanced world. Not only are regional differences ironed out within societies, but societies themselves become more alike, as they 'catch up' with the pace-setters. In short, 'modernisation is the process of change towards those types of social, economic and political systems that have developed in Western Europe and North America from the seventeenth century to the nineteenth and then have spread' (Eisenstadt, 1966, p.2). Contact with more advanced societies initiates a host of changes within the less developed: conversion to new attitudes, emulation of up-to-date behaviour, greater rationality, involvement in the market and its press-ures, adoption of suitable political arrangements. Development is a process of learning new ways, 'acculturation' and assimilation. Within this body of thought belongs the 'diffusion' model of national develop-ment described by Hechter (1975; see also Buttel and Flinn, 1977; Chapter 9, above): as initially isolated and different regions or social systems are brought into contact there is a one-way flow of influences from the dominant, advanced or 'core' system to the subordinate, backward, 'periphery'. As the name suggests, in this model spread effects utterly swamp the backwash and the less developed region is a largely passive recipient of 'bounty' — ideas, innovations, technology — from outside. The moving force making for this whole developmental tendency, at least in Hechter's version, is industrialisation.

Contemporary development theory in its entirety is an onslaught upon the superficiality and inadequacy of these modernisation theses, which share with neo-classical economics the illusion of harmonious gradual evolution towards uniformity. Within the vast alternative literature, the succinct and devastating critique provided by Frank (1971) has not been superseded. His attack is in part empirical, in that he challenges the evidence for the sharp distinctions which modernisation theorists seek to make between systems in terms of their value patterns, ways of life and social structures; he also draws attention to some of the benefits extracted by the more advanced societies, as the price of their 'diffusion' of influences, which are curiously neglected in the balance sheets drawn up by the modernisers. More to the point, his major criticism is theoretical: that the approach sets up a totally misconceived separation between the less developed regions or countries, treated as being in a pristine condition of 'backwardness', and the various modernising forces introduced from outside. This implies that the basis of backwardness – or 'underdevelopment' – is lodged with the values and structures of the 'traditional' pre-existing social order: this, then, joins 'natural' endowment among the conditions which have to be surmounted on the path to development. This very familiar argument, when rehearsed at the international level, is not absent with respect to regionalism. For example, the economic problems of regions such as Appalachia, or the Mezzogiorno, have been attributed to the values of fatalism, particularism, etc., found among the local populations (Weller, 1965; Ball, 1968; Banfield, 1958). Lebas (1977) has suggested that policy makers within the United Kingdom often view at least some of the problem regions as lacking entrepreneurial values, a position close to the one adopted by the Ty Toronto Socio-Economic Research Group with regard to the South Wales valleys (1977). If the full battery of 'pattern-variables' has not been launched against the 'native culture' of Wales, there is no lack of examples, particularly from early in this century and before, of attempts to account for the economic deficiencies of Wales in terms of the retarding effects of the Welsh language and a Welsh 'way of life': a view made notorious as early as 1847 in the 'Treachery of the Blue Books' (the Report of the Royal Commissioners of Inquiry into the State of Education in Wales, 1847).

There is little to be salvaged from modernisation theory, other than its elementary recognition of differences in the occurrence of development between parts of a system. The stress it places upon convergence as the result of integration, particularly within the bounds of developing national unification, leaves it unable to account for the stubborn quality of regional distinctions. As Hechter (1975, p.29) points out, it is implausible to seek the explanation of regional variation within old-established national formations such as Britain, France or Spain in the 'isolation' or insufficient integration of the relatively backward regions. Evidently, integration is perfectly compatible with sustained differences of fortune – the point Frank was making concerning the world system.

Regional Imbalance

We need some further purchase on the sources of unbalanced growth and disequilibrium beyond what Myrdal offers. So far 'regions' have been left wholly unspecified, treated as internally homogenous, while spread and diffusion have been regarded as continuous processes. In reality, elements in a pattern of development are more likely to cluster into mutually sustaining complexes, while whatever diffusion occurs will probably be patchy and discontinuous: development is 'lumpy' and has focal points, as suggested by the concept of 'growth centres'.

We do well to bear in mind the implications that regions can themselves be regionalised (as Wales very clearly can, with its extraordinary concentration in the industrial south) and that space is problematically related to economic and social patterns. Both indicate that 'region' is not something which can be taken for granted. These points will be considered below. The growth pole concept highlights the existence of agglomeration economies and the role of externalities in concentrating activity. Factors like reduction of transport and communication costs, lower levels of risk, access to markets, the benefits of high levels of activity, and familiarity with established centres tend to draw new enterprise into areas which have already achieved successful growth. Many of these benefits play an important part in the over-all distribution of welfare, yet they fall outside the pricing mechanism of the market: crucially they include the provision of public goods (see Chapter 5, above, for a discussion of health facilities). Size in itself can allow thresholds for service provision to be passed, thereby adding new incentives for concentration. There are, naturally, diseconomies such as congestion costs which also come into play, but they point equally to the need to consider the issue in terms of a space economy.

Once these factors are considered, it becomes questionable whether convergence will occur. Even when activity is dispersed away from the agglomeration because diseconomies outweigh attractions, it tends in practice not to be a 'propulsive' activity but some relatively marginal element of the central system: for instance, branch plants which export their product to other levels of the parent organisation and with it most of the potential multiplier effects. Meanwhile the growth centre goes on pulling in new generative activity. If the process continues, the relationship becomes one of dominance; the diffusion model is thrown into reverse, with most of the benefits being drawn out of the region which is already behind. We enter a qualitatively new perception of the problem, expressed in these words of Friedman and Alonso:

the remainder of the country is . . . relegated to a second class, peripheral position. It is placed in a quasi-colonial relationship to the centre, experiencing net outflows of people, capital, and resources, most of which rebound to the advantage of the centre where economic growth will tend to be rapid, sustained, and cumulative. (1964, p.3)

Core, Periphery, Internal Colony

A periphery is here defined in terms of its dependence upon a central or core area. It is important to signal the shift which has taken place. Up to now we have been dealing with processes occurring within regions or across regional boundaries. This is compatible with a basically empirical conception of what these regions are, since they merely provide convenient containers for processes and a rough way of characterising their results. Now, however, we have a stronger assertion of relationship between regions, in which the regions themselves figure as actors: regions are 'dependent upon' other regions, or even 'oppress' one another. The risk of reification is acute and the illumination given by this new conceptualisation may be more than outweighed by the mystification of the processes it seeks to capture; in particular, it opens the way to a variety of ideological distortions. The problem is wider than the question of the specific terms, core/periphery: it besets the field of regionalism as a whole and can be objected to on the grounds that 'the collapsing of social relations and spatial relations into the same vocabulary denotes a lack of concreteness, or in other words that a substantial residue remains to be properly explained' (Booth, 1975, p.79).

Indeed, wherever a social phenomenon is identified with a spatial territory, a danger of reductionist explanation of the social as an effect of space exists: the inner city, ghetto, or deprived community comes to be seen as the source of its own problems; attention is diverted from its location within a wider structure, and the real nature of the processes at work remains unexplored. The expression 'regional problem' is guilty of mis-specification, if it encourages us to look for explanation within the region as such. As Castells states, 'there is no theory of space that is not an integral part of a general social theory, even an implicit one' (1977a, p.115). However, there is no easy translation from social process to spatial pattern; witness Harvey's conclusion that 'each form of social activity defines its space; there is no evidence that such spaces

are Euclidian or even that they are remotely similar to each other'
(1973, p.30). Only lately has this topic of the articulation of space
with society been given serious thought. While the question 'what is a
region?' has generated a considerable literature, most discussions of
the regional problem are content to begin from predefined regions.
This is justifiable to some extent in terms of convenience (e.g. availability of statistics) and policy (when planners and others who already
have a system of regions to work with are being addressed), but not as
a basis for analysis, particularly not if it leads to the region being
treated as a thing-in-itself. Instead, regions must be constituted as an
effect of analysis (Massey, 1978).

This could be done in various ways. The core-periphery model sets
about it by locating structures of domination: a core can exercise
autonomy, whereas the periphery is subject to central control and
experiences development geared to metropolitan interests (Richardson,
1978). Such a power relationship might be based upon external ownership of resources (see Chapter 9, above), reliance upon skills and knowledge monopolised at the centre, or political structures. In the version
offered by Hechter (1975) it is the nature of the state which is fundamental; he brings politics and culture to the fore.

The role of the state is as controversial in discussions of regional
development as it is elsewhere (Holloway and Picciotto, 1978b). It
occupies a very marginal position within the purer versions of neo-
classical theory, but obviously has a significant place in Keynesian
models in which its role is to moderate the unfettered workings of the
market and compensate for regional inequalities. This may entail
correcting imperfections and easing frictions, or modifying relative
prices: subsidies to capital and labour, carrying of social costs, provision of infrastructure, and so on, are now part of the conventional
arsenal of regional policy. Within Britain, the numerous interventions
by the state both nationally and locally have centred on the problem of
shifting the balance of forces which are believed to influence location
decisions of particular firms, workforces, etc. The state stimulates
spread effects and modernisation theories, the state may act to encourage the convergence process: through the educational system, for
example, it will sponsor the appropriate values, train the elites and
promote social mobilisation (see Chapter 4, above). As befits the
generally consensual assumptions of these approaches, there is no
question as to why the state should act as it does: since there is no
conception of any interest behind imbalance, it is self-evident that the
state merely acts to regulate 'obvious' social anomalies. This neutral

view of the state is taken over into some of the would-be radical formu-
lations of the problem: for example, Holland (1976a, 1976b) traces
current failures in regional planning to the impact of large corporations
which have become immune to the existing state policies, and therefore recommends ways of restoring the state to its position as umpire.
Hechter's standpoint is quite different. Adopting the core-periphery
distinction, he identifies the axis of the relationship as the responsibility
of the state: given initial inequality, 'the superordinate group, or core,
seeks to stabilize and monopolise its advantages through policies aimed
at the institutionalization of the existing stratification system' (1975,
p.9); therefore, 'national development has less to do with automatic
social structure or economic processes, and more with the exercise of
control over government policies concerning the allocation of resources' (1975, p.34). Again, we note the ambiguity as to whether the
phenomenon is spatial or not: a superordinate 'group' or area? Hechter
writes freely of regions which are 'exploited', and in justification performs the conjuring trick which equates space and society: the region
is held to contain a distinct social group, which is defined by its possess-
ion of unique social markers of 'ethnicity'. The mechanism which perpetuates the unequal relationship is a *'cultural* division of labour', and
the peripheral region is laid bare as an 'internal colony'. This separates
backward regions which display the necessary cultural symbols —
language, way of life, religion, etc. — from others which do not. Within
Britain, Wales and Scotland qualify as internal colonies, the North East
does not; and Wilding's stress (1977) on the comparability of their
situations comes about only because he fails to include tests of cultural
impoverishment in his battery of measures of deprivation, whereas
Hechter regards them as decisive.

For all its shortcomings, Hechter's thesis does pose absolutely
squarely the question whether or not Wales properly belongs within a
discussion of regionalism. Indeed, the salience given to ethnic factors
ties up neatly with the potential for conflict which is inherent in core-
periphery power relations to provide an explanation of nationalism: if
the source of backwardness rests with the political integration of the
periphery with a dominating core, rather than directly in economic
relationships, then the answer is to fracture those ties and develop on a
basis of political autonomy. Thus, the state is redefined from arbitrator
of the common good into agent of core interests, actively furthering
exploitation, pushing the internal colony deeper into backwardness.
Even where the full burden of the internal colonial model is rejected,
this evaluation of the state's involvement may be retained, as in

Rawkins's assertion (1978) that 'British regional policy has served only to perpetuate the economic dependency of peripheral regions on the centre and on the social provisions of the welfare state'.

The political appeal of the internal colonial thesis is obvious, but its effectiveness is greatest at the level of a mobilising ideology (for example, Hayward, 1977; Khlief, 1978; Williams, 1977), while the analytical value − at least, in relation to Britain − is doubtful. Without a far more precise specification of the cultural division of labour, which at present is no more than a loose hypothesis (Hechter, 1978), it is unclear how its use as a central concept would actually identify the 'colony'; its bearing is more obvious in rural Wales ('Welsh Wales') than in the industrial centres where ethnic markers are less assertive. What is quite clear is that distinctions on both sides of the Welsh/English, peripheral/core boundary are far more subtle than Hechter allows (see Chapter 9, above) and that he circumvents these problems simply by adopting the ready-made distinction between Wales and England. If, however, this conceals vital divisions within each of those countries, then it neither enhances our understanding nor contributes to effective political practice. That it does obscure key considerations has been convincingly argued by Lovering (1978b; see also Day, 1979) who criticises the lack of rigour in the use made by Hechter and his followers of the term 'exploitation', which is a necessary reflection of their failure to specify clearly who (or what) is exploiting whom − given that an area cannot 'do' anything. Lovering also highlights the naive reversal performed in the analysis of the state, which shifts from serving no particular interest at all to become the chief villain, entirely mobilised to benefit a ruling 'core'.

What then is lacking from the internal colonial model? It starts from what seems to be an accurate perception, of peripheral regions which are 'increasingly reduced to economic backwaters disadvantaged by stagnant economic structures, producing lower income levels, higher unemployment, inferior public facilities and amenities, and substantial net emigration' (Esman, 1977, p.374). Lovering's answer is that, despite its 'convincing summary' of the situation, it fails in that its own specific theoretical content deflects attention from a correct approach through the analysis of class relations and uneven development. In this, it would be fairly typical of a variety of 'development' analyses which attribute backwardness or 'underdevelopment' more or less exclusively to the impact upon the relevant system of external forces, thus failing to examine the constitution of the system itself, and the ways in which it is penetrated by structures of dependence (see Day,

1978). The point is well put by Castells:

> From an analytical point of view, the main thing is not the political
> sub-ordination of the 'underdeveloped' countries . . . but the
> expression of this dependence in the internal organisation of the
> societies in question, and, more concretely, in the articulation of
> the system of production and class relations. (1977a, p.43)

Uneven Development

All the efforts to comprehend the nature of regional inequalities that
we have examined so far have had to begin with the recognition of the
unevenness of development. For some, this is no more than an original
condition which is steadily removed; others argue there is more to it
than a lucky 'head-start', since definite steps are taken to reproduce
relative advantages through the exercise of power. Unevenness itself is
unaccounted for. As Massey (1978) has noted, this sets a task of going
beyond general references to uneven development to provide some kind
of explanation. Theories of agglomeration and growth poles take us a
little further; but what is required is a reconstruction of the underlying
logic which dictates both spatial and social distributions. With Lovering
(1978a) we can agree that this is best sought in terms of 'tendencies
inherent in the way the economy is organised, as something endogenous
to capitalism as a mode of production'. There have been some recent
attempts systematically to develop this theme: the spatial consequences
of advanced capitalism (Harvey, 1975; Massey, 1978; Friedman, 1977;
see also Chapter 10, above).

These analyses take as fundamental that the driving force of capitalism is its need continually to expand upon the accumulation of capital
and to maximise the extraction of surplus value. This is made obligatory
by competition between individual capitals, each of which is forced to
take advantage of economies of scale and to seek out new opportunities
for profit. This will include reduction of the costs of circulation and
realisation, such as transport, and may therefore induce spatial concentration. Growth comes about via spontaneous, unregulated expansion of the different capitals and is endemically unbalanced. From
time to time it meets the limits of existing methods, labour supplies or
other barriers and is thrown into crisis, expressed as overproduction,
underinvestment or falling profit rates, and this necessitates periodic
restructuring of the balance of production to enable accumulation to

begin again at a higher level. The solution may be found, temporarily, by raising productivity through new techniques of production or labour control, reduction of the costs of labour, extension of markets or the destruction and replacement of capital. Included in this is the possibility of geographical reshaping, to take advantage of openings toward greater profit. Seeking out the path of least resistance, 'capitalism by its nature drives beyond every spatial barrier' (Marx, 1973, p.524).

During the course of development, the general conditions of production will change, dependent upon technological innovation and alterations in the balance of class relations; this allows a periodisation within the mode of production. Yet at each given moment, the conditions to which investment must respond will include the results of earlier historical stages, such as the existing spatial distribution of the means of production. As Massey argues:

> the process of accumulation within capitalism continually engenders the desertion of some areas, and the creation there of reserves of labour-power, the opening up of other areas to new branches of production, and the restructuring of the territorial division of labour and class relations overall. (1978, p.106)

The end result is a pattern of regional effects in which 'the social and economic structure of any given local area will be a complex result of the combination of that area's succession of roles within the series of wider, national and international spatial divisions of labour' (1978, p.116). The 'regions' that we would derive from the logic of accumulation, and its expression in particular sectors and branches of industry, would be quite different from those which are given in administrative boundaries and official statistics. Space would be redrawn according to the precise phase and aspect of development with which we were most concerned. This is not to rule out the value of empirical case-studies, particularly historically based, which uncover the real effects of particular combinations as they occur in specific, conventionally defined, localities: these have a very great significance in the explanation of such phenomena as variations in local subcultures and forms of political action (Foster, 1974, gives a classic demonstration of this).

Uneven development as the outcome of the logic of accumulation, therefore of the very nature of the economic order, provides a material base for the study of regions; but the analysis is not purely economic. Relationships between social classes are not an extra factor to be added in, since the balance of forces between classes shapes the direction taken by accumulation, while alterations in the dominant tendencies of production, with their spatial consequences, generate new class configurations. Some versions of the 'development' or dependency approach have displaced the study of class from the centre of attention, as part of their tendency to adopt spatial or national definitions of the elements in the system: core/periphery and metropolis/satellite models follow suit (Laclau, 1971). This can induce a kind of fatalism, in which underdevelopment in one place is the inevitable penalty for development elsewhere; it also fixes development in space, in a way which contradicts the essentially dynamic nature of accumulation. While the theoretical analysis of capitalism as a mode of production will tell us in general terms how development is likely to proceed, understanding its actual outcomes requires a more historical and sociological emphasis on the variety of conditions — economic, political, ideological, etc. — which determine its effects (Harvey, 1975). As Brenner puts it (1977, p.91), the weakness of many dependency models rests with their failure to spell out 'the particular, historically developed class structures through which these processes actually worked themselves out and through which their fundamental character was actually "determined"'.

Analysis on these lines brings into clearer focus features of Wales mentioned so far in this chapter only in passing: the sharp internal differences of condition, which give the appearance of totally distinct problems (Chapters 2-11, above; Wilding, 1977), and the transformations of condition over time, which cannot be collapsed simply into a single process of regression into underdevelopment. Both can be regarded as effects of the same underlying process. With respect to historical variation, a first approximation to analysis would distinguish three major stages (Day, 1979; Lovering, 1978a).

1. The gradual penetration into Wales during the late eighteenth and nineteenth centuries of the capitalist mode of production. Its impact was significantly different in the various parts of Wales, some of which became inextricably tied to external markets and controllers. While in some instances the interests of capital were better served in the short run by the preservation of pre-capitalist social relationships, rather than their wholesale destruction, the great achievement of this period was the creation of the massive industrial-urban centres of South Wales and, to a much lesser extent, the North. At the start of this century, Wales was a leader in industrialisation (see Chapter 10, above).
2. The collapse of this economy during the depression, the vast waste of resources and long-drawn-out stagnation of the Welsh economy.

3. The post-war revitalisation of aspects of economic life in Wales, some of which are currently as 'advanced' as anywhere in Britain.

As Cooke's examination of Welsh development in Chapter 11 indicates, these are no more than surface expressions of fundamental changes. They make sense only when related to the wider history of the British economy: the expansive thrust of capitalist industrialisation, which created specialised centres of production to exploit raw materials; the enormous restructuring which had to take place in the 1930s as emphasis switched from a derelict heavy industrial base towards the provision of mass consumer goods, revolutionising the industrial geography of Britain (see Branson and Heinemann, 1971; Carney, Hudson Ive and Lewis, 1976) at the same time as it witnessed the regrouping of capitals into monopolistic concentrations; and the contemporary phase of an evolving international economy (Murray, 1975) in which distinct stages of production contained within the bounds of giant corporations are able to occupy separate spatial locations, given advances in transport and communications. Modern road transport and electricity have contributed greatly to the homogenisation of space and the capacity of industry to follow the logic of profit independently of the fixed constraints of geography and natural endowment (Castells, 1977a, pp.131-7). The emergence of multi- and trans-national corporations further limits the relevance of any predefined demarcation of regions. According to Poulantzas (1975, p.80), the internationalisation of capital which they represent initiates 'a tendency to the internal disarticulation of the European social formations and of their economies (the accentuation of "poles of development") which can even lead to cases of domestic colonisation under various labels of regional planning'. Here, the ghost of internal colonialism reappears, but as a result of an analysis of the current conditions of accumulation rather than an assertion about political processes within national frontiers.

Each of the stages sketched above would be characterised by its own distinctive class co-ordinates, typical forms of state intervention and differing bases of poverty. Any continuity displayed by the relative backwardness of Wales would have to be seen in the light of the changing conditions producing it. Thus, the emergence of capitalism within Wales was dependent upon the existing social relations between classes within Welsh society and their response to the pressures and opportunities arising from developments in England. 'Foreign' capital played a vital role in opening up industry in Wales, but existing aristocratic and landowning families were quick to seize upon new sources of wealth and become capitalist entrepreneurs. The main changes in Welsh society during this period concern the creation of a proletariat and the rise of middle-class and bourgeois elements. Poverty at this stage of development was the consequence of the drive to cheapen labour and preserve certain areas of subsistence production (Jenkins, 1971). When, in the inter-war period, Wales joined the list of Britain's industrial graveyards, the Welsh working class became part of the industrial reserve army: its labour-power was not required, temporarily, as the focus of production moved to southern England and the Midlands. Poverty was associated with this role as surplus population, i.e. with unemployment.

In the contemporary period, the rejigging of the industrial base has complicated repercussions for class patterns. The internal movements of population which accompany the changing occupational structure are associated with the destruction of the proletarian communities which grew up in the first period and survived the 1930s, and with them the political cultures to which they gave rise (Rawkins, 1978), the 'embourgeoisement' of other areas (Rees and Lambert, 1979) and the formation of new professional and middle-class fractions. In his discussion of rural Wales, Williams (Chapter 9, above) draws attention to some of the strains associated with the last of these. He also joins other contributors to this volume (see Chapters 2, 7, 8, 10) in identifying a larger process whereby contemporary industrial development creates a growing separation within the working class, between those who find a niche in the productive and technologically advanced branches of the economy and the rest who are increasingly confined to the 'marginal' sphere of small business, service industry, self-employment or underemployment. This pattern, with its marked spatial effects, is far from peculiar to Wales: it represents the general tendency under monopoly capitalism for economic activity to be dominated by a concentrated nexus of large corporations, providing security and relatively good rewards to their employees, surrounded by an expanding 'low-wage peripheral sector' which is oriented towards servicing the corporations by providing the less profitable, more risky inputs they are unable or unwilling to provide for themselves (Community Development Project, 1978; Friedman 1977). Contemporary poverty to a great extent reflects the insecurity and low rewards of employment in this 'secondary' labour market.

In the very broadest terms, this is a history which has been replicated elsewhere — perhaps especially in the North East of England (Carney *et al.*, 1976). Up to the present, these aspects of the developmental history of Wales have drawn remarkably little attention from social scientists, and there is nothing approaching a detailed and systematic examination of recent patterns of class formation and their implications for future change within Wales. In the absence of such studies, and the illumination they would provide as to the kinds of interest which are at stake and how these affect the possible resolution of some of the strains of uneven development, ultimately unsatisfactory theories of core-periphery opposition and internal colonialism are able to fill the gap (for an exception, see Lovering, 1978a).

The Role of the State

Emphasis on the material contradictions of development, and the multiple divisions of interest and conflicts between classes to which they give rise, points to a more complex conception of the role of the state than those we have so far considered. Given the fragmentary quality of development, at both the social and spatial levels, we must abandon any notion of a polar opposition (ruling class/working class; core/periphery) in which the state acts purely and simply as the agent of one interest against the other. The increasing range and activity of the state, at both national and local levels, with respect to the 'regional problem' (summarised in Community Development Project, 1977), cannot be equated with a consistent drive to 'exploit' the problem areas. If, as Cooke argues (Chapter 11, above), state action served to consolidate dependence at the periphery, it is equally true that poverty would be far greater if the state did not intervene in the economic arena. In fact, the record is one of growing and irreversible state involvement, to the point where Cooke depicts the state as mediating the entire process of future development.

The state has the task of maintaining the social order and regulating the pace of change. This means that it seeks as far as possible to reproduce existing conditions of accumulation: basically, to maintain capitalism in its contemporary form. Each of the preceding essays confronts some aspects of its subsequent tasks. The state acts directly within the sphere of production: it contributes towards the central restructuring of industry, helping to mobilise investment, sponsor 'rationalisation' and merger, restore profitability and regulate labour relations. Where activity vital to production is not viable without state intervention, governments step in to run nationalised industries, provide transport and communications, subsidise private provision, or create infrastructure. More fundamentally, the state concerns itself with the reproduction of the labour force and the provision of means of collective consumption. People must be housed, educated, kept healthy and provided with social services: these constitute the heart of the welfare system and are necessary to ensure a fit, capable labour force. Even if the population of a particular region is currently 'marginal' to the mainstream of economic life, it cannot be left to rot, since it may one day have to be mobilised again. Further, it can still play a role as a market, provided income is available for the creation of effective demand. Finally, if there are no measures to deal with the deterioration of conditions, the state may find itself facing a political challenge, which could threaten the maintenance of stability in the conditions it seeks to uphold.

This conception of the tasks undertaken by the state (see Cockburn, 1977; Ziemann and Lanzendorffer, 1977) does not imply that they are performed automatically because they serve 'ruling interests'. The classes which benefit from the continuation of the existing social order are neither perfectly informed about what will best serve their ends, nor united in their interests; if left to themselves, they would pursue various short-term and particular aims. The dominated classes are not passive either: they will act to compel attention to their problems, pose political threats and secure gains. Hence the state 'can perpetuate existing social relations only through a whole series of compromises which maintain the unstable equilibrium of the classes' (Poulantzas, 1973b, p.283). Poulantzas therefore advocates a conception of the state as a political force with relative autonomy from specific, limited class interests, able to play off different interests in a way which maintains the stability of the social order in the long run. It is an approach which permits us to recognise the real success which has been achieved by regional policies in limiting the extent of inequalities, creating a supply of new jobs and maintaining standards of living in the problem areas, yet also the limitations on what the state can do, or will even attempt to do. Thus, as the earlier chapters in this book show, the current relative deprivations of Wales, especially rural Wales, exist despite quite considerable efforts by the state to remedy them. Certain means adopted (such as the concentration of population into growth centres) may have aggravated the difficulties of the most deprived areas — as the two essays on housing demonstrate (see Chapters 3 and 6, above) — but the issue is less one of the vindictiveness of 'metropolitan' state agencies against the regions, than that of the limited scope available to the state in counteracting the effects of an economic and social system which it is intended to maintain.

The state administers massive welfare payments, endeavours to re-locate employment, builds roads and sponsors development agencies within Wales. It is at least arguable that Wales derives more in benefits from these interventions than is taken out in return, even if the way these receipts are distributed within Wales, by area and by social group, is not the most equitable. As Lovering stresses (1978a), these consequences of integration within the unitary state of an advanced economy are what most distinguish Wales from a dependent Third World country, making it more like an English region. There are no customs barriers, currency restrictions or impediments to the free movement of labour and capital between England and Wales; nor is the flow of transactions greater within Wales than across its borders, since the 'enclave' style development of the advanced sector is almost wholly geared to exports. For these reasons, there is no very obvious means of drawing a boundary around a distinctive Welsh economy. There is so little commonality of condition within Wales that it is as meaningful to consider South Wales a 'core' to the rest of Wales's 'periphery' as it is to locate such a relation between Wales and London/England. On the grounds of economic interdependence, it can be contended that Wales falls apart into sectors oriented to Merseyside, the Midlands and Severnside. Thus, Wales exemplifies very well Brookfield's category of the region with 'no corporate existence except as a collective of parts and a disaggregation of wholes' (1975, p.193).

The Nationalist Response

It is here that the articulation between the economic, and the social and political, becomes decisive. To the extent that state intervention already acknowledges a Welsh economy, it has provided an answer to this problem, since it addresses itself to questions which are seen as having a 'Welsh' dimension. Links are created, in terms of institutions and policies, which begin to generate a 'corporate existence': thus, if and when a North-South motorway is finally built across Wales, it will confirm the existence of the problem which it is designed to 'solve' — that the real unity of Wales is thwarted by poor communications, geography and so on. Such an outcome will, however, be the consequence of a political process, just as the recognition of Wales as an economic planning unit and the establishment of the Welsh Office have been; and it will reflect precisely that balance of forces and class interests which has been identified as an integral element in the economic developments affecting Wales. Again, there is nothing 'automatic' involved, no sense in which the 'natural' unity of Wales must assert itself. When we make Wales a focus of separate attention, we do so because political and social processes, with their 'relative autonomy' from economic forces, over-determine the course of economic development. Wales has a unity because it has a history of its own, which is documented by the presence of distinct political and administrative arrangements. There is within Wales a pervasive 'nationalism', far wider than that represented by formal political movements, which colours what Nairn refers to as 'civil society', namely 'its most characteristic non-political organisations, its religious and other beliefs, its "customs" or way of life, its typical jokes and so on' (1977, p.132). It would lead perhaps the majority of the Welsh to lay claim to a degree of separate recognition and self-administration which is far removed from the local patriotisms of Yorkshire or the North East. But there is no easy coincidence of these characteristics with territorial frontiers.

That there *is* such a fit is, of course, the basic assertion of nationalism. In recent work on the origins and implications of nationalism within the advanced societies, Nairn has pursued many of the threads of the argument from uneven development. He adopts a widely employed analogy of development pushing out from a relatively fixed centre in a series of concentric waves, each ripple causing new disruptions and instabilities (cf. Gellner, 1964; Hechter, 1975; Rawkins, 1978). As we have seen already, this model of a single diffusing influence fails to do justice to the changing spatial patterns resulting from accumulation over time. It does, however, lend itself to the reassertion of certain of the themes of core-periphery and internal colonialist analyses, since it suggests the impact of modernisation upon some preconstituted reality, the latent 'nation'. Thus Nairn argues:

> The process of capitalist industrial development is so blind, so uneven in impact and so metropolitan-centred that left unresisted it will crush all less-developed regions into some kind of prolonged colonialism. (1977, pp.228-9)

> One area, one nationality, one well-situated urban region always obtained the upper hand — found its centrality, its powers of domination, magically augmented by the new forces of production. The others found themselves, by the same token, 'deprived'. (1977, p.318)

Nationalism is, therefore, an historically necessary response by areas which are in danger of being forced into backwardness, or held back from potential advances, against the dominant centres. An indefinite series of regroupings is set in motion until (presumably) all the potential nations have fought their way out of metropolitan control into separate existence. So far as Welsh nationalism is concerned, it is 'a fact of general developmental history, that at a specific time the Welsh land and people are forced into the historical process in this fashion' (Nairn, 1977, p.337).

The fuzziness of the expression 'the Welsh land and people' conceals all the issues of spatial and social differentiation within Wales that this essay has discussed. Undeniably, Nairn's analysis would command widespread sympathy: nationalism currently presents a way of challenging deprivation within certain peripheral areas. By assuming so explicitly the responsibility for obtaining equity between regions, the state has triggered demands for justice which bring regional minorities into confrontation with it. Mobilisation of these interests entails the creation of ideologies, organisations and alliances. In principle this might be attempted almost anywhere, given the presence of what Coulon (1978, p.80) refers to as 'regional forms of political culture articulated with specific local configurations of the class system'. In fact, it may be possible to get plausible 'regionalist' movements off the ground only where some sense of ethnic identity and national aspiration can be proclaimed (Esman, 1977; Burgess, 1978). Since this involves a choice of political direction, made in the political arena, Nairn is contributing to the formulation of ideology as much as offering an analysis of the origins of Welsh nationalism.

That Welsh nationalism as now constituted provides a way out of the predicament of uneven development is highly questionable (Rees and Lambert, 1979); the contribution of 'nationalism' is always doubtful, in that it seeks to unite the most disparate social classes and presents political solutions to what are often economic problems, grounded in the organisation of production. Identifying the issue of 'nationhood' as the crux of the problem may breed a false optimism that a transformation of political machinery will solve all the difficulties. In documenting the existence of deprivation and poverty in contemporary Wales, in its manifold forms, the preceding essays also demonstrate the complexity of the pattern which must be explained. They agree in locating this pattern within the broad economic and social structure of Wales, as it has developed over time, although they disagree as to the role of national differences in the course taken by development and in their suggestions (explicit or implicit) concerning possible remedies. Poverty itself changes character with different phases of development, emerging now, for example, directly out of measures taken to deal with some of its earlier manifestations. The combined effect of the essays is strongly to suggest that within the present structure neither spontaneous developments nor policy interventions will solve poverty: they simply move it around. Tackling poverty would require far-reaching alterations to the structure itself, of a kind which none of the political options currently canvassed appears to contemplate.

BIBLIOGRAPHY

Abel-Smith, B. and Townsend, P. (1965) *The Poor and the Poorest*, Bell, London

Alden, J. (1977) 'The extent and nature of double job holding in Great Britain', *Industrial Relations Journal*, 8, 3, pp. 14-30

Alonso, W. (1964) *Location and Land Use*, Harvard University Press, Cambridge, Mass.

Andrisani, P. (1973) 'An Empirical Analysis of the Dual Labor Market Theory', unpublished Ph.D. thesis, Ohio State University

Bachrach, P. and Baratz, M. (1970) *Power and Poverty: Theory and Practice*, Oxford University Press, New York

Ball, R. (1968) 'A Poverty Case: The Analgesic Subculture of Southern Appalachians', *American Sociological Review*, 33, pp. 885-95

Banfield, E. (1958) *The Moral Basis of a Backward Society*, Free Press, Glencoe

Barker, R. (1972) *Education and Politics, 1900-51: a study of the Labour Party*, Oxford University Press, Oxford

Barnes, J.H. and Lucas, H. (1974) 'Positive discrimination in education: individuals, groups and institutions', in T. Leggatt (ed.), *Social Theory and Survey Research*, Sage, London

Bell, D. (1973) *The Coming of Post-Industrial Society*, Basic Books, New York

Bell, R. and Grant, N. (1977) *Patterns of Education in the British Isles*, Unwin, London

Benn, C. and Simon, B. (1970) *Half Way There*, McGraw-Hill, London

Blackburn, R. (ed.) (1972) *Ideology in Social Science*, Fontana, London

Blaxter, M. (1976) 'Social Class and Health Inequalities', in C. Carter and J. Peel (eds), *Equalities and Inequalities in Health*, Academic Press, London

Bluestone, B., Murphy, W.M. and Stevenson, M. (1973) *Low Wages and the Working Poor*, Institute of Labor and Industrial Relations, The University of Michigan, Michigan

Boaden, N. (1971) *Urban Policy Making: influences on County Boroughs in England and Wales*, Cambridge University Press, London

Bollom, C. (1978) *Attitudes and Second Homes in Rural Wales*, Board of Celtic Studies Social Science Monographs 3, University of Wales Press, Cardiff

Bonacich, E. (1978) *U.S. Capitalism and Korean Immigrant Small Business*, paper presented at International Sociological Association Conference, Upsala, 1978

Booth, D. (1975) 'Andre Gundar Frank: an Introduction and Appreciation', in I. Oxaal *et al.* (eds), *Beyond the Sociology of Development: Economy and Society in Africa and Latin America*, Routledge and Kegan Paul, London

Bosanquet, N. and Doeringer, P. (1973) 'Is there a Dual Labour Market in Great Britain?', *Economic Journal*, vol. 83, pp. 421-35

Bourdieu, P. (1974) 'The School as a Conservative Force: scholastic and cultural inequalities' (translated by J. Whitehouse) in J. Eggleston (ed.), *Contemporary Research in the Sociology of Education*, Methuen, London, pp. 32-46

Bradshaw, J. (1972) 'The Concept of Social Need', *New Society*, 496, pp. 640-3

Branson, N. and Heinemann, M. (1971) *Britain in the 1930s*, Weidenfeld and Nicolson, London

Brenner, R. (1977) 'The Origins of Capitalist Development: a Critique of Neo-Smithian Marxism', *New Left Review*, 104, pp. 25-92

Briggs, A. (1963) *Victorian Cities*, Penguin, Harmondsworth

Brookfield, H. (1975) *Interdependent Development*, Methuen, London

Brotherston, J. (1976) 'Inequality: is it inevitable?' (The Galton Lecture, 1975), in C. Carter and J. Peel (eds), *Equalities and Inequalities in Health*, Academic Press, London

—— (ed.) (1978) *Morbidity and its Relationship to Resource Allocation*, Welsh Office, Cardiff

Buchanan, C. (1963) *Traffic in Towns*, Penguin, Harmondsworth

Burgess, M. (1978) 'The Resurgence of Ethnicity: Myth or Reality?', *Ethnic and Racial Studies*, 1, 3, pp. 265-87

Butt, Philip A. (1975) *The Welsh Question*, University of Wales Press, Cardiff

Buttell, F. and Flinn, W. (1977) 'The Interdependence of Rural and Urban Environmental Problems in Advanced Capitalist Societies', *Sociologica Ruralis*, XVII, pp. 255-81

Buxton, M. and Craven, E. (eds) (1976) *The Uncertain Future: demographic change and social policy*, Centre for Studies in Social Policy, London

Byrne, D., Williamson, R. and Fletcher, B. (1975) *The Poverty of Education: a study in the politics of opportunity*, Martin Robertson, London

Cain, G. (1976) 'The Challenge of Segmented Labor Market Theories to Orthodox Theory: A Survey', *Journal of Economic Literature*, vol. 14, pp. 1215-57

Cardoso, H. and Faletto, E. (1969) *Dependencia y desarrollo en América Latina*, Siglo Veintiuno, Mexico

Carney, J., Hudson, R., Ive, G. and Lewis, J. (1976) 'Regional Underdevelopment in Late Capitalism: a Study of the Northeast of England', in I. Masser (ed.), *Theory and Practice in Regional Science*, Pion, London

—— and Lewis, J. (1978) 'Accumulation, the Regional Problem and Nationalism', in P. Batey (ed.), *Theory and Method in Urban and Regional Analysis*, Pion, London

Carr, J.P. and Morrison, W.I. (1972) *A Survey of Second Homes in East Monmouthshire – Report No. 7*, Enfield College of Technology, Enfield

Carter, C. and Peel, J. (eds) (1976) *Equalities and Inequalities in Health*, Academic Press, London

Carter, H. (1965) *The Towns of Wales*, University of Wales Press, Cardiff

Carter, I. (1974) 'The Highlands of Scotland as an Underdeveloped Region', in E. de Kadt and G. Williams (eds), *Sociology and Development*, Tavistock, London, pp. 279-311

Cartwright, A. and O'Brien, M. (1976) 'Social Class Variations in Health Care and the Nature of General Practitioner Consultations', in M. Stacey (ed.), *The Sociology of the NHS*, Sociological Review Monograph 22, London

Castells, M. (1975) 'Advanced Capitalism, Collective Consumption and Urban Contradictions: New Sources of Inequality and New Models for Change', in L. Lindberg, R. Alford, C. Crouch and C. Offe (eds), *Stress and Contradiction in Modern Capitalism*, D.C. Heath and Co., Lexington, Mass.

—— (1977a) *The Urban Question*, Edward Arnold, London

—— (1977b) 'Towards a Political Urban Sociology', in M. Harloe (ed.), *Captive Cities*, John Wiley, London

Central Advisory Council for Education (England) (1963) *15 to 18* (Newsom Report), HMSO, London

—— (1967) *Children and Their Primary Schools* (Plowden Report), HMSO, London

Central Advisory Council for Education (Wales) (1967) *Primary Education in Wales* (Gittins Report), HMSO, London

Central Statistical Office (1977) *Regional Statistics*, no. 13, HMSO, London

Central Statistical Office (1978a) *Economic Trends*, 296, HMSO, London
—— (1978b) *Inland Revenue Statistics 1977*, HMSO, London
—— (1979) *Regional Statistics*, no. 15, HMSO, London
Chadwick, G (1971) *A Systems View of Planning*, Pergamon, Oxford
Clark, C. (1966) 'Industrial Location and Economic Potential', *Lloyds Bank Review*, no. 82, pp. 1-17
Coates, B. and Rawstrom, E. (1971) *Regional Variations in Britain: studies in economic and social geography*, Batsford, London
Cockburn, C. (1977) *The Local State: management of cities and people*, Pluto Press, London
Community Development Project (1977) *The Costs of Industrial Change*, CDP Inter-project Editorial Team, London
—— (1978) *North Shields: Living with Industiral Change*, The Russell Press, Newcastle-upon-Tyne
Coulon, C. (1978) 'French Political Science and Regional Diversity', *Ethnic and Racial Studies*, 1, 1, pp. 37-59
Culyer, A.J. (1976) *Need and the National Health Service*, Martin Robertson, London
Cymdeithas yr Iaith Cymraeg (no date) *Byw yn y Wlad: Ceredigion*, Aberystwyth
—— (1977) *Tai yng Ngwynedd*, Aberystwyth
Dahl, R. (1961) *Who Governs?*, Yale University Press, London
—— and Lindblom, C. (1976) *Politics, Economics and Welfare*, University of Chicago Press, Chicago
Dahrendorf, R. (1959) *Class and Class Conflict in Industrial Society*, Routledge and Kegan Paul, London
Daniel, W.W. (1974) 'A National Survey of the Unemployed', Political and Economic Planning Broadsheet, 546, London
Daunton, M. (1977) *Coal Metropolis: Cardiff 1870-1914*, Leicester University Press, Leicester
Davies, B.P. (1968) *Social Needs and Resources in Local Services*, Michael Joseph, London
Davies, E. and Rees, A.D. (1960) *Welsh Rural Communities*, University of Wales Press, Cardiff
Davies, G. and Thomas, I. (1976) *Overseas Investment in Wales: the welcome invasion*, Christopher Davies, Llandybie
Davies, J. (1974a) 'Secondary Education and Social Change in the Rhondda 1870 to 1923', in K. Hopkins (ed.), *Rhondda: Past and Future*, Rhondda Borough Council, Porth
—— (1974b) 'The End of the Great Estates and the Rise of Free-

hold farming in Wales', *Welsh History Review,* vol. 7, no. 2, pp. 186-212

Davies, P. (1976) 'A Descriptive Study of the Special Development Areas of South Wales', *Home Office/West Glamorgan CDP Research Team Working Paper No. 14,* Department of Town Planning, UWIST, Cardiff

—— (1978) 'Employment and Unemployment in Wales', *IRD Unit Working Paper No. 78/7,* Mid Glamorgan County Council, Cardiff

Davies, R.B. and O'Farrell, P.N. (1978) 'Second Home Distributions and Their Evolution Over Time in Cemaes, West Wales', *Cambria,* vol. 5, no. 1, pp. 70-4

Davies, T. (1976) 'The Arfon Quarries', *Planet,* 30, pp. 7-22.

Davies, T.M. (1978) 'Capital, State and Sparse Populations: The Context for Further Research', in H. Newby (ed.), *International Perspectives in Rural Sociology,* Wiley, New York, pp. 87-107

Davies, W. and Musson, T. (1978) 'Spatial Patterns of Commuting in South Wales 1951-1971: a factor analysis definition', *Regional Studies,* 12, pp. 353-66

Day, G. (1978) 'Underdeveloped Wales?', *Planet,* 45/6, pp, 102-10

—— (1979) 'The Sociology of Wales: Issues and Prospects', *Sociological Review,* vol. 27, no. 3, pp. 447-74

Department of Employment (1977) 'The Wages Inspector Cometh', *D.E. Gazette,* vol. 85, February 1977, pp. 107-10

—— (1978a) 'Occupational Analysis of unemployed persons and notified vacancies at employemnt offices by region', *D.E. Gazette,* vol. 86, no. 2, February 1978, pp. 186-8

—— (1978b) 'Unemployment Summary Analysis: Great Britain', *D.E. Gazette,* vol. 86, no. 7, June 1978, p. 851

—— (1978c) 'Wages Councils', *D.E. Gazette,* vol. 86, September 1978, p. 1061

Department of the Environment (1976) *Research Report No. 3 – The Value of Standards for the External Residential Environment,* Department of the Environment, London

Department of Health and Social Security (1978) 'Social Assistance – a review of the supplementary benefits scheme in Great Britain', DHSS, London

Department of Industry (1975) *Regional Development Incentives* (Government Observations on the Second Report of the Expenditure Committee), Cmnd. 6058, HMSO, London

Deutsch, K. (1961) 'Social Mobilization and Political Development', *American Political Science Review,* 55, pp. 493-514

De Vane, R. (1975) 'Second Home Ownership — A Case Study', *Bangor Occasional Papers in Economics No. 6*, University of Wales Press, Bangor

Doeringer, P. and Piore, M. (1971) *Internal Labour Markets and Manpower Analysis*, D.C. Heath and Co., Lexington, Mass.

Douglas, J. (1964) *The Home and the School*, MacGibbon and Kee, London

—— Ross, J. and Simpson, H. (1968) *All Our Future*, Peter Davies, London

Dowie, R. (1978) 'Demographic and Socio-economic Indices and Sickness Absence Statistics: their relevance as morbidity indicators', in J. Brotherston (ed.), *Morbidity and its Relationship to Resource Allocation*, Welsh Office, Cardiff

Drakakis-Smith, D.W. (1970) 'Substandard Housing in Welsh Towns', in H. Carter and W.K. Davies (eds), *Urban Essays: Studies in the Geography of Wales*, Longman, London

Dumbleton, R. (1977) *The Second Blitz: the Demolition and Rebuilding of Town Centres in South Wales*, Dumbleton, Cardiff

Duncan, S. (1974) 'Cosmetic Planning or Social Engineering? Improvement Grants and Improvement Areas in Huddersfield', *Area*, 6, pp. 259-71

Dunleavy, P. (1977) 'Protest and Quiescence in Urban Politics: a critique of some pluralist and structuralist myths', *International Journal of Urban and Regional Research*, 1, 2, pp. 193-218

Durkheim, E. (1951) *Suicide*, Free Press, New York

—— (1957) *Professional Ethics and Civil Morals*, Routledge and Kegan Paul, London

Easton, D. (1965) *A Framework for Political Analysis*, Prentice Hall, Englewood Cliffs

Edwards, J. (1975) 'Social indicators, urban deprivation and positive discrimination', *Journal of Social Policy*, 5, pp. 275-87

Edwards, R. (1976) 'Individual Traits and Organisational Incentives. What Makes a Good Worker?', *Journal of Human Resources*, vol. 11, pp. 51-68

—— , Reich, M. amd Gordon, D. (1975) *Labour Market Segmentation*, D.C. Heath and Co., Lexingtom, Mass.

Eggleston, J. (1967) 'Some Environmental Correlates of Extended Secondary Education in England', *Comparative Education*, 3, pp. 85-99

—— (ed.) (1974) *Contemporary Research in the Sociology of Education*, Methuen, London

Eisenstadt, S. (1966) *Modernization: Protest and Change,* Prentice Hall, Englewood Cliffs

Emmett, I. (1964) *A North Wales Village: A Social Anthropological Study,* Routledge and Kegan Paul, London

Engels, F. (1968) 'Origin of Family, Private Property and the State', in *Marx Engels Selected Works,* Lawrence and Wishart, London

Esman, M. (ed.) (1977) *Ethnic Conflict in the Western World,* Cornell University Press, London

Evans, G. (1975) *A National Future for Wales,* Plaid Cymru, Cardiff

Evans, L. (1971) *Education in Industrial Wales 1700-1900: a study of the Works Schools system in Wales during the Industrial Revolution,* Avalon, Cardiff

Eyles, J. (1979) 'Area-based policies for the inner city: context, problems and prospects', in D.T. Herbert and D.M. Smith (eds), *Social Problems and the City: Geographical Perspectives,* Oxford University Press, London

Field, F. (1977) *The Conscript Army,* Routledge and Kegan Paul, London

Fisk, M.J. (1978), 'Social Change, Attitudes and Statutory Services in Rhondda Fach', *Social and Economic Administration,* vol. 12, no. 3, pp. 182-96

—— , Radford, D. and Roberts, G. (1979) Report in preparation for Shelter (forthcoming)

Floud, J., Halsey, A. and Martin, I. (1956) *Scoial Class and Educational Opportunity,* Heinemann, London

Foot, M. (1975) *Aneurin Bevan 1945-1960,* Paladin, London

Ford, J. (1969) *Social Class and the Comprehensive School,* Routledge and Kegan Paul, London

Foster, J. (1974) *Class Struggle and the Industrial Revolution: Early Industrial Capitalism in Three English Towns,* Weidenfeld and Nicolson, London

Frank, A. (1971) *Sociology of Development and Underdevelopment of Sociology,* Pluto Press, London

Frankenberg, R. (1957) *Village on the Border: A Sociological Study of Religion, Politics and Football in a North Wales Village,* Cohen and West, London

Friedman, A. (1977) *Industry and Labour: Class Struggle at Work and Monopoly Capitalism,* Macmillan, London

Friedman, J. and Alonso, W. (eds) (1974) *Regional Development and Planning,* MIT Press, Cambridge, Mass.

Friedman, M. (1962) *Capitalism and Freedom,* University of Chicago

Press, Chicago

Gellner, E. (1964) *Thought and Change,* Weidenfeld and Nicolson, London

Gittus, E. (1969) 'Sociological aspects of urban decay', in F. Medhurst and J.P. Lewis (eds), *Urban Decay,* Macmillan, London

Glastonbury, B. (1971) *Homeless Near a Thousand Homes – A Study of Families Without Homes in South Wales and the West of England,* Allen and Unwin, London

Glyncorrwg Community Development Project (1973) *Abercregan Housing Study,* Glamorgan County Council, Cardiff

Gonzales Casanova, P. (1974) *Sociologia de la Explotacion,* Siglo Veintiuno, Buenos Aires (6a edición)

Gordon, D. (1972) *Theories of Poverty and Underemployment,* D.C. Heath and Co., Lexington, Mass.

––––, Edwards, R. and Reich, M. (1973) 'Labour Market Segmentation in American capitalism', mimeo paper, Harvard University

Gramsci, A. (1977) 'The Historical Role of Cities', in *Selections from Political Writings 1910-1920,* Lawrence and Wishart, London

Grant, G. (1979) *Social Atlas of Gwynedd,* Social Services Department, Gwynedd County Council, Caernarfon

Gray-Jones, A. (1970) 'A History of Ebbw Vale', Gray-Jones, Ebbw Vale

Halsey, A. (1972) *Educational Priority: Volume 1: E.P.A. Problems and Policies,* HMSO, London

Hannan, D. (1978) 'Patterns of Inter-Generational Replacement in Traditional Irish Agriculture', *Proceedings of the Fourth Annual Conference, Irish Sociological Association,* Queen's University, Belfast, pp. 56-62

Harrison, R.M. (1976) 'The Demoralising Experience of Prolonged Unemployment', *D.E. Gazette,* vol. 84, April 1976, pp. 339-48

Hart, J.T. (1970) 'The Distribution of Mortality from Coronary Heart Disease in South Wales', *Journal of the Royal College of General Practitioners,* 19, pp. 258-68

–––– (1971a) 'The Inverse Care Law', *The Lancet,* 27 February, pp. 405-12

–––– (1971b) 'The Health of the Coal Mining Communities', *Journal of the Royal College of General Practitioners,* 21, pp. 517-28

–––– (1976) 'General-Practice Workloads, Needs and Resources in the NHS', *Journal of the Royal College of General Practitioners,* 26, pp. 885-92

Harvey, D. (1973) *Social Justice and the City,* Edward Arnold, London

–––– (1975) 'The Geography of Capitalist Accumulation: a Reconstruc-

260 Bibliography

tion of the Marxian Theory', in R. Peet (ed.), *Radical Geography: Alternative Viewpoints on Contemporary Social Issues*, Methuen, London
Hayward, J. (1977) 'Institutionalized Inequality Within an Indivisible Republic: Brittany and France', *Journal of Society for Conflict Research*, 1, pp. 1-15
Hechter, M. (1975) *Internal Colonialism: The Celtic Fringe in British National Development 1536-1966*, Routledge and Kegan Paul, London
—— (1978) 'Group Formation and the Cultural Division of Labour', *American Journal of Sociology*, vol. 84, no. 2, pp. 293-318
Herbert, D.T. (1975) 'Urban deprivation: definition, measurement and spatial qualities', *Geographical Journal*, 141, pp. 362-72
—— (1976) 'The study of delinquency areas: a social geographical approach', *Transactions, Institute of British Geographers*, 1, pp. 472-92
—— and Johnston, R.J. (eds) (1976) *Social Areas in Cities, vol. 1, Spatial Processes and Form*, John Wiley, London
Hill, M.J. (1977) *The Social and Psychological Impact of Unemployment*, Tavistock Institute, London
—— , Harrison, R.M., Sargeant, A.V. and Talbot, V. (1973) *Men Out of Work*, Cambridge University Press, Cambridge
Hindess, B (1973) *The Use of Official Statistics in Sociology: a critique of positivism and ethnomethodology*, Macmillan, London
—— (1976) 'On Three-Dimensional Power', *Political Studies*, 24, 3, pp. 329-33
Hirsch, J. (1978) 'The State Apparatus and Social Reproduction: Elements of a Theory of the Bourgeois State', in J. Holloway and S. Picciotto (eds), *State and Capital: A Marxist Debate*, Edward Arnold, London
Hirschman, A. (1958) *The Strategy of Economic Development*, Yale University Press, New Haven
—— (1977) 'A Generalized Linkage Approach to Development with special reference to Staples', in N. Manning (ed.), *Essays on Economic Development and Cultural Change in Honour of Bert F. Hoselitz, Economic Development and Cultural Change*, vol. 25, Special Supplement, University of Chicago Press, Chicago, pp. 67-98
Hobsbawm, E.J. (1968) *Industry and Empire*, Weidenfeld and Nicolson, London
Holland, S. (1976a) *The Regional Problem*, Macmillan, London
—— (1976b) *Capital versus the Regions*, Macmillan, London

Holloway, J. and Picciotto, S. (1971) 'Capital, Crisis and the State',
 Capital and Class, 2, pp. 76-101
——— ——— (1978a) 'Introduction: Towards a Materialist Theory of
 the State', in J. Holloway and S. Picciotto (eds), *State and Capital:
 a Marxist Debate*, Edward Arnold, London
——— ——— (eds) (1978b) *State and Capital: a Marxist Debate*, Edward
 Arnold, London
Holman, R. (1978) *Poverty: Explanations of Social Deprivation*, Martin
 Robertson, London
Hopkins, K. (1974) *Rhondda: Past and Future*, Rhondda Borough
 Council, Porth
Howe, O. (1972) 'Some Aspects of Social Malaise in South Wales',
 International Journal of Environmental Studies, 4, pp. 2-20
Howell, D.W. (1978) *Land and People in Nineteenth Century Wales*,
 Routledge and Kegan Paul, London
Humphrys, G. (1972) *Industrial South Wales*, David and Charles,
 Newton Abbot
Hurstfield, J. (1978) 'The Part-time Trap', *Low Pay Pamphlet No. 9*,
 Low Pay Unit, London
Jacobs, C.A.J. (1972) *Second Homes in Denbighshire*, Denbighshire
 County Council Planning Department, Ruthin
Jenkins, D. (1971) *The Agricultural Community in South-West Wales at
 the Turn of the Twentieth Century*, University of Wales Press,
 Cardiff
Jones, P.N. (1969) 'Colliery Settlement in the South Wales Coalfield
 1850 to 1926', *Occasional Papers in Geography*, no. 14, University
 of Hull, Hull
Keeble, D. (1976) *Industrial Location and Planning in the UK*, Methuen,
 London
Keller, S. and Zavalloni, M. (1964) 'Ambition and Social Class: a
 respecification', *Social Forces*, 43, pp. 58-70
Kelly, F. and Wintour, J. (1977) *The Housing Crisis Nationwide*,
 Shelter, London
Keynes, J. (1936) *The General Theory of Employment, Interest and
 Money*, Macmillan, London
Khlief, B. (1978) 'Ethnic Awakening in the First World: the Case of
 Wales', in G. Williams (ed.), *Social and Cultural Change in Contem-
 porary Wales*, Routledge and Kegan Paul, London
Knox, P.L. and MacLaren, A. (1978) 'Values and perceptions in descrip-
 tive approaches to urban-social geography', in D.T. Herbert and
 R.J. Johnson (eds), *Geography and the Urban Environment*, vol. 1,
 pp. 197-247

Laclau, E. (1971) 'Feudalism and Capitalism in Latin America', *New Left Review*, 67, pp. 19-38

Layard, R. *et al.* (1978) *The Causes of Poverty* (Royal Commission on the Distribution of Income and Wealth, Background Paper no. 5), HMSO, London

Lebas, E. (1977) 'Regional Policy Research: Some Theoretical and Methodological Problems', in M. Harloe (ed.), *Captive Cities*, John Wiley, London

Lefebvre, H. (1970) *La Revolution Urbain*, Gallimard, Paris

Lenin, V.I. (1965) *The State and Revolution*, Progress Publishers, Moscow

Lewis, E. (1975) 'Attitude to Language among Bilingual Children and Adults in Wales', *Linguistics*, no. 158, pp. 103-25

Liddell, F. (1973a) 'Morbidity of British Coal Miners in 1961-1962', *British Journal of Industrial Medicine*, 30, pp. 1-14

—— (1973b) 'Mortality of British Coal Miners in 1961', *British Journal of Industrial Medicine*, 30, pp. 15-24

Lojkine, J. (1977) 'Big Firms' Strategies, Urban Policy and Urban Social Movements', in M. Harloe (ed.), *Captive Cities*, John Wiley, London

Lovering, J. (1978a) 'Dependence and the Welsh Economy', *Economic Research Papers Reg 22*, Institute of Economic Research, University College of North Wales, Bangor

—— (1978b) 'The Theory of the Internal Colony and the Political Economy of Wales', *The Review of Radical Political Economics*, 10 pp. 55-67

Lowe, R. (1978) Address to journalists attending Annual Meeting of British Medical Association, Cardiff (reported in *South Wales Echo*, 13 July 1978)

Lukes, S. (1974) *Power: A Radical View*, Macmillan, London

Mackay, R.R. (1974) 'Evaluating the Effects of British Regional Policy', *Economic Journal*, vol. 84, pp. 367-75

Maclean, M. and Jefferys, M. (1974) 'Disability and Deprivation', in D. Wedderburn (ed.), *Poverty, Inequality and the Class Structure*, Cambridge University Press, Cambridge, pp. 165-79

Mandel, E. (1975) *Late Capitalism*, New Left Books, London

Manpower Services Commission (1975) *Vocational Preparation for Young People*, MSC, London

—— (1977) 'The Costs of Unemployment', in *MSC Review and Plan 1977*, MSC, London, pp. 88-9

—— (1978) 'The Long Term Unemployed: a Discussion Document', unpublished paper

Manson, T. (1979) 'Health Policy and the Cuts', *Capital and Class*, 7, pp. 35-45

Marriott, O. (1969) *The Property Boom*, Pan, London

Marx, K. (1959) *Capital*, Vol. III, Lawrence and Wishart, London

—— (1973) *Grundrisse*, Penguin, Harmondsworth

Massey, D. (1978) 'Regionalism: Some Current Issues', *Capital and Class*, 6, pp. 106-25

—— (1979) 'In What Sense a Regional Problem?', *Regional Studies*, 13, pp. 233-44

—— and Catalano, A. (1978) *Capital and Land*, Edward Arnold, London

Mid Glamorgan County Council (1977a) *County Structure Plan Report of Survey Vol. 2: Employment*, Mid Glamorgan County Council Planning Department, Cardiff

—— (1977b) *County Structure Plan Report of Survey Vol. 3: Housing*, Mid Glamorgan County Council Planning Department, Cardiff

Miliband, R. (1978) 'A State of De-subordination', *British Journal of Sociology*, 29, pp. 399-409

—— (1969) *The State in Capitalist Society*, Weidenfeld and Nicolson, London

Ministry of Housing and Local Government (1969) *Housing Act 1969: Area Improvement*, Circular 65/69, HMSO, London

Moore, B. and Rhodes, J. (1975) *Regional Policy and the Economy of Wales*, Welsh Office, Cardiff

—— —— (1976) 'Regional Economic Policy and the Movement of Manufacturing Industry to the Development Areas', *Economica*, 43, pp. 17-31

Moore, R. (1974) *Pit-men, Preachers and Politics*, Cambridge University Press, Cambridge

—— (1978) 'Sociologists Not at Work – Institutionalised Inability: a case of research funding', in G. Littlejohn, B. Smart, J. Wakeford and N. Yuval-Davies (eds), *Power and the State*, Croom Helm, London, pp. 267-302

Morris, J. and Williams, J. (1958) *The South Wales Coal Industry 1841-1875*, University of Wales Press, Cardiff

Murray, R. (1975) *Multinational Companies and Nation States*, Spokesman Books, Nottingham

Myrdal, G. (1957) *Economic Theory and Underdeveloped Regions*, Duckworth, London

Nairn, T. (1977) *The Break-up of Britain: Crisis and Neo-Nationalism*,

New Left Books, London

NALGO (1979) 'Public Expenditure: The role of the public sector in a depressed region', NALGO, London

Nash, R. (1978) 'Perceptions of the Village School', in G. Williams (ed.), *Social and Cultural Change in Contemporary Wales,* Routledge and Kegan Paul, London, pp. 76-86

National Economic Development Council (1963) *Conditions Favourable to Faster Economic Growth,* HMSO, London

Neave, G. (1975) *How They Fared,* Routledge and Kegan Paul, London

Newby, H., Bell, C., Rose, D. and Saunders, P. (1978) *Property, Paternalism & Power: class and control in rural England,* Hutchinson, London

Newport Borough Council (1976) *Strategy for Area Improvement in Newport,* Newport Borough Council, Newport

North Tyneside Community Development Project (1978) *In and Out of Work,* North Tyneside CDP, Newcastle

O'Connor, J. (1969) 'Scientific and Ideological Elements in the Economic Theory of Government Policy', *Science and Society,* 33, 4, pp. 385-414

—— (1973) *The Fiscal Crisis of the State,* St Martin's, New York

Offe, C. (1976) 'Political Authority and Class Structures', in P. Connerton (ed.), *Critical Sociology,* Penguin, Harmondsworth

OPCS (1971) *Handicapped and Impaired in Great Britain,* HMSO, London

—— (1974) *Morbidity Statistics from General Practice: Second National Study,* HMSO, London

—— (1975) *General Household Survey 1972,* HMSO, London

—— (1978) *General Household Survey 1976,* HMSO, London

Opinion Research Centre (1967) *Housing Problems, Priorities and Preferences,* ORC, London

Osmond, J. (1977) *Creative Conflict: the politics of Welsh devolution,* Routledge and Kegan Paul, London

Pahl, R. (1975) *Whose City?,* Penguin, Harmondsworth

Parliamentary Debates (1975/6) vol. 913, oral answers, c. 127

—— (1976/7a) vol. 934, written answers, c. 367-8

—— (1967/7b) vol. 936, written answers, c. 482-3

Parsons, T. (1966) 'The Political Aspect of Social Structures and Process', in D. Easton (ed.), *Varieties of Political Theory,* Prentice Hall, Englewood Cliffs

Payne, G. (1973) 'Typologies of Middle Class Mobility', *Sociology,* vol. 7, pp. 417-28

Peate, I. (1940) *The Welsh House,* The Honourable Society of Cymrodorion, London

Perroux, F. (1955) 'Note sur la notion de pôle de croissance', *Economie Appliquée*, 8, pp. 307-20

Pickvance, C. (1977) 'Marxist Approaches to the Study of Urban Politics: divergences among some recent French studies', *International Journal of Urban and Regional Research*, 1, 2, pp. 219-55

—— (1979) 'Policies as Chameleons: an interpretation of regional policy and office policy in Britain', in M.J. Dear and A. Scott (eds), *Urbanization and Urban Planning in Capitalist Societies*, Maaroufa, Chicago (forthcoming)

Pinch, S.P. (1978) 'Patterns of local authority housing allocation in Greater London between 1966 and 1973: an inter-borough analysis', *Transactions, Institute of British Geographers*, 3, pp. 35-54

—— (1979) 'Territorial justice in the city: a case study of social services for the elderly in Greater London', in D.T. Herbert and D.M. Smith (eds), *Social Problems and the City: Geographical Perspectives*, Oxford University Press, London

Piore, M. (1970) 'Jobs and Training', in S.H. Beer and R.E. Barringer (eds), *The State and the Poor*, Winthrop Publishers, Cambridge, Mass.

Poulantzas, N. (1972) 'The Problem of the Capitalist State', in R. Blackburn (ed.), *Ideology in Social Science*, Fontana, London

—— (1973a) 'On Social Class', *New Left Review*, no. 78, pp. 27-56

—— (1973b) *Political Power and Social Classes*, New Left Books, London

—— (1975) *Classes in Contemporary Capitalism*, New Left Books, London

—— (1976) *Critica de la Hegemonia del Estado*, Editorial Cuerro, Buenos Aires

Presthus, R. (1971) 'Pluralism and Elitism', in F. Castles *et al.* (eds), *Decisions, Organisations and Society*, Penguin, Harmondsworth

Quijano, A. (1973) 'Redefinición de la Dependencia y Proceso de Marginalizacion en America Latina', in C. Weffort and A. Quijano (eds), *Populismo, Marginalizacion y Dependencia*, Editorial Universitaria Centroamericana, San Jose, Costa Rica, pp. 171-229

Rawkins, P. (1978) 'Nationalist Mobilization in Scotland and Wales', in A. Cottrell and J. Ross (eds), *The Mobilization of Collective Identity: Comparative Perspectives*, University Press of America, Washington

—— (1979) 'The Implementation of Language Policy in the Schools of Wales', *Studies in Public Policy No. 40*, Centre for the Study of Public Policy, Univeristy of Strathclyde, Glasgow

Rees, A.D. (1950) *Life in a Welsh Countryside*, University of Wales Press, Cardiff

Rees, G. and Lambert, J. (1979) 'Urban Development in a Peripheral Region: some issues from South Wales', paper presented to the CES Urban Change and Conflict Conference, University of Nottingham

Rees, G. and Wragg, R. (1975) *A Study of Passenger Transport Needs of Rural Wales*, Welsh Council, Cardiff

Rees, T. (1974) 'Evaluation of Transport Schemes 1970-1973', *Home Office/West Glamorgan CDP Research Team Working Paper No. 3*, Department of Town Planning, UWIST, Cardiff

—— (1976a) 'A Demographic and Socio-Economic Profile of Migrants To and From the South Wales Valleys with special reference to the Upper Afan Valley', *Home Office/West Glamorgan CDP Research Team Working Paper No. 16*, Department of Town Planning, UWIST, Cardiff

—— (1976b) 'The Origin and Destination of Migrants to and From the South Wales Valleys, with special reference to the Upper Afan Valley', *Home Office/West Glamorgan CDP Research Team Working Paper No. 17*, Department of Town Planning, UWIST, Cardiff

—— (1977) 'The Non-Movers of the Upper Afan Valley: A Comparison with in-migrants and out-migrants', *Sociological Research Unit Working Paper No. 2*, University College, Cardiff

—— and Smith, G. (1979) 'The Transition from School to Work in Wales', Sociological Research Unit, Department of Sociology, University College, Cardiff

Report of the Chief Medical Officer (no date) *Health Services in Wales 1976*, Welsh Office, Cardiff

Report of the Royal Commissioners of Inquiry into the State of Education in Wales (1847), HMSO, London

Revell, J. and Tomkins, C. (1974) *Personal Wealth and Finance in Wales*, Welsh Council, Cardiff

Rex, J. and Moore, R. (1967) *Race, Community and Conflict*, Oxford University Press, Oxford

Richards, J.H. and Lewis, J.P. (1969) 'House Building in the South Wales Coalfield 1851-1913', in E. Minchington (ed.), *Industrial South Wales 1850-1914: Essays in Welsh Economic History*, Frank Cass and Co., London

Richardson, H. (1978) *Regional and Urban Economics*, Penguin, Harmondsworth

Roberts, C. (1979) 'The Sociology of Education in Wales', paper presented to the BSA Sociology of Wales Study Group Conference,

Gregynog Hall, Powys,

Rotman, A. (1974) *Dependencia, Estructura de Poder y Formacion Regional en America Latina*, Siglo Veintiuno, Buenos Aires

Roweis, S. and Scott, A. (1978) 'The Urban Land Question', in K. Cox (ed.), *Urbanisation and Conflict in Market Societies*, Methuen, London

Royal Commission on the Distribution of Income and Wealth (1975) *Report No. 1*, Cmnd. 6171, HMSO, London

—— (1977) *Report No. 5*, Cmnd.6999, HMSO, London

—— (1978) *Report No. 6*, Cmnd.7175, HMSO, London

Runciman, W.G. (1966) *Relative Deprivation and Social Justice*, Routledge and Kegan Paul, London

Scottish Development Department (1963) *Central Scotland: a programme for development and growth*, Cmnd.2188, HMSO, Edinburgh

Simon, B. (1960) *Studies in the History of Education 1780-1870*, Lawrence and Wishart, London

Sinfield, A. (1968) *The Long Term Unemployed*, OECD, Paris

South Glamorgan County Council (1976) *County Structure Plan Report of Survey*, South Glamorgan County Council Planning Department, Cardiff

South Wales Echo, 13 November 1965, 30 January 1973

Stacey, M. (ed.) (1976) 'The Sociology of the NHS', *Sociological Review Monograph 22*, London

Standing Conference of Rural Community Councils (1978) *The Decline of Rural Services*, National Council for Social Service, London

Steele, G. (1974) 'Industrial Accidents: an economic interpretation', *Applied Economics*, 6, pp. 143-55

Sunday Times, 10 September 1978

Swansea City Council (1975) 'Multiple Occupation', *Housing Subject Plan – Interim Planning Statement Pt. 3*, Swansea City Council Planning Department, Swansea

Tai Nos (1978) *I Ended Up On My Own With A Torch*, Tai Nos, Cardiff

Taylor, G. and Ayres, N. (1969) *Born and Bred Unequal*, Longman, London

Thane, P. (ed.) (1978) *The Origins of British Social Policy*, Croom Helm, London

Thomas, R. (1966) *Industry in Rural Wales*, Welsh Economic Studies no. 3, University of Wales Press, Cardiff

Tomkins, C. and Lovering, J. (1973) *Location, Size, Ownership and Control Tables for Welsh Industry*, Welsh Council, Cardiff

Touraine, A. (1977) *The Self-Production of Society*, University of

Chicago Press, Chicago

Town, S. (1978) *After the Mines: changing employment opportunities in a South Wales valley,* Board of Celtic Studies Social Science Monograph no. 4, University of Wales Press, Cardiff

Town and Country Planning Association (1976) *A Regional Strategy Plan for South Wales* (Press release), TCPA, London

Townsend, P. (1976) *The Difficulties of Policies based on the Concept of Area Deprivation,* Barnett Shine Foundation Lecture, Queen Mary College, London

The Treasury (1977) *The Government's Expenditure Plans,* Cmnd. 6721, HMSO, London

Tuck, C.J. (1973) 'Second Homes', *Merioneth Structure Plan Subject Report No. 17,* Merioneth County Council Planning Department, Dolgellau

Tuck, M. (1974) 'The Effect of Different Factors on the Level of Academic Achievement in England and Wales', *Social Science Research,* 3, pp. 141-50

Ty Toronto Socio-Economic Research Group (1977) *A Socio-Economic Strategy for the Valleys of South Wales,* Ty Toronto, Aberfan

Tyler, W. (1977) *The Sociology of Educational Inequality,* Methuen, London

Wachter, M. (1974) 'Primary and Secondary Labor Markets: A Critique of the Dual Approach', *Brookings Papers on Economic Activity,* vol. 3, pp. 637-80

Wales TUC (1977) *A Note on the Shortage of Training Opportunities for Young People in Wales,* Wales TUC, Cardiff

—— (1978) 'Unemployment: the Way Out. A Ten Year Strategy', *Wales TUC Fourth Annual Report,* Cardiff

Waugh, S. (1976) *Needs and Provision for Young Single Homeless People – A Review of Information and Literature,* Campaign for Single Homeless People, CHAR, London

Webber, R.J. (1977) *The National Classification of Residential Neighbourhoods: An Introduction to the Classification of Wards and Parishes,* PRAG Technical Papers TP 23, CES, London

Weber, M. (1964) *The Theory of Social and Economic Organisation,* The Free Press, New York

Wedderburn, D. (ed.) (1974) *Poverty, Inequality and the Class Structure,* Cambridge University Press, Cambridge

Weller, J. (1965) *Yesterday's People,* University of Kentucky Press, Lexington

Welsh Committee of the National Union of Teachers (1975) *Quali-*

fications for Entry into Sixth Forms in Secondary Schools in Wales,
NUT, Cardiff
—— (no date) 'Absence in Secondary Schools in Wales: the comments
of the Welsh Committee of the National Union of Teachers on the
Welsh Education Office Paper "Absenteeism in the Schools of
Wales" ', unpublished paper, Cardiff
Welsh Consumer Council (1976) *Council Housing: A Survey of Alloca-
tion Policies in Wales*, Welsh Consumer Council, Cardiff
—— (1979a) *Whose Homes?*, Welsh Consumer Council, Cardiff
—— (1979b) *Getting Primary Care on the NHS*, Welsh Consumer
Council, Cardiff
Welsh Council (1971) *A Strategy for Rural Wales*, Welsh Council,
Cardiff
—— (1976) *Services for the Elderly in Wales*, Welsh Council, Cardiff
Welsh Education Office (1978) *Primary Education in Rural Wales*
(Education Survey no. 6), Welsh Office, Cardiff
—— (1979) *Literacy and Numeracy and Examination Achievements in
Wales: a further commentary*, Welsh Office, Cardiff
—— (no date) *Literacy and Numeracy and Examination Achievements
in Wales: Report of a Conference held at Mold, March 1978*, Welsh
Office, Cardiff
Welsh Housing Associations Committee (1978) *Housing in Wales*,
National Federation of Housing Associations, London
Welsh Office (1967) *Wales: the Way Ahead*, Cmnd.3334, HMSO,
Cardiff
—— (1971) *Inspector's Report of Higher Education Precinct Public
Inquiry*, Welsh Office, Cardiff
—— (1972) *Inspector's Report of Centreplan Public Inquiry*, Welsh
Office, Cardiff
—— (1973) *Welsh House Condition Survey 1973*, HMSO, Cardiff
—— (1975a) *Health and Personal Social Service Statistics for Wales
No. 2*, HMSO, Cardiff
—— (1975b) *Note for Guidance on Employment/Industry and Population*, Welsh Office, Cardiff
—— (1976a) *Proposed All-Wales Policies and Priorities for the Planning and Provision of Health and Personal Social Services from
1976-77 to 1979-80*, Welsh Office, Cardiff
—— (1976b) *Welsh House Condition Survey 1976*, HMSO, Cardiff
—— (1977a) *Welsh Social Trends*, no. 1, HMSO, Cardiff
—— (1977b) *Welsh Economic Trends*, no. 4, HMSO, Cardiff
—— (1977c) *First Report of the Working Party on Housing Finance in*

Wales, Welsh Office, Cardiff
—— (1978a) *Second Report of the Working Party on Housing Finance in Wales*, Welsh Office, Cardiff
—— (1978b) *Report of Steering Committee on Resource Allocation in Wales*, Welsh Office, Cardiff
—— (1978c) *Welsh Economic Trends no. 5*, HMSO, Cardiff
Welsh Office/Department of Health and Social Security/Local Authorities in the Administrative County of Glamorgan and the Cardiff and Swansea County Borough Councils (1972) *Report of the Joint Working Party on the Situation in the South Wales Survey Area referred to by Mr Bryan Glastonbury in 'Homeless Near a Thousand Homes'*, Welsh Office, Cardiff
Wenger, C. (1980) *Mid Wales: Development of Deprivation*, Board of Celtic Studies Monograph, University of Wales Press, Cardiff (forthcoming)
Westergaard, J. (1978) 'Social Policy and Class Inequality: some notes on welfare state limits', in R. Miliband and J. Saville (eds), *The Socialist Register*, Merlin Press, London
—— and Resler, H. (1975) *Class in a Capitalist Society: a study of contemporary Britain*, Heinemann, London
Western Mail, 27 May 1966, 24 January 1977, 12 October 1978
Wilby, P. (1977) 'Education and Equality', *New Statesman*, 16 September, pp. 338-40
Wilding, P. (1977) *Poverty: The Facts in Wales*, Child Poverty Action Group, London
Williams, G. (ed.) (1978) *Social and Cultural Change in Contemporary Wales*, Routledge and Kegan Paul, London
—— (1978) 'Industrialization and Ethnic Change in the Lower Chubut Valley, Argentina', *American Ethnologist*, vol. 5, no. 3, pp. 618-31
—— (forthcoming) 'La Imagen de America Latina en Gales del Siglo XIX', *America Latina*
—— and Howell, J. (no date) 'Quarrying for Water: a study of employment in the Dinorwic hydroelectric project', unpublished manuscript
Williams, L.J. and Boyn, T. (1977) 'Occupation in Wales, 1851-1971', *Bulletin of Economic Research*, 29, pp. 71-83
Williams, P. (1977) 'The Internal Colony', *Planet*, 37/38, pp. 60-5
Williams, R. (1978) *The Welsh Industrial Novel*, Gwyn Jones Lecture, Cardiff
Williams, W. (1970) 'A Study of General Practitioners' Work Load in South Wales 1965-1966', *Reports from General Practice No. 12*, Royal College of General Practitioners, London

Winkler, J. (1977) 'The Corporatist Economy: Theory and Administration', in R. Scase (ed.), *Industrial Society: Class, Cleavage and Control*, George Allen and Unwin, London

Zeimann, W. and Lanzendorffer, M. (1977) 'The State in Peripheral Societies', *Socialist Register*, pp. 143-77

NOTES ON CONTRIBUTORS

Philip Cooke is a lecturer in planning theory and urban politics at the University of Wales Institute of Science and Technology. His research interests include the theory of development in peripheral regions and state intervention in urban problems.

Graham Day teaches sociology at University College of Wales, Aberystwyth. He has done research on community patterns and religious organisation in Central Wales and is currently interested in the relevance of development theories and class analyses for Wales, and the scope for a sociology of regions. He is convenor of the BSA Sociology of Wales Study Group.

Malcolm Fisk lives in Rhondda and works for the Secondary Housing Association for Wales. He is responsible for the setting up of housing associations and housing co-operatives in Wales, notably in the valleys, and has undertaken research into Welsh housing problems for voluntary agencies such as Ty Toronto, the Centre for Valleys Concerns and Shelter.

Denis Gregory is Research Officer, Trades Union Research Unit, Ruskin College, Oxford, currently working with the Wales TUC. He is employed on a research project sponsored by the Manpower Services Commission on the effectiveness of a trade union response to interventionist labour market policies.

David T. Herbert is Reader in the Department of Geography at University College, Swansea with research interests in the field of urban-social geography.

Robert McNabb is a research fellow in the Department of Economics, University College, Cardiff. His research interests include labour market problems in South Wales.

Gareth Rees is a lecturer in urban sociology and urban policy at the University of Wales Institute of Science and Technology, Cardiff. He is interested in state intervention in urban and regional development, particularly in peripheral regions.

Teresa L. Rees is a research officer in the Sociological Research Unit, Department of Sociology, University College, Cardiff. Her research interests centre on problems of industrial decline in South Wales, such as migration, youth unemployment and redundancy. Editor of the BSA Sociology of Wales Study Group *Newsletter.*

Paul Wilding taught at the University of Nottingham from 1967 until 1975. Since then he has been Senior Lecturer in Social Administration at University College, Cardiff.

Glyn Williams is a lecturer in the Department of Social Theory and Institutions, University College of North Wales, Bangor and editor of *Social and Cultural Change in Contemporary Wales,* Routledge and Kegan Paul, London, 1978.

INDEX

For Product Safety Concerns and Information please contact our EU
representative GPSR@taylorandfrancis.com
Taylor & Francis Verlag GmbH, Kaufingerstraße 24, 80331 München, Germany

www.ingramcontent.com/pod-product-compliance
Lightning Source LLC
Chambersburg PA
CBHW071353290326
41932CB00045B/1787